Other Titles in the Smart Pr~ ~~~~~

GETTING LOST

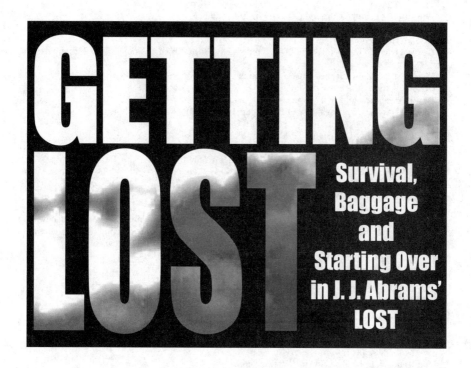

GETTING LOST

Survival, Baggage and Starting Over in J. J. Abrams' LOST

EDITED BY

ORSON SCOTT CARD

BENBELLA BOOKS, INC.

Dallas, Texas

BenBella Books, Inc.
6440 N. Central Expressway, Suite 617
Dallas, TX 75206
www.benbellabooks.com
Send feedback to feedback@benbellabooks.com

Printed in the United States of America
10 9 8 7 6 5 4 3 2 1

Library of Congress Cataloging-in-Publication Data

Getting Lost : survival, baggage, and starting over in J.J. Abrams' Lost / edited by Orson Scott Card.
    p. cm.
    ISBN 1-932100-78-4
    1. Lost (Television program) I. Card, Orson Scott.
    PN1992.77.L67G48 2006
    791.45'72—dc22

2006012226

Proofreading by Stacia Seaman & Jennifer Thomason
Cover design by Todd Michael Bushman
Text design and composition by John Reinhardt Book Design
Printed by Victor Graphics, Inc.

Distributed by Independent Publishers Group
To order call (800) 888-4741 • www.ipgbook.com

For media inquiries and special sales contact Yara Abuata at yara@benbellabooks.com

Contents

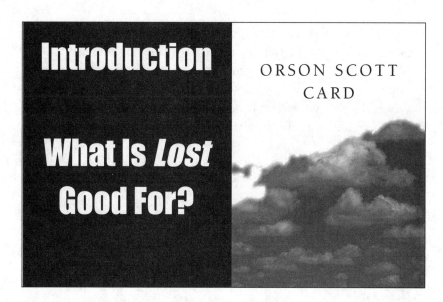

Introduction

ORSON SCOTT CARD

What Is *Lost* Good For?

Back in 1998, my son Geoffrey and I came up with a group of proposals for television series to pitch to various producers and networks. At the time, Geoffrey was writing under the name "Rob Porter" to try to avoid son-of-better-known-author syndrome. One of Geoffrey's ideas was expressed in a mere two paragraphs:

LOST
ROB LEE PORTER AND ORSON SCOTT CARD

One hour drama series (fantasy adventure): Survivors of the crash of an L.A.-to-New-York flight soon realize that they are not where they ought to be—maybe not even on Earth. Jungle, desert, medieval villages, modern towns where people have never heard of America—they want only to go home, but it's the one place they can't find. Robinson Crusoe in Oz.

This idea is dangerous—it could easily degenerate into Gilligan's Island or Lost in Space. But if properly developed, this story would allow an ensemble of characters to grow, develop relationships with each other, and face important moral dilemmas as they struggle to understand where they are each week and how to get back to reality. Star Trek *with civilians—and without having to fake any space stuff.*

We even copyrighted this little prospectus, back in 1997.

No, I'm not claiming that we had even a trace of influence on the Lindelof/Lieber/Abrams TV series that this book explores and celebrates; nobody's going to get sued. My point is merely that what makes this series work is not the idea—or at least not *just* the idea. Because the idea was "in the air." Indeed, one might even say that it was obvious.

But not so obvious that just anybody could have done it. In fact, there are so many ways to do it badly that I made the decision not to push this idea or pursue it beyond the handful of people we showed those paragraphs to. I knew enough about writing to know that this would be almost impossible to pull off, not just for me and Geoffrey, but for anyone.

That's why it seems almost a miracle that it has been done so well in the series *Lost*.

How Television Series Work

When television began, it sounded the death knell of the fiction magazine. People turned from the quick read of the *Redbook* or *Argosy* short story to the equally quick, but much cheaper and easier-to-absorb, half- and one-hour episodes of television. The trouble was that, until recently, television simply didn't deliver the full range of what newspaper and magazine fiction used to give its audience.

That's because what triumphed in television was the series.

There had been fiction series before—indeed, America had long supported the Nancy Drew, Hardy Boys, and other series aimed at kids. But when a story had to be broken up into once-a-week episodes on television, it forced certain structural decisions.

There was no way to build a word-of-mouth audience for a one-shot teleplay. In those days before videotape, when something aired, it was over. If you saw it and loved it, good for you—and too bad for any of your friends you might tell about it, because it would never be aired again.

Introduction

The only way to build a loyal, predictable, continuing audience (which is what advertisers craved) was either to create a brand name (*Hallmark Hall of Fame*) or . . . a series.

What worked was repetition. People who liked a series could expect to tune in week after week and see the same characters living through very similar stories. So people could tell their friends and they could tune in and have the same experience. Continuing viewers got a story each week that was at least marginally new, but word of mouth could help the audience grow.

The only time the characters changed in any meaningful way was as a reflection of business decisions outside the storyline. Like on the *Andy Griffith Show,* when Gomer Pyle (Jim Nabors) left Mayberry to join the Marines and was replaced at the local garage by his cousin Goober Pyle (George Lindsey), who played the same buffoon but with a different face. The real motivation for the change was so that Jim Nabors could star in the spin-off TV series *Gomer Pyle, USMC*— which was based on the play and movie that made Andy Griffith a star, *No Time for Sergeants*.

Or the weird transformation that struck the character of Darrin Stephens on *Bewitched*, when, instead of being a hapless pantaloon who looked very much like the actor Dick York, he became a hapless pantaloon who looked very much like the actor Dick Sargent.

The good thing about repetitive series starring unchanging characters is that if the audience takes them to heart, they get to return week after week to the warm embrace of a "family" that doesn't quarrel with them or make surprising demands or become estranged.

The bad thing about those unchanging characters is that, after a while, they cloy. We tuned in and glanced at the screen for a few moments and then sighed and said, "Oh, yeah. This again."

Very few series had real staying power. *Andy Griffith* was one; *Gunsmoke* and *Bonanza* held up the traditions of westerns. *Dragnet* represented cop shows and *The Rockford Files* and *Magnum, P. I.* took care of private-eye adventures. *Dallas* was the glitzy soap opera, and *The Waltons* served as America's country soap.

Other shows that lived for many years in syndication were relatively short-lived in their original runs: *Star Trek* and *Gilligan's Island* barely got through the magical three-year run that made syndication even possible. Why? Because, for the general public, the novelty had worn off. We got tired of them. The cast of continuing characters was too small, their relationships were too predictable, the writers were clearly straining to come up with new plotlines, and the flaws began to be more annoying to an audience that was no longer surprised by anything.

Both of them continued to appeal to an audience of fanatics who memorized the episodes and for whom they became more a way of life than an entertainment. But that's another matter entirely; for the networks, as they seek to put series on the air that will draw a large audience for many years, the numbers weren't there and it was time to pull the plug.

As it is time to pull the plug on most series—sometimes after their first episodes have barely had time to air.

The Problem of Weekly Television

One can argue that this is the reason television is such a bad artistic medium—for in the endless search to have not just a good large audience, but the *best* and *biggest* audience on any given weeknight, the networks regularly jettison series which have high quality in favor of series that, in a word, suck, but in a very popular way.

And yet I believe that in the long run, it is quality that lasts. While the economics of it demand that all television series aspire to as large an audience as possible, this in no way implies that these series *must* be bad or even *should* be bad. (Except, of course, in the eyes of elitists for whom it is an article of faith that any entertainment that is beloved by millions must be not just inferior, but downright pernicious, the enemy of "real art." But elitists are only happy when they're reading or watching something that only they and their friends appreciate, so we need hardly concern ourselves with them and their private pleasures.)

There are truly excellent series that disappear too soon—*Firefly*, for instance, which might have appealed to a much larger audience than it got if we had had a chance to hear of it before it was canceled.

But by and large, the series that last for many years are the ones that:

Introduction

1. *Create a situation a lot of people can believe in,*
2. *Create a cast of characters that a lot of people care about, and*
3. *Are productive of many engaging and fresh-seeming storylines.*

Fresh-seeming storylines. Ay, there's the rub!

How do you keep coming up with new storylines without changing the characters to such a degree that the audience stops liking them? Yet how do you keep people caring about characters who never seem to learn or grow or change?

That's the worst problem with family-centered series. The children grow up! John-Boy leaves the mountain! The cute kids aren't cute anymore!

That problem of aging characters was the death, ultimately, of *Family Ties* and *Growing Pains*. Both series tried the "have a baby" gambit, and it was kind of sad watching Leonardo DiCaprio try to breathe new life into *GP* as a semi-adopted street kid. *Full House* lasted forever mostly because they had such a young cast of first-rate child actors. Even the twin babies who were cast as infants grew up to be passably talented—pure luck, but it paid off: a seven-year run, instead of the six that *FT* and *GP* had to settle for.

We've also watched series kill themselves—or nearly kill themselves—by fiddling with a romantic relationship. *Moonlighting* famously self-destructed when they finally let Maddie (Cybill Shepherd) and David (Bruce Willis) get together (though there were other reasons as well). And *Cheers* nearly met the same fate when Sam (Ted Danson) and Diane (Shelley Long) were allowed to, er, mate. The answer, of course, was to dump Diane, first out of the relationship, and then out of the show entirely; bringing in Kirstie Alley, as Rebecca Howe, gave the series six more years of life.

How can the producers of a series find a balance between the hunger of the audience for a repetitive experience, and the equally fierce hunger for novelty and change?

Soap operas have always thrived on change—but traditionally these are daily shows, and their progress through the storylines is incremental. Generally speaking, if you miss a day or two, you haven't missed anything at all, since half of every episode consists of characters telling each other what happened to them or others in previous episodes.

But prime-time series have only one episode a week—they can't advance quite so incrementally. And if they make big changes, then they are practically demanding that the audience *never* miss an episode or they'll become confused or completely left behind.

Let's look at how *Moonlighting* worked. We might have forgotten now, but when it came out in the mid-eighties, it had the most sparkling writing and the most entertaining love-hate relationship on television (yes, even more than *Remington Steele*, on both counts, though clearly *Moonlighting* was *Remington Steele*'s love child).

The characters changed. The relationship developed. But it killed the series, for two reasons. First, as with Sam and Diane in *Cheers*, once the two admitted they were in love and hopped in the sack, the romantic tension was over. Second, and perhaps more importantly, the writers spent so much time and effort on the ongoing relationship between the characters, they forgot that it was a *one-hour mystery drama*—they began to treat the weekly mysteries as virtual throwaways.

And that was a mistake. Because prime-time television is *not* just an incremental soap opera. Each episode must also stand alone—we have to care not just about the main characters, but also about *this week's episode*. Otherwise, we learn to think of the series as missable. I remember my wife and me saying to each other, "No point in staying home to see it, it's just Maddie and David fooling around again."

The Evolution of a Solution

Friends got ten years of life, but not necessarily because they solved the problems I'm talking about. *Friends* had the benefit of consistently brilliant writing and the most gifted ensemble of comic actors ever assembled into a single television comedy. (And in a world that once saw *Mary Tyler Moore* and *Dick Van Dyke*, that's saying something.)

They had a productive situation, though—a group of engaging but semiloser singles whose friendships with each other were productive of conflict and romance, as well as laughs. They had that thread of soap opera and nursed it delicately along; and when one pairing became unproductive, there was always another one filled with tension. The characters grew and changed.

They also had a history. Not just a joke history, but real backstories that had influence on present events.

Of course, the writers often dipped into the standard bag of tricks—the identical relative played by the same actress, as the most obnoxious example—but they got a good nine years anyway.

Law and Order took the opposite tack. They gave us characters we came to love, but they spent almost *no* time on their personal stories. Rather, they concentrated relentlessly each week on the mystery-and-trial, in a semidocumentary style, so we got caught up in the particular events of the episode, and were almost never distracted from it by the personal troubles and stories of the repeating characters. The only time we saw them as people was when their personal problems influenced the course of events in the investigation or the trial; and then, if a character became too committed to a distracting course of action, they dropped him or her.

Thus Chris Noth ended his long run as Mike Logan by punching out a miscreant in front of the TV cameras. He was the last of the original cast. Sam Waterston is, I believe, the actor with the longest tenure and has emerged as probably the only nondisposable character. But the point is that, with the possible exception of Waterston, the writers have been ruthless with the cast. They made the story structure the star of the show, and kept the characters relatively interchangeable.

This was perceived as realism: we might miss a character, but as in any workplace, people come and go. With good casting and good writing—and only a few missteps in either category—they have made this not only an incredibly long-running series, but have also spun off many daughter-series, each with its own committed audience.

NYPD Blue, despite its much-vaunted blue content, did not last for its eleven seasons because of the occasional butt shot or side view of a breast. Such gimmicks might help attract an initial audience of the curious; *NYPD Blue* lasted because it found its own balance between the episode and the continuing stories. Unlike *Law and Order*, *Blue* put its characters at the center of a strong soap opera. But, unlike *Moonlighting*, the soap opera was not about just one thing, but kept changing as the characters' lives changed.

They did learn one thing from *Law and Order*, though: change the cast. It might not have been their plan from the start (it's doubtful *L&O* started with such a plan, either), but they made it work. When David Caruso pulled a Chevy Chase and jumped ship after the first season, *LA Law* alumnus Jimmy Smits proved just as strong, as did Rick Schroder after him. There was practically a revolving door for the women—and yet we cared about all of them.

Watching these excellent shows, one could almost believe that the prime-time series had evolved about as far as it could go.

Dickens and the Serial

But no. Because outside of the television genre, there was another great tradition that had seemingly died: the serialized novel.

The master of that form, the first author we think of when it's mentioned, was Charles Dickens. In a way, he and the other creators of serialized fiction were the first to face the challenges now faced by the writers of weekly TV series. But unlike movie series, which were intended to be spun out indefinitely, Dickens created weekly series that built together into a single coherent whole. When the serial was complete, it was a novel. It could be read from beginning to end, whereupon it would reach a conclusion and all the plot threads were resolved.

Not only that, but Dickens created characters so memorable that we could keep track of them week after week even if there were several installments in which they did not appear (though he was deft about reminding his readers of them from time to time, so they never slipped entirely from memory).

Dickens's trick was to imbue his characters with entertaining eccentricities, tag them with memorable and evocative names, and then involve them integrally in the life of the protagonist.

The protagonist himself, however, was the almost nondescript viewpoint character: He was there to focus our eyes on the action and give us someone to identify with, *not* to be entertaining in himself. Thus we readers are able to identify with David Copperfield or Oliver Twist or Esther Summerson or Phillip Pirrip, appreciating their virtues, and though sometimes we are frustrated when these viewpoint characters are trapped by honor or naiveté or momentary weakness into making their own situation worse, we always find ourselves sliding comfortably back inside their skin, identifying with them easily in their struggle to find their place in the world.

It looks like it should be a formula that could be adapted easily to television.

The problem is that it is *not* a simple formula. It's a *strategy*, and a good one. But it must be coupled with absolutely brilliant storytelling in order to function well. Assigning eccentricities to make lesser characters memorable is fine—*if* you also know how to make them fascinating. Even the unlikable characters must fascinate us—yes, Uriah Heep (like Jonas Chuzzlewit and Mr. Tulkinghorn and Bill Sykes) is repulsive, but he is also dangerous and seemingly untouchable.

And the storyline must be endlessly surprising. It can be thick with archetypes, and it must have a central skeleton upon which everything else is built, but you don't know how *any* of the individual storylines are going to play out. For instance, in *Bleak House*, Tulkinghorn looks like the central villain of the piece—and then he is murdered long before the end of the story, and suddenly we're dealing with a murder mystery in which a cop, whom up to now we have disliked, becomes the agent of justice as he keeps first one, then another of our favorite characters from being wrongly executed for the crime. No one could have guessed that *Bleak House* would suddenly, at least in several of its plotlines, become a detective story.

More importantly, the key events all depend on complicated moral decisions, in which two good choices compete with each other, or two bad ones. In other words, the hero isn't just dealing with bad guys, he has to try hard not to *be* a bad guy himself. And even good people make terrible decisions and have to live with the consequences. This is what makes the characters more than their eccentricities. Their own sense of honor or decency keeps them from doing things they desperately wish they could do; or, having violated their own honor, they have to find some way to make things right again. It is this, more than any other single element of the Dickensian story, that raises it above the level of all the other newspaper serials of the day and makes these stories live on in public memory.

Still, each novel has its central story thread, which binds all aspects of the tale together. In *Great Expectations* Pip has an unknown benefactor who is not at all the person he expected, and must attempt to become worthy of this unearned gift. *Bleak House* is built around a court case and the story can't resolve until the case does; *Chuzzlewit* has the question of where the title character intends to bestow his money; we can't be content until young Oliver Twist safely attains his rightful place in society.

The moral choices therefore do not take place in a vacuum. The readers hold to a thread of story as they wind their way through the maze of eccentric characters and complicated moral dilemmas.

Few prime-time series have even attempted to use the Dickensian strategy of serialization, and fewer still have succeeded.

Attempts at Single-Thread Series

Murder One was an attempt to tell a single coherent story in one season—twenty-two episodes. There would be a single court case, and we would follow the lawyers through its ups and downs. Unfortunately, the clear (but inaccurate) impression was given that if you didn't watch every single episode from the start, you would never be able to catch up. It felt like too much of a commitment, and discouraged many from starting.

Still, the series had its audience, primarily, I believe, because of the brilliant Daniel Benzali as the lead detective. He was a character of mythic proportion. Unfortunately, the network thought that *he*, being bald and middle-aged, must be the reason people weren't watching in appropriate numbers. The more likely reason was that the character of the defendant was so utterly unsympathetic and uninteresting. So when they dumped Benzali, they unwittingly dumped the series.

The X-Files did not begin as a single coherent story, but by the end it had evolved into one. Unfortunately, the continuing cast was too small, too enigmatic, and too unknowable to evoke the kind of passion that lifts a serial to Dickensian heights.

24 was (and remains) the first truly successful attempt to tell a season-long story—and then to tell another, and then another, using the same casts. In essence, each *year* is like an episode in a traditional series; but each *week* is like an installment of a Dickensian serial. The writers are brilliant and ruthless—anyone (except Kiefer Sutherland) can die, and probably will. And the moral dilemmas are every bit as cruel (and rarely as uplifting) as any in Dickens's work.

The trouble is that because, as the concept requires, each season takes place entirely within a single day, there is no time for characters to grow. They can have epiphanies, but they cannot evolve over time. Nor do they have time to reflect, or even, really, to learn. Decisions must all be made in an instant. There can be no turning back. Thus 24 is Dickensian in some ways, but remains a thriller at its core. And ultimately, the viewer is bound to see the stitching pop here and there where the writers, talented as they are, were unable to make it *really* believable that all this could have happened in a single day.

Which brings us back, at last, to *Lost*.

The Perfect Television Series?

It is impossible to call anything perfect until it is complete—because *Lost* is still in process, we know it can still collapse in ruins. Those who doubt this possibility have only to remember how hopeful we all were after *The Matrix* debuted, only to watch all those profound questions get such tedious or ridiculous answers that the second and third installments were only marginally watchable.

But let's assume that the executive producers, who are mature storytellers, know exactly what they're doing and have the capacity to deliver answers worthy of the questions they have raised. How are they doing right now, in midstream, at creating what Dickens created: a serialized story that, when it is completed, will stand as an admirable, memorable, satisfying whole?

In other words, how are they doing at taking a core idea that *anyone* could have thought of—that some of us *did* think of—and turning it into something that has never been achieved on television before?

For there is no way they can do what 24 has done so well—complete the story and then go on for another round. The folks at 24's CTU headquarters can resolve their crisis and then go about their business until the next season's crisis propels them into yet another near-fatal day of frenzied world-saving.

But once *Lost* reveals its secrets—what really is going happening on the island, what it's all *for*—what are they going to do? Crash another plane the next season? Or—I know!—they'll do *Lost* with a cruise ship that crashes on a *dry* island with lots of ancient gods around. Or...do *Lost* in a moon colony when suddenly and inexplicably their supply ships stop coming and they hear no more communications from Earth! Or how about *Lost* right in the middle of Kansas when a train derails and...

I know, it's nauseating *me*, too. It reminds me of those horrible "Let's do *Speed* on a train!" meetings that infested Hollywood for a few years. Though when you consider that *Speed* began as "Let's do *Die Hard* on a bus!" you have to admit that sometimes derivative thinking can lead to something pretty good.

Usually, though, it leads to the artistic equivalent of Ebola—bleeding everywhere and no hope of survival.

No, *Lost* cannot be spun out indefinitely, with a new set of castaways every few years. It must reach an ending, and the ending must satisfy us. It *can't* turn out to be Bobby Ewing's long nightmare, because the writers surely know we would find them and kill them, and no jury would convict us. If all the seeming magic turns out to have realistic causes, then those had better be not just convincing but *thrilling*, because losing the magic will just about kill us. But if the magic is too far-fetched, we will again turn away in disgust, because it will feel like the problems weren't solved, they were just made to disappear in a cheap trick with mirrors.

We'll assume, though, that the writers know what they're doing and the answers will make us laugh with *delight* or cry with *relief*—rather than with, respectively, scorn or disappointment.

Here, midway through the second season (I just saw Sayid, Ana Lucia, and Charlie return with the tale of what they found in the grave of Henry Gale's wife), how successful are these writers at coming up with something truly Dickensian?

The Situation

It's not just a plane crash. As I already proved, anyone can think of that. It's not even the island, for even though the Robinson Crusoe aspects of the story were fascinating at first, that wouldn't have kept the series going even to the end of the first season.

Introduction

What a serial needs is a situation that is productive of interesting stories, and we have that. Partly it's because every person who lived through the crash (and every person they meet on the island) is a source of relationships, which is where stories come from. Mostly, though, it's because of the mysteries.

Some of them point to fantasy—the mystical numbers, the way Walt's interests keep turning real, Locke's healing (and his sudden momentary relapse just at the moment when it can cost someone's life), the way people are sometimes nothing but whispering apparitions.

Some of them point to science fiction—the laboratory where Claire and her baby were obviously about to be the victims of a mad-scientist plot, the serum that the previous tender of the hatch was injecting himself with, the mechanical explanations that keep turning up for otherwise fantastical events. (Ah, there are polar bears in the training film! Ah, the monster is a *machine!*) The Dharma conspiracy looks like it might hold all the answers. After all, supplies are still being parachuted in. Who built this vast mechanism? Is anyone still in charge?

Some of them point to religion—Locke's mystical belief that all of this is happening for the island's own purpose, the hint that only the *good* were taken from the beach where the tail-section survivors ended up, the sense that everyone is being morally tested and given a chance to reform or grow up or heal or find hope—whatever it is they most needed. This leads to metaphysical speculations about whether they're alive or not, or whether the Others are evil or merely a phantasm. Whoever is in charge, is it God or the devil?

Some of them point to allegory—it is almost pathetically easy to find real-world analogues of all the storylines. "They are civilization in the midst of barbarians"; "they are ignorant people arrogantly assuming that whatever they don't understand must be evil"; "they play golf while the world is collapsing around them"; "humans are here, so polar bears have to die!"; "look how their first recourse is to weapons"; "isn't Charlie just like America after 9/11 when he preemptively kills Ethan instead of learning from him?" Such allegorical readings generally tell more about the observer than about any intent on the part of the writers of *Lost*.

All these mysteries work together to create the overall thread of the story, the skeleton that holds it all together. What we care about week by week are the stories of the individual characters and their relationships with each other. It's way cool when the heavy metal doors come crashing down in the hatch and a mysterious map is projected on the door where only the injured-and-bleeding Locke can see it; but it's far *more* important to us, at the moment anyway, to see how the Locke/Jack conflict will play out, and to find out who Henry Gale really is and what team he's playing for. (We're reasonably sure now that he does not have a farm in Kansas and a niece named Dorothy.)

The Characters

Other essays in this book will be exploring some of the characters in detail. For my purpose it is enough to note that out of the chaos on the beach right after the crash, we had several characters emerge. Initially, Jack Shephard was our neutral observer character—which is precisely what we needed. He took bold action to save others, he had suffered his own wound—he was the hero we needed to identify with.

The other characters, for the first few weeks, were generally marked, as Dickens marked his characters, by their eccentricities. John Locke is the quiet bald guy with the incredible knife collection who knows everything about survival. Sawyer is the cynical, jeering scrounge who seems to want everyone to hate him. Kate is the pretty woman with the criminally dark past.

And the even simpler ones: Jin and Sun, the Korean couple who speak no English. Charlie, the druggie rock star. Hurley, the big guy. Michael, the single dad of a reluctant son, Walt. Claire, the pregnant girl. Sayid, the Iraqi ex-soldier.

These obvious markers kept them separable and memorable in our minds until, week by week, we were given a chance to come to know them as real people with complicated pasts.

Backstory—that's been a key element in the brilliance of *Lost*. Flashbacks are usually deadly—but the writers have used them here as the best novelists do. We *only* get a flashback that is (a) interesting in and of itself and (b) pertinent to the present action, so that we don't resent the interruptions.

Introduction

It's not just that these characters all have troubled pasts (who doesn't, as long as you define "troubled" broadly enough), it's that their pasts help shape their moral decisions now. Because of what they've been through before, they either do or refrain from doing things that would ordinarily have seemed inexplicable. By the time we find out Sun actually speaks fluent English, we have a good idea why she keeps this information from her husband.

At the same time, the backstories help us comprehend things that otherwise would have been inexplicable. Why is Jin able to fish when no one else can, and yet seems such a dangerous guy? Why is Sawyer so egregiously offensive to everyone, when he surely can see that it's only going to make them hate him? Why does Jack have to ruin everything, even though in his heart he clearly thinks he's only doing what "must be done"? Why is Kate so emotionally fragile and yet so stubborn, not at all like the kind of person who needs to be transported in handcuffs?

The most difficult characters to flesh out are the ones with the most trite eccentricities. Charlie—how do you make a drug addict ex-rock star *interesting* again, when we've had the same story over and over again in the tabloids? And Hurley—when you see writers trot out a fat guy, it usually means that they're desperate, willing to trade their brains in for a cheap laugh. Instead, they have each become strong individuals, whose aspirations we share and whose demons we understand.

Thus when Hurley runs yelling for them *not* to blow open the hatch, it isn't so we can laugh at the fat guy running. In fact, by that point he has been so well created as a character that we don't really even *think* of him as the fat guy anymore (and we resent Sawyer when he does!). He's *Hurley*, our incredibly lucky/unlucky friend whose terror at seeing those numbers on the hatch casing is completely understandable.

And by the time Claire has her baby, she's long since ceased to be the pregnant girl, just as Sayid is far more to us than the Iraqi interrogator. And the doomed characters whose incestuous-seeming relationship had led to overlapping layers of resentment and devotion had become so much more than clichés that many of us wept with those who loved them when they died.

Heck, even a throwaway character was made rather endearing before people started getting bits of Arzt on them.

This is like Dickens at his best. No opportunity for interesting characterization is discarded unused.

Even the single (but huge) flaw in the characterizations in *Lost* is shared with Dickens:

The cast of characters is too small. Out of forty-odd survivors of the crash, how many do we actually know? Arzt made his little joke about not being part of the "merry little band of adventurers," but it's not really a joke. Why don't these guys ever talk to any of the other people?

I won't say, "What would it cost them to let them talk to minor characters now and then?" because I know the answer: every actor who speaks must be paid union scale, and the budget for *Lost* is already sky-high, thank you very much. Producers of TV shows don't make profits until syndication, usually, and they have to watch pennies during the actual run of the show. (Thank heaven for the DVD sales...but more on that later.)

Still, they're following right in Dickens's footsteps on this one. Even though his novels take place all over England, or at least all over London, and he populates them with a dazzling array of characters, you can be sure that if any character is given more than a couple of words to say, he's going to end up being connected in some weird way or another to the main threads of the storyline. The nice ex-soldier who owns a shooting range in *Bleak House* has to be somebody else's long-lost son; the street urchin who takes a veiled lady to her husband's grave is *also* the reason that same lady's long-lost daughter gets smallpox, and then when he dies, he does so in the aforesaid ex-soldier's establishment, cared for by the doctor who is in love with the lady's smallpox-scarred daughter, and...can a world get any smaller than that?

By Dickens's standards, the cast of characters is positively huge, because in the backstory sequences we are constantly introduced to new characters played by interesting guest stars.

Those backstory guest stars are where the budget for cast members goes, and it's the right choice. Use them once, send them away until you decide to write another sequence where they pop up again.

But introduce another minor character on the island, and the audience starts trying to find reasons why they're going to be important to the plot. Like that shrink who came with the tail-section group—very minor, but Hurley has a crush on her and she has to help Claire recover her lost memories. Once introduced, these minor characters refuse to stay minor. Even the dead ones keep cropping up in backstory and other revelations—Ethan is turning out to be a major player, a year after Charlie plugged him. They can't end this series until we know *all* their stories.

A Hundred Little Epiphanies

The real secret of *Lost* is the secret of Dickens's serials: These aren't really "episodes" or "installments" we're watching. They are really a single, continuous story. Yet we leave each episode satisfied, even thrilled, not because we've been given grand adventures, but because we have been shown at least one character's epiphany—a realization, a flash of light, a glimmer of understanding or resolution—immediately followed by a tongue of fire, a glimmer of danger or deception that functions like, but actually is not, the traditional cliffhanger.

In other words, each week we get a *chapter*. Nothing is actually resolved. But something is understood, even as something else is made more mysterious. And as long as each of those epiphanies feels important and truthful to us, we will keep tuning in for another dose.

Meanwhile, though, the engine driving the story is more than the writers' understanding of human relationships—though these are often deep and rarely smack of case studies out of half-remembered soc or psych classes. In addition, the writers are—unconsciously, I hope—tapping into deep archetypes.

The Others sometimes function as Behemoth, at other times as the prophet(s) of the Beast of Revelation—they do evil things, but now we understand that they are themselves afraid of an even greater evil. In this they are rather like Saruman in *Lord of the Rings*, always aware of Sauron but trying to get away with stuff behind his back. Because somewhere, even deeper in the background, there is the "him" that even Ethan was afraid of—someone pulling the strings.

We have all the character types, and all the story types as well.

At times Sawyer is the cynic, Hurley the buffoon, Jin the pantaloon; Locke and Jack alternate as the father figure to others, to be rebelled against and resisted—while they also play the same role to each other.

We get the archetypes that hide in all powerful stories:

Crossing the sea, out of which Leviathan rises.

Going down into the labyrinth under the earth, where the monster lurks and sometimes the doors slam down and you must crawl through even narrower tunnels to get out.

Going to the *Black Rock*, which turns out to be an echo of the sea in the form of a wooden ship stranded high above sea level, which contains within it a deadly dragon's "cave" out of which the heroes must extract terrifying treasure without being blasted—which, of course, one of them is.

There is a boundary which cannot be crossed.

There is the ritual death of the plane crash.

There is the injured hero—indeed, a plethora of injured heroes.

There is the missing father, and also the hated or dangerous father.

There is the person in disguise, and the revelation of true identity—it happens over and over again, in different ways, as all kinds of masks are stripped away.

There are the Fair Folk, at once fascinating and terrifying yet another aspect of the Others. After all, weren't the fairies reputed to carry off a human child from time to time? We lack only the changeling that they leave in its place.

There are the dead, literally in their graves near the beach, and legendarily in the story of the Frenchwoman's dead compatriots. The dead sometimes come out of their graves, as Jack's father did, leading Jack into the jungle to where he found the water the survivors needed so desperately.

There is the huntress Diana, though French, not Greek, was her first language. The messenger Hermes, though he is known to them as Walt. Astarte, the goddess of love and fertility, who judges men— sorry, Charlie. Or watch her tend her garden in her earth-mother guise. And check out the prankster, Loki/Puck/Sawyer. See how Jack plays cards with the devil and wins at the devil's game, bringing healing back to the people who depend on him. And who is the god of war?

I believe—or at least *hope*—that *none* of these archetypes has been consciously inserted into the story. The result of *that* sort of thing is usually a mess. Archetypes work only when they are so deeply believed by the storyteller and the audience that they merely *feel* right. As soon as an archetype is deliberately inserted in order to convey a deliberate meaning, it is stripped of most or all of its power.

When archetypes are working properly, they do not follow some careful program. Rather, they come out of nowhere, striking hard below the belt and then disappearing again. We feel each impact, but do not know what it was or where it came from.

But that is always a part of storytelling that moves us enough to shape our view of the world around us. In *Boston Legal,* David E. Kelley writes all his moral lessons out in the open, where his self-deceptions are merely pathetic and he ends up preaching only to the choir—but can feel quite smug about having taught that audience a thing or two. In *Lost*, the writers trust their instincts, their sense of what is true and important, to reveal deeper things, in a longer-lasting way, without their having to intervene consciously at all.

They aren't trying to score points in a debate. They aren't trying to convert people to a religion or political camp. They're trying to tell stories that feel important and true to *them*—and therefore they have a much better chance of winning their audience over, to see the world through their eyes and be, sometimes a little and sometimes profoundly, changed.

Which is the point of it all, isn't it? Cultures and communities are created and sustained by stories that tell us why people do the things they do, show us which actions and motives are noble and which are contemptible, and light in our minds the memory of having done great deeds and suffered great calamities.

They become our shared memory. And those of us who have watched and cared about the stories in *Lost* are, I believe, better people for having done so; better people because we are likelier to behave in ways that will make our communities and cultures the better for our having lived through the experience of *Lost.*

For art can be technically good without ever becoming good *for* us; can we not measure technical quality in art by its effectiveness in transforming or affirming the values of a worthy community? Lost is good medicine, even if the physicians who administer it cannot themselves explain just how it works.

Game Theory

JOYCE MILLMAN

*Anyone who has ever become immersed in an all-consuming comput-
er game knows what it's like when you surface and return to the real
world. Mere reality can seem so tame and pointless. Plus, nobody's
keeping score. Then again, reality can also seem dangerous and uncertain compared to a game. In the real world, you never know when
you've cleared a level and the bad guys will stop coming at you.*

*And even when you "win," there's always another level ahead of you
that you can't possibly beat. Oh, wait...that's true of games and reality.
Are we sure there's really a boundary between them?*

BLAME IT ON THE POLAR BEARS. They're the reason why I can't commit
to any of the usual theories of *Lost*.

Oh, it's not that the theories are bad. I mean, there are times when
you can almost convince me that the castaways are dead but they
don't know it. These people are obviously lost souls—all those un-
resolved past relationships, all those deaths (both premeditated and
accidental) on their consciences. They could easily be in some kind
of island purgatory, waiting at the karmic baggage claim for their re-

demption or damnation to come around. And my respect for the afterlife theory of *Lost* only increased with the opening of the hatch and
the discovery of the wiggy Desmond living in a biosphere that once
belonged to a scientific experiment called the Dharma Initiative. Is
Desmond a figure of divinity, or a demon of the demimonde? And
what about the enigmatic task—inputting Hurley's numbers into a
computer and hitting the Execute key every 108 minutes—that Desmond stuck the castaways with when he abandoned his post? That
possibly meaningless button-pushing sure looks like another form of
purgatory (or hell) to me, more punishment for our castaways as they
float in the ether of eternity.

Then again, there are times when I am equally susceptible to the
theory that the survivors of Oceanic Flight 815 are alive and everything that is happening to them, however bizarre, is really happening. Remember, we are within the elastic boundaries of SF storytelling
here. So the island could be, as the grainy Dharma Initiative "Orientation" film stated in the third episode of season two, a hot spot of electromagnetism, presumably wreaking havoc with any plane or boat that
wanders into its pull. And the shadowy Initiative may have seriously
screwed up the island to the point where an "incident" really will happen if that Execute button isn't pushed at the appointed times—as the
film so vaguely and ominously cautioned. Yes, either theory is sound,
and I could have chosen a side and rooted for the team if not for one
problem: I couldn't stop thinking about the polar bears.

Yes, I know, they were finally explained (sort of) in the "Orientation" film; the Dharma Initiative included zoology experiments,
which were signified by a brief scene of two polar bears merrily wrestling on an ice floe. So the polar bear that Sawyer shot in the pilot of
Lost was apparently neither a group hallucination nor the animal you
meet in hell. But even if the polar bear really did exist (on a Pacific
island), it still perplexed me so much that I turned to Google for an
explanation. Hey, did you know that polar bears symbolize reawak-
ening in dream imagery? Thanks, Google! I have come to realize,
however, that the Arctic beasts' symbolism is beside the point. Rather, it's their mere presence that is so nagging and intriguing. They are
just so disturbingly...*whimsical*. The polar bears are an odd, random detail—why not tigers or gigantic poisonous snakes, something

more jungle-like? And that randomness is what makes *Lost* so creepy, so weird, and so great. *Lost* sustains a chilling sense of normality skewed, of something not quite right with this picture. My flesh still crawls thinking about the scene in the first-season finale, when the fishing trawler appeared out of nowhere and the grizzled geezer at the helm eyed Walt and told Michael, in a terrifyingly amiable tone, "The thing is, we're gonna have to take the boy." This was definitely not the Gorton's fisherman bringing everyone some nice fish sticks.

And if you add the geezer and the polar bears to the show's other odd, random details (the monster, the hatch, Ethan Rom, the whispering voices on the wind), a vaguely familiar scenario emerges. Now, where have you seen hapless protagonists endlessly beset by random, inexplicable events and torments? Well, one place is the Bible—you know, plagues, disembodied voices, frogs falling from the sky, the sea parting. So maybe the castaways are at the mercy of a whimsical, cruel, polar-bear-loving God, or, at least, of someone with a serious God complex. But there's another, more mundane context in which characters are yanked around by someone who's having a big bunch of fun controlling their destinies and putting obstacles in their path just to watch them jump. And, frankly, here's where the polar bears led me down the slippery slope to weirdo-Theoryville. Because I can't let go of the idea that *Lost* is all a game—to be precise, a computer game.

Think about it. References to games, game-playing, and computers are sprinkled throughout *Lost*. Locke taught Walt how to play backgammon. Walt was also seen playing a hand-held computer game on the plane in the final flashback of season one. Hurley became a millionaire playing the lottery with his "cursed" numbers; on the island, he mapped out a makeshift golf course so the castaways could have some quality leisure time. And, of course, season two introduced us to the computer that must be obeyed in Desmond's lair. Are these references intended to be mischievous signposts pointing to the show's hidden premise? Then there's the fact that games seem to come up a lot in *Lost* co-creator J. J. Abrams's work. His spy show *Alias* is plotted like a chess game played with human lives; it also revolves around a gigantic puzzle, as the good guys try to figure out the ultimate purpose of the playful, otherworldly gadgets created by fifteenth-century inventor/seer Milo Rambaldi.

But for an even more startling hint about what sort of tricks Abrams might have up his sleeve for *Lost*, consider the "Help for the Lovelorn" episode Abrams wrote in 2000 for his old WB series *Felicity*. A surreal black-and-white homage to *The Twilight Zone*, "Help for the Lovelorn" climaxed with the show's heroine, college sophomore Felicity Porter, awakening to find herself trapped inside a smooth, stark box with her school pals Ben, Noel, Elena, and Julie. Boosted up on her friends' shoulders, Felicity bravely climbed the slippery walls and pushed off the lid, whereupon she fell over the edge. The scene shifted to a little Felicity doll lying face down on the floor. The camera pulled back to reveal Felicity's Goth roommate, Meghan, picking up the doll and scolding it ("How did that happen?") with a nasty little smirk. Throughout the series, nobody had ever been allowed to touch or look inside Meghan's most prized possession, her mysterious trinket box. But, finally, in this episode, we were shown what Meghan kept in the box—Felicity and her friends.

Yes, this was a larky, one-time-only episode of *Felicity*, but it gives you an idea of what's going on inside Abrams's brilliant, diabolical mind. If *Felicity* could be reinvented as a sadistic punkette playing with voodoo dolls, and if *Alias* is a never-ending game of strategy, then it's quite possible that *Lost* could be taking place in a virtual world, with the castaways as characters in a game controlled by unseen players. Once you consider this alternate explanation for what might really be going on in *Lost*, the random, freaky aspects of the show suddenly start to make sense. All things become plausible if they're happening in a virtual realm with no limits, if their function is to test the skill of the game's player, not to test the castaways' mettle. And, as of this writing (three episodes into season two), the most elegantly simple evidence that it's all a computer game is right before our eyes. The numeric code must be entered into the biosphere's computer and the Execute button pushed every 108 minutes or the program will crash. And what happens when you're playing on the computer and it crashes? Right—the game is over.

Lost is, in many ways, structured more like a computer game than a TV series. The show's storytelling is nonlinear, jumping around between real time and flashback. With mythology-rich and densely detailed episodes that can't be mastered in a single viewing, *Lost* was made to be replayed; it demands that viewers pay closer attention than they normally would to many other TV series, to be on the alert for clues and connections. "We're gonna have to watch that again," Locke told Jack after viewing the puzzling, overstuffed Dharma Initiative "Orientation" film; it was a sly commentary on the intense scrutiny with which *Lost* fans greet each episode.

Lost is an interactive TV experience in the tradition of *The X-Files* and *Buffy the Vampire Slayer*, except it has one huge advantage over those past series: time has created a more Internet-savvy viewership. And *Lost* fully embraces and plays to Web culture. ABC's official *Lost* Web sites, thelostexperience.com, thehansofoundation.org, and oceanicflight815.com, are strewn with hidden clues that extend *Lost* beyond one hour of TV time a week. And after each episode, fans gather on numerous *Lost* message boards, like thefuselage.com and lost-tv.com, to compare theories about The Meaning of It All. No detail is too tiny to escape the microscope—moments after the season two premiere aired, the boards were buzzing with heated debates about the brand of obsolete computer found inside the hatch. (The consensus seems to be that it's an Apple II tricked out with a Commodore keyboard.) *Lost* is the perfect show for a wired age in which most of us have become, out of necessity, a little bit techno-geeky.

And a little bit gamer-geeky as well. *Lost* bears more than a few similarities to the popular 1990s computer game *Myst*, largely in the way both borrow from Jules Verne's classic SF novel *Mysterious Island*. In *Mysterious Island*, a group of shipwreck survivors is marooned on a deserted island that seems to have a strange power of its own; it turns out that the island is the secret hideout of Captain Nemo (hello, Desmond), who functions as a deus ex machina in the survivors' lives. *Myst* begins with the player (also called "The Stranger") suddenly and cluelessly transported to Myst Island via the pages of a magical book which eventually reveals the island's history. The cold start of *Myst* was paralleled in the very first shot of *Lost*—Jack's eyes opening as he was sprawled on his back on the ground after the crash. Like *Myst* players, *Lost* viewers (and the show's characters) were plunged into the action with no preamble, left to negotiate a disorienting environment that has its own murky rules and logic.

In *Myst*, the player navigates through the game by figuring out the meaning and function of obtuse symbols and incongruous landmarks. *Lost* has the hatch; *Myst* has a spaceship, a clock tower, a giant gear, a log cabin, and an old sailing ship that has been split in two by a huge rock (it may have been the inspiration for the abandoned slave ship the *Black Rock* which the *Lost* castaways discovered in the season one finale). Caverns and tunnels are another important part of *Myst*, leading players to ancient subterranean cities filled with artifacts of past civilizations—much like the Dharma Initiative's underground biosphere on *Lost*, which is furnished with objects from the 1970s (turntable, vinyl record albums, lava lamp) and 1980s (the early-model personal computer) that had been left by previous inhabitants.

There is one major difference between *Lost* and *Myst*: there are no people in *Myst* (the island's godlike founder Atrus and his two sons make their presence felt mostly through words, with occasional holograms or voices). *Myst* is all atmosphere, a pervasive eerie emptiness punctuated by haunting electronic music and sound effects. But if you populated *Myst* with the lifelike virtual humanoids of, say, the computer game *The Sims*, you would have something very close to *Lost*. In *The Sims*, players control the daily lives of characters (named Sims) that are imbued with individual personalities, needs, wants, fears, and aspirations. (Players can also customize their Sims along these lines.) As *Lost* unfolded in season one, we were introduced to the main castaways, who were Sims-like in the array of ages, races, ethnicities, nationalities, personalities, belief systems, and the socioeconomic classes they represented. Each survivor has a backstory that ends with them boarding the doomed flight. But if they have backstories, doesn't this mean they had lives independent from the game? Not necessarily.

The backstories are told in flashback; we don't see the castaways' pre-crash lives in real time. And each backstory is triggered by an object of significance. For Kate, it's a toy airplane that belonged to the man she loved and killed. For Jack, it's his dead father's coffin, which he was escorting home from Australia. For Hurley, it's his cursed lottery numbers. For Sayid, it's a photograph of the woman he loved back in Iraq when he was a member of the Republican Guard and she was a freedom fighter. All of these objects of significance in *Lost* function the way "Easter eggs" do in computer and video gaming.

Easter eggs contain hidden information or new levels of a game; a player must figure out where the Easter egg is, as well as the code to open it. On *Lost*, each Easter-egg flashback gives the viewer more insight into what motivates the characters, provides more pieces to the larger puzzle, and more fuel for the various theories about the castaways' ordeal.

There are Easter eggs buried in the island's physical landscape as well. Sayid stumbled upon a trip wire in the sand that led to the hideout of Danielle Rousseau, the crazed lone survivor of a research team that washed up on the island sixteen years earlier. The discovery of Danielle provided the castaways with some information about the island (none of it good), as well as the location of a handy cache of dynamite. Boone found another Easter egg, a crashed two-seater airplane perched in the jungle trees, and it brought about his death. And, of course, Locke found the metal hatch on the jungle floor and blew it open in the first season's finale to reveal a thirty-foot-long tunnel. Season two opened with Locke and Kate entering the tunnel to discover Desmond's world below; in an ingenious blend of computer-game structure and TV storytelling, the tunnel had literally advanced the game, and the show, to the next level.

In *The Sims*, you can interfere with your Sims' everyday lives out of benevolence or sadism; you can make them work hard to achieve their aspirations (writing a novel, gaining a promotion) and move on to greater levels of physical and financial comfort, or you can torture them out of boredom or curiosity (have your Sims forget to take out their garbage or ignore the smoke coming out of the toaster and see what happens). The appeal of *The Sims* game is not hard to figure out—it lets you play God. But who is playing God on *Lost*? Who is at the keyboard with a Red Bull and a bag of Cheetos, showering the castaways with crises (illness, birth, death, clashes, natural, and man-made predators), or guiding them through their choices?

In the strictest sense, the many-headed deity behind *Lost* would be co-creators Abrams, Damon Lindelof, and Jeffrey Lieber (and the show's writers). In the metaphoric sense, though, the show's clue-scouring viewers are the ones playing the game. But within the fantastic realm of the show itself, there are several tantalizing possibilities about the true nature of the game and the players.

With a nod to the twist ending of Abrams's *Felicity* episode (as well as to the famous finale of *St. Elsewhere*, in which the hospital series was revealed to have taken place in the imagination of an autistic child), *Lost* could be a game playing out on the computer screens of Hurley and his fellow inmates at the psychiatric ward. Or maybe the game is metaphysical—after all, Desmond told the castaways that by inputting the code and executing the computer program, he was "saving the world." That computer in the biosphere could be the source of life, the hard drive at the end of the universe—a homage, perhaps, to Douglas Adams's concept of Earth as a powerful supercomputer built by an otherworldly intelligence. (It has probably not escaped the notice of *Hitchhiker's Guide to the Galaxy* readers that one of Hurley's magical, mystical lottery numbers is 42.) Did the Dharma Initiative write the program? Or could it have been running long before the scientists modified it for their own arcane purposes?

Then again, *Lost* could be spinning a *Matrix*-meets-*TRON* scenario, in which the castaways are humans trapped inside a dangerously advanced form of virtual reality. What if the "sickness" that killed Danielle's fellow crew members, and which Desmond believes pervades the island, is actually a computer virus? Could Ethan Rom (so close to ROM, "read only memory") and the Others be infected with the virus, and have mutated into malicious code? That would explain the injections Desmond shoots himself up with—they're his antivirus program.

Okay, I realize that I'm starting to sound like a glassy-eyed crackpot ("Dude! I'm not crazy!"). But in a few years, when the camera pulls back in the final scene of the final episode of *Lost* and the big revelation blows your mind, remember this: I told you so.

Joyce Millman is a freelance writer whose essays about TV and pop culture have appeared in the *New York Times*, Salon.com, the *Boston Phoenix*, and *Variety*. She was a finalist for the Pulitzer Prize in criticism in 1989 and 1991 for columns written while television critic for the *San Francisco Examiner*. She has contributed essays to the BenBella Smart Pop Anthologies *Alias Assumed*, *Flirting with Pride and Prejudice*, and *Mapping the World of Harry Potter*. She lives in the San Francisco area with her husband and son.

Staying Lost

CHARLIE W. STARR

There are those who obsessively catalog all the questions and puzzles and anomalies on Lost, *hanging around* Lost *Web sites and arguing over what it meant when Ethan fell this way and not that when Charlie shot him, and is he really dead or just pretending, and is his first name meant to evoke Vermont and the Green Mountain Boys?*

Then there are those of us who have given up on guessing anything. We just lie back in our recliners and let the show wash over us.

THE TAIL GOES ONE WAY and the head another. Locke stands up and helps; then, by firelight, the invisible dino-tron rips trees from the roots and Merridoc cum Charlie says, "Terrific" but isn't very happy. We watch the flashback twenty times or so, letting character thicken plot. The rain—"day turning into night, end-of-the-world type weather"—is a baptism. Forty-eight survivors plus one, not including the captain, who wakes and dies (from one flight too many) so he can get back to *Alias*. And that's only the first hour.

Re:vision

Jack and Kate lead but don't claim to be leaders (after she puts him in stitches on the side), though he sees dead man walking and she's a criminal. Bears and boars hound them though Vincent survives without a scratch and with quite a gloss on his coat. Sayid works on a boom box to capture Rousseau's chart topper—sixteen years and playing strong. Claire dehydrates, so the survivors split—beach from cave. Locke begins his lessons when Charlie becomes a moth. He takes FATE into his own hand (only to lose FAT later one letter at a time à la Hansel and Gretel bread crumbs). And though Shannon can't breathe to save her life, Hurley's greatest huffings and puffings can't lose him a single pound (though they do manage him a nice golf course).

Sawyer is as conniving as his fence-painting namesake Tom, but Locke is more Shaman than was philosopher John, and Sayid is an Iraqi Republican Guard torturer with a conscience and a noble heart. The woman from *Babylon 5* leaves more questions than answers. Claire dreams the truth, not in time for Hurley to make his list and check it twice. It doesn't matter that Ethan Rom (who has no connection to Wharton's *Ethan Frome* as far as I can tell) looks a thirty-something waspy geek—he can kidnap a nuclear family, beat the best trackers, beat Jack to the ground, and put caution in Locke's step.

Jack hates his father, Boone has sex with his sister, Claire is a single mom to a messianic baby, Michael is dad brand new to a preteen psychic son who knows what not to open—the bird flies into the sliding glass door and dies anyway, like Walt's mom, Jack's dad, Kate's love, Sawyer's childhood, Sayid's Muslim beauty (or so it at first seems), and Rousseau's child.

The hatch is Boone's bane and Locke's unlockable puzzle. The numbers are a combination to Hurley's fortunate curse. As for the briefcase Kate finds taking a bath (a *cheeky* ploy for ratings, no doubt), it has a key (buried with the dead marshal, but they are both soon dug up). Now Charlie can blow Ethan away, payback for Ethan's having killed him the first time. Loose Shannon has the hots for a man from a sexist, fundamentalist culture who has lost the love of his life. And he has the hots back? Well, at least she can read French.

Sun and Jin (whose food makes Claire's baby kick) talk in subtitles until she reveals her secret. They had a dog once—payment for a stay of contracted execution. She grows plants while he and Michael beat the crap out of each other, then make up and build a raft twice. They have less trouble communicating in two languages than husband and wife do in one. Jin teaches Hurley to fish but won't pee on him.

Claire saves herself, allowing Charlie to put her diary down which is good since she can't remember a thing. Sawyer shows up in everyone else's flashbacks, even the mystic pig's. His headaches redefine nerd glasses. Locke builds the baby a cradle and himself a trebuchet, loses his kidney to the guy from *Emergency*, almost loses his legs again, and sees the light, though it costs Boone his life after breaking the Madonna and talking to someone else claiming to be the survivors of Flight 815. Then the baby is born and the guy who always plays a sinister spy ring leader in the movies (*Long Kiss Goodnight, The Bourne Identity, X-Men 2*) narrates the recap episode to suck the rest of America in.

There's a moment when everyone wants Locke dead, even Shannon (though before she'd sarcastically referred to her only technically incestuous un-brother as "God's friggin gift to humanity"). Sayid, it turns out, ended terrorism in Australia. Sawyer's reading ends the baby's tears. Walt's the saboteur who has a change of heart. Rousseau sees smoke that warns of the Others, takes them to the *Black Rock*, and takes the baby. Jin and Sun play make-up while Arzt—suddenly a new, old character out of beach-survivor obscurity—plays with dynamite and blows himself up.

The Dark Territory—more questions than answers; Locke loves the security system. The raft is launched. The Others come by sea—turns out it was the wrong child. Everyone got on the plane in some strange way. They blow the hatch and its secret is revealed: a long row of rungs and a cliffhanger.

And that's only the first season.

Q Without A

They began almost immediately: the *Lost* boys (and girls) plunging into the adventure as far from primitive jungles as possible: the *virtual* reality, the Internet superhighway. Labeled "Losties," they've plumbed the mysteries and pointed out the inconsistencies together on the World Wide Web. Some have said the survivors didn't—they're all dead and the island is purgatory or limbo (or worse). After all, Jack says, "Three days ago we all died" and therefore doesn't want to know what Kate did before the crash. How could polar bears survive there, and why didn't they eat the one they killed? Australians keep correcting Americans on accents, idioms, spellings, geography, and which side of the road to drive on. How can people who've survived a crash be so healthy and healed?

The dead couple at the bottom of the lagoon couldn't still be holding hands. The camera crew appears in brief, freeze-frame-and-you'll-see-them shots (as noted by the truly anal retentive) all throughout the series. Perhaps Walt's supernatural abilities are the origin of the strange island phenomena: he reads a Spanish comic book with a polar bear in it and then is attacked by one (and that comic has aliens in it too!). Did Vincent survive the crash (or return to life) by Walt's power? The baby is named "Aaron" in the season finale titled "Exodus"—they haven't wandered the island wilderness forty years, but it has been forty days.

Dino-tron is actually (or apparently) a whiff of black cloud—is it a collection of nano-bots? The island may be a government experiment gone terribly wrong, a kind of Area 51 left on automatic to run its out-of-control experiments. Or it may be Captain Nemo's *Mysterious Island*—the base from which he launched the *Nautilus* 20,000 leagues ago. Or perhaps it's a Disney theme park gone awry (who names their kid "Walt" anymore?), the hatch a doorway to *Tomorrow Land*, the *Black Rock* a prop for *Pirates of the Caribbean* (where the dynamite is live and unstable). They could be caught in a parallel universe, a recurring time loop, a limbo-place between times—perhaps that's what Michael means when he says, "Time doesn't matter on a damn island!" Is it an alien experiment, an ark created by God to preserve a group of people from a worldwide apocalyptic disaster—alien attack, meteor strike, plague?

I like the various virtual-reality theories: while their bodies are held in technology-induced comas, their minds experience the island—when they die, they return to their bodies and wake up; or it's all a dream, or it's a VR game, or it's a game show—*Survivor* gone *Twilight Zone* in which the players don't know they're playing a game. But many Losties insist that it's all real, sometimes adamantly so: "It's all real; real, Real, Real!"—forgetting, I guess, that it's actually only a TV show.

The island may be moving, may be a Japanese stronghold from World War II, a refuge for survivors of a nuclear war—sent by some benevolent, though conspiratorial government, or even an old forgotten European mining colony wherein the miner's descendants have somehow become technologically more advanced than the rest of the world. There have been connections to Coleridge's "Rime of the Ancient Mariner" (the plane an albatross?), Saint John's *Apocalypse* (baby Aaron the Antichrist?), and Disney's *Finding Nemo* (Rousseau's song, "La Mer"). And let's not forget *Watership Down*, which figured prominently in *Donnie Darko*, which suggests maybe the parallel-universe theory isn't so strange after all. As for the numbers, they have more connections than can be counted—but someone on the Net did.

What's up with Ana Lucia, the box next to Locke's bed (called "Locke's Box" on the Internet, and no one misses the fact that he worked for a box company before the crash)? And what's the deal with the cable Sayid finds, with there being any survivors from a plane falling from 30,000 feet in the first place, and with the Others? My favorite *Others* theory has them as telepathic telekinetics, drawing people like themselves (i.e. Walt) to the island. And the most interesting insight to me is the point that all the survivors are either fatherless or have severe issues with their dads, a theme at the heart of American storytelling since the colonials flew from the lands of their fathers for an ocean voyage to an unknown place.[1]

There's the hatch, the child, the Others, the numbers, the monster, and the island's seeming sentient will (hmm...six numbers, six mysteries...) and in the end we're left with nothing certain but 4, 8, 15, 16, 23, 42 and the one theory that hasn't yet been suggested.

Surrender

Nearly two hundred years ago, the English poet John Keats discovered the secret to *Lost*:

---

[1] Think of *The Scarlett Letter*, where little Pearl wants the Reverend Mr. Dimmsdale to confess he's her father; of Huckleberry Finn, who runs away from his abusive, alcoholic dad; of *Moby-Dick* and its famous first line: "Call me Ishmael"—Ishmael the rejected son of Abraham; of Jay Gatsby, who rejects his father's life and name; of that great movie of the American myth, *Field of Dreams*, where Ray Kinsella builds a baseball field so he can have a catch one more time with his dead father.

"... at once it struck, what quality went to form a Man of Achievement especially in Literature & which Shakespeare possessed so enormous-ly—I mean Negative Capability, that is when man is capable of being in uncertainties, Mysteries, doubts, without any irritable reaching after fact & reason.... This pursued through Volumes would perhaps take us no further than this, that with a great poet the sense of Beauty overcomes every other consideration, or rather obliterates all consideration."

The secret to *Lost* is surrender. *Negative Capability* is the secret to all mystery: the ability to surrender our demand for answers and revel in the beauty of the experience, to even playfully enjoy when things stop making sense. The one theory that no one seems to be taking seriously is the theory that we're not meant to know the an-swers to the island's mysteries (at least not now). We're supposed to enjoy the journey. That is how I've decided to approach the show. I'm not giving up; I'm giving in—going along for the ride.

Surrender is the key to all true knowledge. To Charlie Starr the teach-er, this truth came years ago as a momentous revelation. Those of us not teaching our students to conform to the rest of society are constantly teaching them to think for themselves, to ask questions, to doubt. Such thinking has its place, but it has incredible limitations as well. I know of few teachers instructing their students in the value of surrender. A high-school senior of mine (this was a millennium ago) doubted, ques-tioned, and probed everything I tried to teach her for two years until, one day two weeks before her graduation, she said, "So what you're say-ing is..." and she beautifully summarized the theory of literature I'd so long been trying to get her to understand. I said, "Yes, that's it exactly," and I saw the light turn on in her eyes, the guard fall in her smile. In the next three months, by e-mail, I was able to teach her more than I ever could in person the previous two years. Granted the questioning, prob-ing, and doubting were what she needed to do before she could learn from me; nevertheless, it got in the way for a very long time.

My best students have never been the self-thinkers and doubters who confused true learning with thinking for themselves and doubting things. Only those brave enough to risk trust, to go past mere ideas and *experience* what I would teach them in a dynamic relationship have ever really learned from me or the literature and movies I share with them.

Only those willing to surrender. It *is* a risk, no doubt. But it's one I've taken myself, finding that there's no other way to survive the island of mystery without going mad. Let analysis and doubt come later—they should. What has to happen first, though, is the experience of wonder and mystery—coming to truth through the beauty of surrender.

As Seen on TV

It's the lesson of the island from the very beginning: don't try to find out what the monster is; don't fight or run from it at all (and whatever you do, don't poke your head out of the cockpit window to get a look at the thing!). Don't go looking for Ethan on his turf; Claire will come back on her own (though the intensity of the experience will keep her from being able to recall what happened). Forget about torture—you can't demand answers to the island's mysteries. At best, all torture will get you is a cheesy pick-up line ("Baby, I'm tied to a tree in a jungle of mystery,") and a kiss from Kate.

The light from the hatch suggests that it's meant to be opened; the numbers suggest it's not. But to force knowledge through violence or violation rather than surrendering to locked mysteries will doubtless prove perilous. In a poem by the German poet Friedrich von Schiller,[2] a youth who would have all knowledge comes to the temple of Isis at Sais where a great statue of the goddess stands, her face covered with a veil. According to the temple priests, the one for whom the goddess lifts the veil will learn all truth, but woe to him who comes to knowledge by guilt. Unable to wait for the understanding that comes through the long process of contemplating the mystery of the veiled form, the youth sneaks into the temple at night and lifts the veil. The result: he loses the joy of living for the remainder of his days, and the anguish in his heart leads him to an early grave.

Pardon the pun, but Locke is the key, even if he violates his own understanding in leading Boone to his death and then blowing the hatch open. He teaches Charlie to surrender addiction, Boone to surrender his sister, Michael and Claire to surrender their suspicions—and always by some experiential method that demands surrender, a way of

---

[2] "Das verschleierte Bild zu Sais."

learning that is indirect, unclear to the rational mind, but crystal clear in the impact of what it reveals. He understands, even if he can't always follow the way of surrender himself,[3] that the island's mysteries cannot be discovered; they must be revealed. Boone learns this lesson from Locke so well that he dies with it: he teaches Jack to surrender control when Jack is so adamant about saving Boone that he pumps his own blood into him and almost cuts off his leg. Says Boone: "Let me go, Jack. I'm letting you off the hook." Jack had to surrender.

And so must we all. Locke tells Charlie, "The island can give you what you're looking for, but you have to give something back." And he's telling us: we must wait and see and, until subsequent seasons take us further along, stop, surrender, and revel in the mystery. Don't go on the raft, out on the sea of Internet trivia-lizing, desperately searching to be rescued from the frustrations of questions without answer. Wait. Just wait. The island will show us the way. It's showing us its most important mystery right now. The secret is in staying lost.

Charlie W. Starr teaches English, humanities, and film at Kentucky Christian University in Eastern Kentucky, where he also makes movies with his students and family. He writes articles, teaches Sunday school, and has published three books: one on Romans, the second a science fiction novel, and the third, *Honest to God*, was released by Navpress in the summer of 2005. His essay "The Silver Chair and the Silver Screen" is the lead chapter in the book *Revisiting Narnia*, released by BenBella books in October 2005, and his essay "Of Gorillas and Gods" appears as a chapter in another BenBella Book: *King Kong Is Back!*, released in November 2005. He enjoys writing, reading classic literature, watching bad television, and movies of every kind. His areas of expertise as a teacher include literature, film, and all things C. S. Lewis. Charlie describes his wife Becky as "a full of life, full-blood Cajun who can cook like one, too." They have two children: Bryan, a high-school senior who wants to be the next Steven Spielberg, and Alli, a seventh grader who plays a pretty mean piano. You can find more on Charlie's books and look at some of the movies he's made at his Web site: http://campus.kcu.edu/faculty/cstarr.

---

[3] Or else he knows that sometimes the moment where knowledge of the truth must be demanded has its place.

The Same Damn Island

ADAM-TROY CASTRO

I have long been of the opinion that Lost *is an obvious rip-off of a certain television series from another decade, which also featured an island. In both, the visitors to the island arrived by airplane. In both, there were already people on the island who might or might not be dangerous. But the biggest problems were always brought by the visitors themselves, who had to resolve their private issues before they could go home. You know the series I'm talking about. Just close your eyes and imagine you can still hear Hervé Villachaize crying out, "De plane, boss! De plane!"*

THE NAYSAYERS WHO CONDEMNED Lost prior to its first-season success were fond of claiming that it was "just like" a certain *other* television show, from some forty years in our cultural past, that it added nothing to the mythos established by that *earlier* phenomenon, and that it was impossible to watch *Lost* without thinking of that *other* show and its set of similar contrivances.

As fans, we can deride the short-sightedness of those facile voices all we want.

After all, *Lost* is a drama, whereas the previous series was a comedy. *Lost* has moments of terror and suspense, whereas the previous show had pratfalls. *Lost* has some four dozen castaways, whereas the previous show had only seven.

Add to these obvious differences the fact that the other show reveled in its stupidity, while *Lost* has moments of undeniable brilliance, and the charge is revealed as a ridiculous canard, barely worth mentioning.

Except.

When you take a closer look, you find that the naysayers might just have a point.

A few words of orientation, first, for the benefit of those readers more familiar with the survivors of that ill-fated Oceanic Flight 815 crash, and not the prior band of unlucky travelers.

There were these seven people, see.

They all boarded a fishing boat, in Hawaii, for a three-hour excursion. Within those three hours, a freak storm came out of nowhere, battered the little boat to and fro, and left it in ruins on the shore of an uncharted desert island.

With no boats, no lights, no motorcars, and not a single luxury, the survivors had to make do, forming a little gang that often had to band together to ward off communal threats.

Of course, the two groups of survivors have nothing in common.

Or do they?

The earlier survivors included an absurdly wealthy man.

The current group has Hurley.

The earlier survivors included a spoiled woman who found the whole thing a huge inconvenience.

The current group had Shannon.

The earlier island had a movie star who defined herself solely in terms of her celebrity.

The current group has Charlie.

The earlier survivors included an unflappably wise figure who seemed to have all the answers.

The current group has Locke.

The earlier survivors included beautiful women who continued to look like models after the cosmetics ran out.

The current group has . . . well, pick one of several.

The earlier survivors had a guy who attracted disasters.

Again, Hurley. Or, if you don't want to name him twice, Arzt.

But these are just shallow similarities, easy to find if you separate characters into their broadest possible archetypes. It may be that any survival situation involving a number of random human beings will provide opportunities to pick out equally resonant patterns.

The true phenomenon only appears when you examine the characteristics of their respective environments.

And come to the unmistakable conclusion that both sets of castaways landed on the same damn island.

What do we know about the island that imprisons the castaways of *Lost*?

We know that despite its "uncharted" status, it is far from uninhabited, and it is home to crazy French ladies, guys buried in underground chambers, and mysterious Others.

We also know that the castaways can wander to and fro, forever, and somehow never run into any of these people until the plot demands it.

What about the earlier show?

In Episode 5 of that show, the castaways discovered that a pilot named Wrong-Way Feldman had been stranded on the island for ten years.

In Episode 15 they found a Japanese Soldier still fighting World War II.

In Episode 19 they found a feral Jungle Boy.

In Episode 34 they discovered the famous painter Alexandri Gregor Dubov, also after he'd lived on the island ten years.

There are a number of other examples.

Dozens, actually.

Both reputedly deserted islands hide these people until they're needed, then produce them.

Since, in both cases, the castaways stick to a relatively small geographical area and rarely venture to "the other side of the island," there's plenty of room for such people to be hiding.

Indeed, both groups might even be hiding from each other.

What else do we know about *Lost's* island?

Well, we know that strange, paranormal events take place there. (This happened on the previous island as well.)

Various stories hinge on telepathy, clairvoyance, voodoo, prophecies, vampirism, and visits from mad scientists. (The other island seems to attract the same such forces.)

The island's plentiful supply of caves include not only ancient hieroglyphics, but also strange radioactive elements like the previously unheard-of Supremium.

There are more mysteries on this one island than on a world filled with continents.

What are the odds of there being two such islands?

Five to one? More?

Castaways marooned on *Lost's* island tend to have complex backstories which connect in odd ways unknown to them. Thus we have Locke working for Hurley, Sawyer sharing a drink with Jack's dad, and so on.

The odds of this happening off the island are minimal. The show is quite open about these hidden connections and how they defy the laws of probability.

By the time *Lost* completes another season or two, the coincidences will multiply even more.

Does the previous show have anything in the same vein?

The answer is lots and lots and lots. . . .

For instance, at least two castaways had exact physical duplicates who visited the island and were mistaken for the people they resemble.

The odds of that have got to be, at least, ten to one.

And the castaways were constantly overhearing news reports about their lives back home.

Maybe four to one?

But let's talk about one extreme example: Episode 52, "Not Guilty."

The castaways discovered, via a Honolulu newspaper that conveniently washed up on shore, that a man named Randolph Blake was murdered shortly before their tiny ship set sail. Authorities suspected one of the passengers was responsible.

The academic among them blamed Blake for plagiarizing a research paper.

The millionaire had caught him embezzling.

The movie star had been two-timed by him.

The small-town girl hated him for forcing her father into bankruptcy.

All of these people, previously unknown to each other, had confronted Blake on the same night, minutes before his accidental death. All were still unknown to each other when they took the charter cruise the next day.

My good pal Joey Green, who wrote a book about this merry band of idiots, summarized this phenomenon about as well as anybody could when he pointed out, "The odds of four people who don't know each other having a common enemy who they each confront the night before sailing on a charter boat are even more remote than the chances of fishing a crate from the ocean that contains a copy of the newspaper reporting that individual's murder."

Unless, as Locke would put it, the island wants it to happen.

Lost's island is a mysterious, protean place that seems to sprawl over many, many square miles of real estate. Its very size—and its population of previous visitors—argues against the likelihood of its uncharted status. This is clearly a place that people keep running into. But why is it unknown, then?

Well, let's talk about the previous island.

Episode 18 placed it 250 miles southeast of Hawaii, at 140 degrees longitude and ten degrees latitude. Episode 21 placed it at 110 degrees longitude and ten degrees latitude.

It also changed shape.

It was mapped three times, in Episodes 58, 75, and 90. The three maps are dissimilar in every detail, failing to agree even in outline.

All we know for sure is that, despite being close enough to civilization to play host to a regular parade of visitors, all of whom left without rescuing our castaways, it remains unmapped, unsuspected, unknown: a catalogue of bizarre miracles just a short cruise from Hawaii.

It's clearly a geographical amoeba, traveling wherever convenient, capturing people for its own alien reasons.

And where is *Lost's* island? Somewhere between Australia and Los Angeles—the exact habitat prowled by the prior land mass.

The conclusion becomes more and more inevitable, doesn't it?

It's the same damn island.

And what's more, these are not the only two times we've heard from it.

Let's talk about another *Cast Away*. The one played by Tom Hanks, in the movie of the same name.

He was a FedEx man whose airplane ran into trouble over the Pacific.

The only survivor of a crash at sea, he made it to the shore of a deserted island.

No boats, no cars. Not a single luxury.

Like the castaways of *Lost*, he soon realized that the plane had been hundreds of miles off course and that any rescue mission was looking in the wrong place.

Fortunately, a whole bunch of packages containing useful tools washed up on shore.

This is the same coincidence that benefited the first set of seven castaways.

And just as fortunately, he found salvation in the form of one package adorned with angel wings that he refrained from opening even in desperation.

Somehow, he knew.

That, too, is the same damn island.

How long has this one freakish outcropping been wandering the world's oceans, scooping up human flotsam and playing with their heads, just for the hell of it? There's no way of knowing. But we already know that the survivors of *Lost* are not the first. Neither are the survivors of *Cast Away* or *Gilligan's Island*. It began long before them, before Gulliver, before Crusoe, before Prospero, before any of the countless *New Yorker* cartoons about two guys on a pimple-sized bump of sand, sharing a punch line that plays on their isolation. One suspects it's been around as long as life on this planet. Sooner or later, somebody will find caveman bones there.

Or a gorilla suit.

Or a cache of Nigerian heroin.

Or anything it bloody well wants you to find.

Crusoe, and Gilligan, and Tom Hanks were all lucky. They all got off, eventually. The island grew tired of them.

How long before it wearies of tormenting the castaways of *Lost*?

As always, only the ratings will tell.

Adam-Troy Castro's short stories have been nominated five times for the Nebula, two times for the Hugo, and once for the Stoker. He has contributed to previous Smart Pop volumes about King Kong, *Hitchhiker's Guide*, *Alias*, and Harry Potter, among others. His next book is *My Ox is Broken!*, a guide to the TV series *The Amazing Race*. He has been assured that the paperback version of his collection *Vossoff and Nimmitz* will be out sometime in 2007. He lives in Miami with his long-suffering wife Judi and a rotating assortment of cats that now includes Maggie, Ralphie, Uma Furman, and Meow Farrow.

The *Lost* Book Club

BILL SPANGLER

The thing about writers is that they are fundamentally lazy. They're doing an episode in which Sawyer gets a headache from eyestrain. But to pull that off, he has to be reading something. "A book!" shouts the prop guy. And some grip or gaffer picks up the book she's been reading between setups and tosses it to the prop guy and lo! Sawyer is seen reading Watership Down.

Either that or the writers created the whole eyestrain business precisely so that they could put Watership Down *on the screen as a significant clue to the deepest meanings of what is going on (i.e., these are all the dreams of bunnies).*

The question is: Does it even make a difference whether a reference is intentional or accidental? The cultural resonances are still the same...aren't they?

THERE'S NO SPA. The cuisine is somewhat limited. The nightlife consists primarily of attacks by a creature that can turn invisible. However, the island where Oceanic Flight 815 crashed does boast one amenity.

There's plenty to read.

Books and literary references can be found regularly on *Lost*. Some books that have been seen are part of the booty Sawyer took from the wrecked plane in "Tabula Rasa (1-3)." Others have been found in Swan Station, the Dharma Initiative bunker. As of spring 2006—roughly two-thirds through the second season—the references have ranged from superhero comics to classic novels to philosophy. Hardcore fans are turning to the books in search of clues to the show's mysteries.

When *The Third Policeman*, a novel by Flann O'Brien, was added to the *Lost* reading list in the second season, it was mentioned in *USA Today* and other national media outlets. The publisher of *The Third Policeman* ordered a new print run of 10,000 copies in order to meet the expected demand. Craig Wright, co-author of the episode that includes *Policeman*, was quoted as saying, "Whoever goes out and buys the book will have a lot more information in their back pocket as they theorize about the show. They will have a lot more to speculate about—and, no small thing, they will have read a really great book."

In addition to possible clues, I think other things can be found by looking at the books shown on *Lost*. It's a way of learning about the writers' influences and getting a different perspective on the events of the show.

One of the first books to make a cameo appearance on *Lost* was *Watership Down* by Richard Adams. Published in 1972, *Watership Down* is an epic fantasy, but there are no dwarves or elves in sight. The cast is made up of the animal denizens of the English countryside, including rabbits, mice, and cats. Inspired by a vision of impending disaster, a group of rabbits is thrown together on a quest for a new home. The cast is nearly as large as the cast of *Lost*, and, over time, the group absorbs rabbits from different warrens, just as the human survivors of Flight 815 merges two different groups together. As the lead character in *Watership Down*, Hazel—who is male, by the way—puts it:

> *"In our situation we can't afford to waste anything that might do us good. We're in a strange place we don't know much about and we need friends."*

The role of human beings in *Watership Down* is very similar to the role of the Others on *Lost*. They appear without warning, bringing death and destruction, while their motives and goals remain mysterious. The rabbits—and other wildlife—can only try to avoid the humans' lethal presence.

Like the island on *Lost*, the setting of Adams's novel is a relatively small piece of real estate. However, it is still the site of epic confrontations. Also, the English countryside is definitely a character in *Watership Down*, just as the island itself is a character in *Lost*. Here's just one of Adams's loving descriptions of the natural world:

> "The sun, risen by the copse, threw long shadows from the trees southwestward across the field. The wet grass glittered and nearby a nut tree sparkled iridescent, winking and gleaming as its branches moved in the light wind. The brook was swollen and Hazel's ears could distinguish the deeper, smoother sound, changed since the day before. Between the copse and the brook, the slope was covered with pale-lilac lady's smocks, each standing separately in the grass, a frail stock of a bloom above a spread of cressy leaves. The breeze dropped and the little valley lay completely still, held in long beams of light and enclosed on either side by the lines of the woods. Upon this clear stillness, like feathers on the surface of a pool, fell the calling of a cuckoo."

47

In the first section of the novel, a rivalry between two rabbits for the leadership of the refugees is reminiscent of the tension between Jack and Locke. However, it's unlikely that the humans were patterned after the rabbits. Hazel resembles Jack in so much as he worries about the problems of leadership and is surprised when others turn to him for guidance. Hazel is, however, different from Jack, as he is a man of faith (rabbit of faith?) in this story, because he depends on the visions of another rabbit, Fiver. Bigwig, like Locke, has impressive survival skills, but he is considered more practical than Hazel.

The tension between Hazel and Bigwig dissolves when the latter is almost killed by a human snare, while the tension between Jack and Locke is increasing.

When the man calling himself Henry Gale is imprisoned in the bunker, he is given a copy of *The Brothers Karamazov* by Fyodor Dostoevsky to read. One of the major themes in this classic novel is faith versus reason. The four brothers—Dmitri, Ivan, Alyosha, and Smerdyakov—represent different points of view on that topic.

In "The Whole Truth (2-16)," Sawyer is seen reading *Are You There God? It's Me, Margaret* by Judy Blume. This is also a book about faith, although it is very different from both *Watership* and *Brothers*. The title character is a girl who speaks regularly and directly with God, despite the efforts of her parents to keep her away from organized religion.

Here's a sample of Margaret's prayers:

"Are you there God? It's me, Margaret. I just told my mother I want a bra. Please help me to grow God. You know where. I want to be like everyone else. You know God, my new friends all belong to the Y or the Jewish Community Center. Which way am I supposed to go? I don't know what you want me to do about that."

Another major question in *Lost* is what role the children—Walt, Aaron, and possibly Alex Rousseau—are going to play in the story. Children also play important roles in *A Wrinkle in Time* by Madeline L'Engle and *The Turn of the Screw* by Henry James, which have both been shown on *Lost*. Confronting invisible forces is a theme in these stories as well. (*Wrinkle* is a young adult novel, while *Turn* is a novella.)

In *A Wrinkle in Time*, three human children are drawn into an interstellar battle against a creature called IT or the Dark Thing. The Dark Thing is spreading from planet to planet, absorbing individuality and independent thought. The children—Meg, Charles Wallace, and Calvin—all have abilities that set them apart from their friends, although their powers are not as spectacular as Walt's seem to be. They also receive a little more guidance than Jack and the others have received so far, in the form of the aliens Mrs. Who, Mrs. Whatsit, and Mrs. Which.

The invisible force in *The Turn of the Screw* may not be paranormal in origin, though. A young governess in Victorian England believes that the two children under her care are being stalked by ghosts. These ghosts, however, might be the manifestations of the governess's own emotional problems. Scholars are still debating whether the ghosts in *Turn* are real—and whether the question can ever be answered satisfactorily.

Watership Down, *A Wrinkle in Time*, and *The Turn of the Screw* are all fairly well-known stories. However, the same thing can't be said of *The Third Policeman*. O'Brien wrote this book in 1939, but it wasn't published until 1967, a year after his death. Denis Donoghue, in his introduction, compares the novel to the surrealistic plays of Samuel Beckett.

The current edition was first published in 1999 and has sold about 15,000 copies as of its first appearance in *Lost*.

(For one feverish moment, I thought about correlating the publication dates of *Policeman* with the known history of the Dharma Initiative, but I sat down for a while and the feeling went away.)

The Third Policeman appears early in the episode "Orientation (2-3)," as Desmond is preparing to leave Swan Station. After reading the book, it's easy to see why Desmond would be interested in it.

The narrator of *Policeman* is a nameless man who gets involved with a robbery and murder. While trying to locate the money from the robbery, he winds up at a rural police station which "did not seem to have any depth or breadth and looked as if it would not deceive a child." The two policemen on duty are obsessed with bicycles and a nearby underground bunker which they call Eternity.

That's right, an underground bunker. And check out this description of Eternity:

> "*The walls of the passage seemed to be made with bolted sheets of pig-iron which looked to me like ovens or furnace doors or safe deposit boxes such as banks have. The ceiling, where I could see it, was a mass of wires and what appeared to be particularly thick wires or possibly pipes. All the time there was an entirely new noise to be heard, not unmusical, sometimes like water gurgling underground and sometimes like subdued conversation in a foreign language....Here and there I saw a dial or an intricate nest of clocks and dials resembling a control board....*"

The phrase "subdued conversation" could be used to describe the whispers that can sometimes be heard on the island in *Lost*.

At the center of the bunker is "a well-lit airy hall that was completely circular and filled with indescribable articles very like machinery but not quite as intricate as the more difficult machines...." This line seems to suggest that some of the machines are outdated or anachronistic, like many of the items in Swan Station.

The exotic machinery inside the bunker can produce anything that a visitor wants, but, naturally, there's a catch: in this case, you really can't take it with you. Whenever somebody uses the elevator that connects the outside world with Eternity, he has to weigh himself first, because the elevator will handle only that much weight on the return trip. The narrator refers to the numbers he sees on the scale before they make the descent. Unfortunately, the digits he sees are 6, 9, 10, and 16, only one of which helped Hugo "Hurley" Reyes win the lottery.

Another chore that the policemen do will sound even more familiar. They constantly monitor the readings on various mysterious devices in the bunker because if the readings go too high Something Terrible will happen.

The narrator searches for answers to all these strange events, but his quest seems doomed to failure. As Sergeant Pluck, one of the policemen, tells him, "The first beginnings of wisdom is to ask questions but not to answer any. You get wisdom from asking and get wisdom from not answering."

Interestingly, there's one plot point in the novel that looks like it's related to *Lost*, but probably isn't. It seems that the narrator of *The Third Policeman* is dead, and that everything he sees and experiences—except for a brief trip back to the world of the living near the end—is actually the afterlife.

The possibility that the castaways are, in fact, dead is a theory that was promoted frequently during the early days of *Lost*. However, the creative staff of the show has definitely ruled that option out. How definitely? In the first issue of *Lost: The Official Magazine*, Javier Grillo-Marxuach talks about how a neighbor asked him if Jack and the rest of the island inhabitants are dead. His answer was a straightforward "No." (Grillo-Marxuach, for the record, is a supervising producer of the show and co-author of "Orientation.")

Also, in the December 30, 2005 issue of *Entertainment Weekly*, Executive Producer Carlton Cuse described the show as a way to explore the question of "how you lead a meaningful life." To me, this is a peculiar statement to make if the characters are all dead and their decisions have no effect on themselves or the world.

Another book in the bunker's library is a collection of short stories by Ambrose Bierce. The collection, seen in "The Long Con (2-13)," was named after Bierce's story, "An Occurrence at Owl Creek Bridge." Like *Policeman*, "Owl Creek" plays fast and loose with the dividing line between life and death, but mentioning the story in *Lost* may be a reminder to the viewing audience not to trust everything they see.

A novel titled *Lancelot*, written by Walker Percy, is shown briefly— very briefly—in the episode "Maternity Leave (2-15)." This may be a reference to Kate's story, because it's about a man who kills his unfaithful wife by blowing up their house.

Along with these books, the creators of *Lost* have referred to comic books and ancient mythology. A polar bear, in a Spanish comic book in the pilot episode, is clearly meant to be connected to a real polar bear that the castaways encounter later in the show. The comic in question is a Spanish version of *Faster Friends*, a graphic novel featuring the DC superheroes Flash and Green Lantern. The book was published in 1997 and Amazon currently lists it as out-of-print.

How did an older comic, not in English, wind up on Flight 815, an airliner leaving an English-speaking country? It turns out that Hurley brought it on board. He is seen taking it out of his carry-on bag after he boards the plane in the second half of "Exodus (1-24)." This is an elegant solution, since Hurley speaks Spanish and it's easy to imagine that he's a comic-book fan.

There are definitely comic fans on the *Lost* staff. Co-Creator Damon Lindelof is now writing for Marvel Comics—in addition to working on the show—and Grillo-Marxuach is writing *The Middleman* for Viper Comics. In addition, Paul Dini, who was on the writing staff during the first season, was one of the driving forces behind the critically acclaimed *Batman* animated series.

Recently, Hurley found something new to read. In "The Long Con," he says he found a manuscript of "a mystery book" in one of the suitcases. This appears to be *Bad Twin*, a hardcover novel published in May 2006. The manuscript has been attributed to a character named Gary Troup. Troup did not survive the crash of Flight 815, but it seems that he sent a copy of this novel to his publishers before he boarded the plane. So a complete copy of *Bad Twin* will be available in bookstores.

The reference to classic mythology comes to the series through an unlikely medium: a crossword puzzle. In the episode "Old Habits (2-8)," Locke is doing a crossword that he found in the Dharma Initiative bunker. One of the clues—42 down, another reference to Hurley's jinxed numbers—is "Enkidu's friend." The friend in question is Gilgamesh, the hero of what some people believe to be the oldest known recorded story.

The saga of Gilgamesh could be described as a study in leadership and in accepting mortality. Gilgamesh was the ruler of the Middle Eastern kingdom of Uruk. Part god and part man, he was a fierce warrior who had made Uruk a wealthy and powerful land. To his subjects, though, he was cruel and ruthless.

Gilgamesh learns compassion and empathy when he meets the beast-man Enkidu. They go on adventures together, but their exploits draw the wrath of the gods. Anu sends down the Bull of Heaven, which leads to seven years of famine in Uruk. Enkidu and Gilgamesh kill the bull, but the gods kill Enkidu in retaliation. (Unlike the Others in *Lost*, the gods of ancient mythology generally have easy-to-understand motivations. They're driven by emotions like jealousy or lust, the same feelings that humans have to deal with.)

After Enkidu dies, Gilgamesh searches the known world for a way to cheat death. Eventually, he obtains a plant that will restore his youth. The plant is stolen before he can use it, but, by this time, the ruler has come to terms with the fact that he will die. The prosperity he brought to Uruk will be remembered throughout the ages and that is all the immortality he needs.

This might not have much to do with the long-range story arc of *Lost*, but it definitely has applications to "Old Habits." This episode details the background of Ana Lucia Cortez, the leader of the tail-section survivors, and provides an opportunity to compare her leadership style with Jack's.

Both Ana Lucia and Jack are nobility of a sort. She followed her mother into law enforcement, while he followed his father into medicine. However, Jack is a reluctant leader who is still learning what he can and can't do. Ana Lucia, on the other hand, doesn't seem to suffer Jack's doubts. She expects to be obeyed quickly and without question.

Like Gilgamesh, dharma has a long history, but it does not refer to a specific person (Jenna Elfman notwithstanding). In Buddhist doctrine, dharma refers to moral principles, such as justice. As I understand it, Dharma, with a capital letter, is another name for the Buddha's collected teachings. Why Gerald and Karen DeGroot chose this name for their project, and whether it was an accurate choice still has to be determined.

Specific philosophy books have not been sighted on the show so far, but they may not be needed, since two of the regular characters are named after noted philosophers. The real John Locke, who lived in the seventeenth century, introduced the idea that our senses could be relied upon when it came to experiencing the world. In his *Essay Concerning Human Understanding*, he writes:

53

> *"The infinitely wise contriver of us, and all things around us, hath fitted our senses, faculties and organs to the conveniences of life and the business we have to do here. We are able, by our senses, to know and distinguish things; and to examine them so far as to apply them to our uses... Such a knowledge as this, which is suited to our present condition, we want not faculties to attain."*

I think the fictional Locke reflects this philosophy when it comes to his general attitude toward the island. He knows what has happened to him. He was confined to a wheelchair; now he can walk. He knows he has experienced a miracle; therefore, the island is a place of miracles.

There's at least one other reference to Locke's writings in *Lost*. The original Locke describes the human mind at birth as "white paper, void of all characters, without any ideas."

This state is sometimes called *tabula rasa,* or a blank slate. As noted earlier, there's a first-season episode titled "Tabula Rasa," although it focuses on Kate rather than Locke. At the end of the episode, Jack suggests that the crash has turned them all into blank slates. "It doesn't matter, Kate, who we were, what we did before this, before the crash," he says. "Three days ago, we all died. We should all be able to start over."

The mysterious French woman is named after Jean-Jacques Rousseau, who was known for the concept of the "Noble Savage." Rousseau argues that every person qualifies as a Noble Savage when he or she is born, with a strong individuality and survival instinct. Institutions such as governments and schools have to be designed in such a way as to do as little damage to this savage state as possible. When Sayid finds Danielle Rousseau in "Solitary (1-9)," she has at least partially reverted back to this state.

Another thing that can be said about these references—what may be the most important thing, in the long run—is that they never get in the way of the human stories on the show. In fact, they are sometimes used to help develop the characters. Sawyer was seen reading often enough in the first season that the creative team decided to turn it into a subplot. He started getting headaches, which Jack diagnosed as needing glasses.

(At first glance, Sawyer does not come across as an avid reader. In "Tabula Rasa" he doesn't acknowledge that he's taken books. He tells Jack that he has "booze, smokes, and a couple of *Playboys*." At that point, though, Sawyer was trying to isolate himself from the other survivors. It's easy to believe that he would grab any books he could find as a form of entertainment that wouldn't require him to interact with anyone else.)

This balancing of elements—and this attention to detail—is part of what makes *Lost* the show that it is.

According to the baby-book compiled by his mother, Bill Spangler wrote his first fan letter to a television show while he was in elementary school. (The show? *Romper Room*.) These days, his fan letters are being published by BenBella Books in volumes such as *Farscape Forever!* and *Star Wars on Trial*, as well as this one. He has also written articles about pop culture for national magazines and original comic-book stories based on science fiction TV shows such as *Alien Nation* and *Quantum Leap*. Bill and his wife Joyce live in Bucks County, Pennsylvania, with two ferrets and a dog. Bill would like to thank his wife, Jon Plante, and Kathy Morrow for their help in pulling this essay together on a relatively tight schedule.

Oceanic Tales

Have You Been Framed?

EVELYN VAUGHN

A skeptic might say that literary critics are likely to find resemblances between Lost *and every book they ever read, just as movie critics can find* Lost *echoing every movie ever made. One might wonder if plumbers find that episodes of* Lost *make them think of unplugging stuck drains or finding a ring in somebody's sink trap. Lawyers find resonances of famous cases, and orthodontists notice that everybody has such even teeth.*

Except that Lost *is written, and therefore has writers who have read things and learned from what they've read. So when we try to figure out how* Lost *does to us the things it does, it's not at all far-fetched to look back at works of literature that have done similar things to their audiences.*

NOT TO WORRY YOU OR ANYTHING, but I teach literature. And I've gotta say, when I consider the popularity of the TV show *Lost* and think "Everything old is new again," I'm not *just* comparing it to 1964's *Gilligan's Island*.

I'm thinking more along the lines of some fourteenth-century classics.

See, *Lost* is an example of a "frame story." It's a narrative that presents a whole series of short tales, often with different tellers, wrapped in the "frame" of one large, extended story. One of the most famous is Boccaccio's *Decameron*, a fourteenth-century Italian work in which ten young nobles flee the plague-ridden city of Florence for the safety of the country. There, they distract themselves by telling ten tales a day for ten days. (All those tens would be the "Deca" part of the title.) But the frame story you're most likely to recognize, possibly by suffering through it in high-school or college English, is Chaucer's *Canterbury Tales*, of the same century.

Yes, that *Canterbury Tales*.

I beg you, put aside any lingering resentment you may still have over being forced to memorize and recite the prologue in its original Middle English. I don't make my students do that (except occasionally for extra credit, and only if they want to). Try to think past the hard-to-read part of Chaucer, past the forced-to-do-it part of Chaucer, to the actual *story*. That's the part I'm pretty sure Geoffrey Chaucer would have wanted you to notice, anyway. In *Canterbury Tales*, a group of travelers, making a pilgrimage to a shrine in Kent, decide to travel together for safety and to tell stories to pass the time. What results (if you can get past the Middle English) is one of the most amusing series of stories by one of the most diverse casts of medieval characters you could possibly want to meet.

Starting to sound like *Lost* yet? Even a little?

True, comparing a twenty-first-century television sensation to fourteenth-century frame stories for mere comparison might sound a bit too publish-or-perish to count as pop culture. But what I've taken away from the startling similarities is no less than a theory about how *Lost* has become one of those rare shows to straddle the line between critical success and popular triumph.

That's quite a coup, you've got to admit. Shows like *Arrested Development* and *Freaks and Geeks* manage to be critical darlings, but too few people tune in to keep them on the air. And as for shows that are huge hits—do you realize what the largest audience for a TV series is? *Baywatch*. 1.1 billion viewers in 142 countries, as of 2002 anyway. Clearly *Baywatch* has a lot of fans. But you can't say that it gets a lot of critical respect.

There's a lot of distance between what *Arrested Development* does and what *Baywatch* does, and yet *Lost* manages to do both. It has won Emmy Awards, Saturn Awards, Golden Globe Awards, SAG Awards, and has even been nominated for a Hugo. Safe to say, the critics approve. And yet it's also done beautifully in the ratings—in its freshman year, the only new show to do better was *Desperate Housewives*. It's shown in Spanish, English, Arabic, French, Korean, and German. So "popular" isn't a reach either.

Network executives can't be the only people wondering how this show about a bunch of plane-crash survivors on a weird island is managing such a powerful one-two punch. So here's at least one possibility.

Lost is doing well because it's following a technique for storytelling that was proven popular (and has stuck around) since the fourteenth century. Really. *Lost* rocks, in part, by being a frame story.

So what's a frame story again?

Per a few paragraphs back: a frame story is a narrative that presents a whole series of short tales, often with different tellers, wrapped in the "frame" of one large, extended story. In the *Decameron*, the frame is the escape from plague-ridden Florence. In *Canterbury Tales*, the frame is the pilgrimage to Canterbury. And in *Lost*, the frame is the crash of Oceanic Flight 815 and all the subsequent island mysteries faced by the survivors. I'll admit, of the three, *Lost* probably has the most enthralling frame. The only classic frame that comes close in drama is Sheherazade's daily risk of death in the *Book of One Thousand and One [Arabian] Nights*...and that one, while it has stories about many different characters, only has one teller, so I'm not focusing on it. Among the classics, the frame of *Lost* is a clear winner.

But is that enough to make it stand out among television dramas?

I think so. Because of its frame structure, each episode of *Lost* doesn't just advance the external plot—every week we also get a full story about one of the large cast of characters—how Sayid became a torturer, how Hurley won his fortune, how Jack found (or later lost) his wife. This inclusion of individual stories is what makes everything else—the island, the Others, the creature some fans call *Lostzilla*—a frame...a solid, engaging frame.

It's the same with the fourteenth-century classics. *Canterbury Tales* isn't just about a bunch of pilgrims riding to southwest England. *Canterbury Tales* is the Wife of Bath's story about what women most want, and the Nun's Priest's Tale about the talking animals, and the Pardoner's Tale about the three drunkards who go off in search of death. The *Decameron* isn't just about a bunch of rich youths sitting around having a storytelling contest. It's about sweet tales of true love, and amusing tales about con artists, and a mind-boggling number of tales about sex outside of marriages and inside of religious orders and everywhere else.

It's the clever combination of the two—the group frame and the individual stories within the frame—that make the classics, and *Lost*, stand out. And here's how.

The Frames Are Often about Journeys

The pilgrims in *Canterbury Tales* aren't the Puritan (or Pilgrim's Pride) kind of pilgrim on a quest for freedom to practice their religion. Heck, even the religious characters in the story are generally pretty shady types. Although their "official" purpose is to visit the shrine of St. Thomas à Becket, it's as much a spring break kind-of-vacation as anything (as those of you who had to memorize the prologue should know. April, remember?). Similarly, the young nobles in the *Decameron* are trying to get away, not only physically but emotionally, from all the death and destruction of the plague. They're all travelers.

Well, so are the characters on Oceanic Flight 815 from Sydney to Los Angeles—all travelers. Some, like the characters in the *Decameron*, are fleeing something. Claire, Sawyer, Sun, and Jin. Others, like those in the *Canterbury Tales*, are on vacations, though of mixed success. Hurley and Locke. But one thing all of them have in common is that they're going from one place to another—and that means they are outside their usual lives.

Think about the dramatic possibilities. All of these characters are betwixt and between. It makes them bolder. It makes them more adventurous. And it sure as heck makes them more interesting. Remember your most enjoyable vacations. Didn't you find yourself doing something you wouldn't have done in your at-home life? Entering a limbo contest? White-water rafting? Sleeping with a sexy Italian tour guide?

We get a little of that in the travel of a frame story, too, romantic or not—don't think there wasn't some flirting going on even among the storytellers of the *Decameron*, and we've all seen the pairings, possible pairings, and former pairings of the *Lost*aways. Do you really think that Charlie and Claire would have ever gotten together in Sydney or Los Angeles? How about Sawyer and Kate (and Jack)? Sayid and Shannon? Their hookups, like those with sexy Italian tour guides, are possible in part because the characters have slipped the surly bonds of Earth... or at least of their usual, earthly self-definitions. The characters also take non-romantic chances they might never have tried before—Michael building the raft, or Arzt helping to fetch dynamite to blow the hatch. (Hey, they aren't all successful chances.)

Travel lets us break out of our usual routine and take those chances. **59**

The Stories Often Reveal Individual Secrets

True, in *Lost* we don't have characters actually sit down and tell their stories to the other survivors—not most of the time—much less make a contest out of it. But through the magic of televised drama, we get individualized stories, via flashback, with every episode. For example, we find out how Sun planned on leaving Jin, or how Kate ended up in custody. But the flashbacks do more than that. They reveal secrets about the characters that, to judge only by their frame, we might not know. Remember the pilot episode, when it only seemed passing strange that Locke was so darned happy to have been in a plane crash? The lingering camera shot showed us his fascination with his own moving feet. But only several episodes in, when we got Locke's first flashback, did we learn the truth: he'd been in a wheelchair, unable to walk, before the crash! The initially strained relationship between Michael and Walt is another example—only once we got the flashback about how Michael had lost and then suddenly regained custody did we fully understand.

Guess what? That's a technique used heavily in the classic frame stories, as well. In the *Decameron*, Dioneo, the punster, tends to tell stories that are witty and rebellious. The older Pampinea's stories tend to have just endings, reflecting her own structured personality. And in the *Canterbury Tales*, the characters' choices of stories reveal themselves even more (as do their prologues). When the Carpenter annoys the Miller, the drunken Miller then tells a bawdy tale about a carpenter whose pretty young wife is cheating on him. When the Wife of Bath tells a tale rife with feminine independence, the misogynist of a Clerk then tells a story about a woman who is rewarded for always trusting that her husband is doing the right thing, even when said husband claims to have their children murdered or to turn her out without a penny.

The stories they tell—or in the case of *Lost*, remember—*are* their characters.

Theme and Variation

By their very nature, frame stories meet two conflicting desires in the audience.

One desire is for *theme*, something familiar enough for audience comfort, returning to the same characters and situation week after week. This is a pretty powerful need for audiences, and probably one reason that big changes in a story's situation (long-awaited weddings, or ensemble high-school students who graduate) threaten to destroy so many shows. Losing a major character (Eric Foreman leaving *That '70s Show* or Dr. Joel Fleischman leaving *Northern Exposure*) shakes the core of normalcy that brought the audience back week after week. It feels like going back to the old homestead after Grampa died.

Just not the same.

Even when shows survive the loss of a major player—*ER* bidding goodbye to Doug Ross, or Mike Logan leaving *Law and Order*—they do so by keeping other things as familiar as possible . . . the emergency room setting, or the great "doink doink" between scenes. If *Charmed* stopped being about witches fighting evil, or *CSI* stopped being about forensic crime solving, this would be an even bigger problem. Audiences want the familiar. When we find something we like, we want more of the same.

Sort of.

Here's the rub. At the same time that audiences want more of the same—want our nighttime soaps to stay soapy, our paranormal thrillers to stay paranormal, and our favorite characters to remain forever—

we also want new twists. Variation. Eventually Ryan and Marissa, on the *OC*, will run out of things to believably argue about. Eventually Dr. Richard Kimble had to find the one-armed man. And eventually, stranded castaways must get off the island.

So how can a show put off that inevitable big change for as long as possible? By mixing things up along the way.

By variation.

The ultimate in TV variation would, of course, be the "variety show." Those series may have recurring actors, but the same characters don't show up every week, certainly not in a continuing plot. *The Carol Burnett Show* was perhaps the best example of this, popular enough to run from 1967–1978. Other variety shows that might immediately come to mind would include *Sonny and Cher*, *The Smothers Brothers*, or *Rowan and Martin's Laugh-In*.

Or wait...they'll probably only come to mind if you're old like me! Most of these were popular in the late '60s or early '70s. Several only lasted for a season or two (Sonny and Cher's *Show* lasted a year, their *Comedy Hour* lasted three).

Okay, how about *In Living Color*? *The Dave Chapelle Show*? *Saturday Night Live*? Current variety shows are more the exception than the rule. And just as many crash and burn, like 2004's *The Nick and Jessica Variety Show*. In any case, variety they may give, but in the form of comedy and music, not drama.

Another way to bring in variation, without the comedy and with more emphasis on the storytelling, would be the anthology series. *The Twilight Zone* and *The Outer Limits* are examples of anthology science-fiction series—while the audience could count on the same kind of story each week, those stories never featured the same characters in a continuing narrative. Instead, one week we had William Shatner freaking out about a gremlin on the wing of his airplane ("Nightmare at 20,000 Feet"), and the next week we had the near-death experience of a Civil War soldier ("Occurrence at Owl Creek Bridge"). But here's the thing...even fewer anthology series have really held the public imagination like those two than have variety hours. Oh, *Tales from the Crypt* did okay, in the '90s. But even the *New Twilight Zone* in the '80s, or *Steven Spielberg's Amazing Stories* (also in the '80s) could only struggle along for a couple of seasons. And they were rarely imitated.

Why aren't anthology series more popular? Because while audiences may want variety, remember that we also want something familiar to return to, week after week. The same cast of characters. The same basic setting.

Frame stories, more than any other kind, manage to meet both desires at the same time. We get the variation of the individual stories: if you don't like the Wife of Bath's tale, you'll enjoy the Clerk's. If you don't want to hear more about Kate, you can come back for some insight into Hurley. And yet we also get the theme of the basic frame—no matter who our point-of-view character is that week, we know that every episode will be set on the island, with the same basic ensemble. We know that every tale will be told en route to Canterbury, in that wacky Middle English.

We know what we're getting. Sort of.

You've got to admit, it's kinda brilliant.

Character, Character, Character

Speaking of variety, another thing that the good frame stories do, and do well, is that they emphasize a wide range of characters. This may be the most significant feature (among many) of *Canterbury Tales*. In Chaucer's classic, you have noblemen like the Knight and the Squire, and you have poorer characters like the Clerk and the Cook. You have men who do physical labor, like the Carpenter and the Miller, and you have men we would currently claim as white-collar—the Doctor and the Lawyer. Almost a third of the pilgrims are in some way religious, the Monk, the Friar, the Parson, and the Abbess with her Priests, among others. Others...not so much.

Because all of them tell their own story, they also have to be very, *very* well-defined characters.

We get the same thing with *Lost*. There's Jack, and then there's Locke. There's Sawyer, and then there's Hurley. Some of our characters are wealthy, not that you'd immediately guess it. Some are almost penniless. Some are addicts, and some are health nuts. They have conflicting belief systems and philosophies and values...and it's all for the good.

The variety of characters also helps satisfy both critics and mass audiences. The more in-depth the character studies, the happier the critics. And the better looking and more easily understood the characters are, the happier the mass audiences. Again, *Lost* pleases both sides.

Risk-Taking

Along with all those other benefits of frame stories, there's the one we don't often talk about in English-Lit classes.

These stories can really push the envelope.

Really. The things that go on in the monasteries and convents of *The Decameron* would make you blush. What Absolom does with that hot poker after he's been tricked into kissing Alison's nether regions in *Canterbury's* Miller's Tale is...extreme, to say the least.

Lost takes its share of chances as well. Shannon and her stepbrother Boone, for example?

But they aren't all sexual chances—*Lost* does appear on network TV, after all. There are also risky characters. Sawyer, whom fans have hoped all along is a redeemable bastard, is increasingly turning out to be just a bastard (though still more attractive than Chaucer's Miller...especially as played by Josh Holloway). Kate, who looked so innocent and cute at the very start, turns out to be a criminal. Charlie, perhaps even cuter, is a drug addict. Or a recovering addict. Hard to tell.

So why is risk-taking so much easier in a frame story than in the usual narrative? Probably because the stories within the frame are so very character driven, it's almost as if the writers can blame Sawyer, or Charlie, for their particularly dark flashbacks. Chaucer isn't to blame for the dirty story about the carpenter, Alison, Absolom, and Nicholas—that one's the drunken Miller's fault.

And in the end, this is probably the frame element that most allows a show like *Lost* to straddle its two worlds, not just between Sydney and Los Angeles, but between popular success and critical acclaim. The audience is more forgiving of the occasional character death, the occasional scene of torture or near incest, because whatever element is distasteful one week probably won't be repeated the next—the variety of alternating the character focus, episode to episode, pretty much promises variety. For whatever reason (probably because it makes us think more than just escape), critics love unlikable characters and deaths of major players. So everyone's happy.

Frame stories. I'm telling you. They're not just for medieval entertainment anymore.

Rita award-winning author Evelyn Vaughn has published fifteen romance and adventure novels (including *A.K.A. Goddess* and *Something Wicked*) and a dozen fantasy short stories in anthologies such as *Constellation of Cats*, *Vengeance Fantastic*, and *Familiars*. She also teaches literature and creative writing for Tarrant County College in Texas. When neither writing nor teaching…oh, who are we kidding? She's almost always writing and teaching. And watching TV (being an addict). It helps her rest up from the writing. And the teaching.

She loves to talk about what she writes, whether that's an attractive quality or not. Check out her Web site at www.evelynvaughn.com.

All Hail Hurley!

NICK MAMATAS

Hurley has been my favorite character right from the start. Maybe that's because I've always had a weight problem, and even though I've been up and down, topping out at over 300 pounds at times and happily within the life insurance company's recommended weight range at others, I always think of myself as the fat guy whose secret vice is always on public display. Poor Hurley—every time he eats anything, other people despise him for it.

But now Mr. Mamatas has a different theory about why so many of us—even skinny people—identify so completely with Hugo "Hurley" Reyes. And I think he's right.

FAT MEN HAVE BEEN A TELEVISION TRADITION since Jackie Gleason twinkle-toed across the screen in glorious black and white, and since those halcyon days character development for fat, nerdy characters hasn't budged an inch. There were two choices: (1) belligerent husband or (2) woebegone scorch, the butt of every joke and cream pie to the face. Occasionally, "sensitive" portrayals were in order, so we might have a young obese boy weep at being called names, only to redeem himself later by winning a pie-eating contest or by being the anchor on the winning tug-o-war team. (The opponents, inevitably bourgeois to a lad, illegally used a tree stump for their anchor.)

On the first episode of *Lost*, Hurley was clearly going to be the fat comic-relief character. He was one of the few to stand out in the first ten minutes of the pilot, filled as it was with people running around and screaming "Aaaaaaah!" while the cameras shook and jittered. What a thrill it was, as the first season of *Lost* progressed, that Hurley ended up being something more.

Of course, there is still plenty of comic relief in the character. His backstory lacks the melodrama of Kate's or Sawyer's, and makes up for it with unadulterated gonzo. His first flashback episode, "Numbers (1-18)," shows us Hurley, going by his real name Hugo Reyes, sitting on a couch, being berated by his mother. Why isn't he going out with his friends, she demands to know. Mothers are blind. We all know exactly why Hugo is sitting at home on a Friday night: he weighs 350 pounds if he weighs an ounce, smells of grease from the fast-food chicken joint he works at, and is still in the stupid uniform. He surely doesn't have a cent to his name, either. And we're saved from the near-inevitable "You just don't understand, Mama!" speech by the announcement that Hugo has won the lottery. He faints, but he still ends up with more dignity than the average television fat man or nerd. Because Hurley is more than just a fat nerd, he is a fan. It isn't necessarily apparent on the show—though hints abound, like his placement in a backgammon tournament—but he is one, nonetheless. Hurley is a tribute to the hardcore fans of science fiction, the guys who prefer the old *Battlestar Galactica* to the new version, the people who start the fan Web sites and initiate the letter-writing campaigns when a new show like *Lost* comes in with low ratings. Hurley's the man who watched the last season of *The X-Files* and he is clearly a stand-in and an object of identification for the fannish segment of the audience.

Ah, dignity. That's what makes Hurley such a compelling character. A grown man working fast food isn't supposed to have any dignity. If Latinos are allowed any, it is either because they're wealthy drug dealers and dripping with sexuality, or they are a violent lumpenprole Other who frightens the white viewers into supporting the War on Drugs. The sort of geek who spends his time at backgammon tournaments certainly cannot be allowed any social intelligence, but Hurley has social skills going spare. He's the one who created the golf course for the castaways, the one who outsmarted Sawyer by simply asking for the passenger manifest rather than negotiating or threatening for it, and the one who decided to do a census of islanders in the first place, thus discovering that Ethan wasn't on the plane.

Hurley's an Everyman hero, one with no special skills or abilities. *Lost* always struck me as a bit far-fetched given the stunning collection of individuals on board: a medical doctor, a box-factory employee turned Great White Hunter, an electronics wiz/torturer, an architect with sufficient secondary ability in naval engineering to create a raft that's more well built than the house I live in, you name it. In the real world, of course, most of the castaways would be deputy shift managers at PaperPush Co. Hell, I write novel essays about television shows for a living. My only role on the island would be as bait for the Invisible Dinosaur. Or, I could be like Hurley.

Hurley is the fan. He says "dude" a lot. He knows that he is looked down upon, but still insists on being taken seriously because he—because *we*—deserve it. As he demands of Danielle when questioning her about his ill-starred winning lottery numbers: "You don't know?! Okay...That thing in the woods? Maybe it's a monster. Maybe it's a...pissed-off giraffe, I don't know. The fact that no one seems to be looking for us? Yeah, that's weird. But I just go along with it...'cause I'm just along for the ride. Good old fun-time Hurley. Well, guess what? Now—I want some friggin' answers!"

Hurley already has some answers, though. Like many fans, he sees the new world in which he now lives as an opportunity to remake himself. "Hurley" is the sort of peculiar name a fan would come up with. It's deracinated, where Hugo Reyes is clearly Latino (actor Jorge Garcia is as well). Hurley is middle-American *sounding* without actually meaning anything. I'm reminded of the number of people I've met at science fiction conventions and Live Action Role-Playing games who call themselves "Tigger" or "Logan," the former based on the Pooh character and the latter after the X-Man Wolverine. Sure, Tigger may be a nickname someone ends up with rather than gives to oneself, but when was the last time you met a person who had that nickname without a self-christening? And certainly there are people who are really named Logan from birth (and Dirk and Clint and Hunter, and with surnames like Stryker or Dark), but, geez, is Dennis Golembiewski so horrible a name?

Well, sometimes it is. My surname is derived from the name of a saint (literally and genealogically), but that hardly meant anything to some snot-nosed fourth-grader who thought it was just the very funniest thing in the world to say "Muh-muh-muh-muh-muh-muh-may-tuhs." Twenty-five years later, Internet wits still come up with some great ones like "Mamat-ass." Brilliant! If I were 200 pounds heavier and worked at Mr. Cluck's, I might abandon my name and ethnicity too, once I had the chance.

Ditto social class. Hurley's something you just don't see very frequently on television. He's poor. Not a struggling college student or a kid, just poor. Born poor, grew up poor, and living an adult life in poverty. So poor that playing the lottery may even seem like a rational economic action. Nor was he one of those bright and shining stars of the ghetto; he isn't the television subject aspiration, a kid who is going to study hard and do his homework at the kitchen table, pencil scratching and tongue hanging out from the corner of his mouth, ready to set the world aflame once some (white) person finally decides to give him a chance. Hugo was the kind of kid where the best thing you could say about him was that he "stayed out of trouble."

At least, we presume he stayed out of trouble. Hugo did spend some time in a mental hospital, and still carries the weight of his past—where he first encountered the cursed numbers—all the way to Australia and then to the island. He says he has a history as a warrior as well. Could he have been a SoCal gangbanger, or just the best Neutral Good Dwarf Fighter his *Dungeons & Dragons*™ group had ever seen? Thousands of fans of the show immediately assumed the latter—the fat-guy stereotypes are that fully ingrained. (For the record, there are plenty of obese gang members. Plenty.)

In managing his millions, he did all the usual aspiring things: he bought a Hummer, a home for his mother, invested some of the money as best he could (in a domestic box factory! Not exactly a growth industry, is it?), but mostly he just tried to be himself, wearing his usual T-shirts to business meetings and the like. But he still wasn't much, even with his newfound (mis)fortune.

Hurley is desexualized as well, like too many fans. Which major character hasn't had at least a smooch, if only in flashback? Locke's disability and attraction to a phone-sex operator was played for pathos and not laughs, but he's a sexy old guy now, with his smirks and long throwing knives. Hurley is the only principal without even a trace of a sex life. Now there's Libby, of course, but she's a shrink and he's crazy—will their kiss be anything other than yet another "inappropriate" attraction that Hurley will have to repress?

Fans, of course, often have very active, even ridiculous sex lives. *Pace* Heinlein, polyamory is a very big thing, and anyone who has ever attended a SF convention has likely seen enough D-cupped boobs shoved into chain mail and/or corsets for a number of lifetimes. For every sexually rapacious fan, though, there are a few who have never had a relationship, have never been kissed, and have never had any sexual relations with anyone. And these include people well into their thirties, people perhaps a decade older than Hurley.

One of the common coping mechanisms the habitual isolate takes up is an acceptance of the role. I've met many a person, some a little more unattractive than average, to be sure, but all warm and kind and no less attractive than the millions of us who manage to find partners, who have simply declared themselves non-sexual. They're incapable, they say, of experiencing limerance, that mad rush of hormonal head-over-heels love that keeps the species procreating despite how annoying we can be to one another. Too many people have the instinct for it just beaten out of them.

Hurley may well be one of these people. Even as a millionaire, he didn't rush out and claim a bunch of loose women to accompany him everywhere, and he was living in Los Angeles at the time. How hard could it have been? On the island he mostly hangs around with Jack and Charlie, with few scenes involving him and any of the female castaways. (His confrontation with Rousseau is hardly the stuff of heavily sexualized fan fiction.) He even spends time with the kid, Walt, playing backgammon (and losing, and racking up an $83,000 debt) in social situations better suited for equals than an adult and a child.

But where does Hugo end and Hurley begin? On the island, it seems. The former wallflower was already rallying the troops with his easy manner and seemingly newfound social skills. He even became a bit of an action hero, dodging the booby traps littered around the island and finding the battery for Sayid. The Dwarf Fighter seems to have taken a couple of levels in Rogue for just such a contingency. Island life wouldn't be a crisis, but an opportunity (much as it is for Locke, Charlie, and Kate), if not for those damned numbers.

The question is, will we see more? Hurley fans were already aggrieved that the character got the short shrift. *Lost*, with its large ensemble cast of fourteen "main" castaways and a number of minor characters, spends a lot of time on flashbacks of the characters' preisland lives. Hurley only had one major flashback episode in season one, while Charlie and his damn photocopy-thing had two. Jack seems to get flashback episodes every other week, and he's already devilishly handsome, wise, a leader, a medical doctor, and is a player in one of the main romantic subplots. So many of our stereotypes and popular conceptions are born of media representations, so it's no surprise that even in airtime, the smart jock wins and the fat nerd loses, but what about the theme of change and growing into oneself that Hurley represents?

Hurley did get more action in the second season. "Everybody Hates Hugo (2-4)," was, unfortunately, more of the same. We got to see some wackiness—Hurley quitting his job thanks to his lottery winnings, and having a mini-adventure with his equally nerdy pal, but there were problems of pure realism. Why was Hugo berated by the manager for eating chicken on the job? Feeding yourself is one of the very few perks of a food-service job. Back in my McDonald's days, I'd wrap cheese slices around McNuggets and fry 'em up. For the no-collar poor, often the only reason to take such a job is a guarantee of at least one free meal, albeit from "timed out" foods, a day. I guess such concerns are far away when you're writing a hit show.

The rest of "Everybody Hates Hugo" was diverting, but not special. He plays a trick on his former boss, he asks out a girl, and she says yes—and that thread is quickly dropped. There was more sexual tension between Hurley and the African American senior citizen Rose (an asexual Mammy character; she is even the island laundress!) than we were allowed to see between Hurley and an attractive woman of his own age. Instead, we're given a few scenes that culminate in a contrivance: Hugo's pal drives him to the convenience store where Hugo bought his winning ticket, and there happens to be a news crew out front, and the cashier happens to recognize Hugo from across a dark parking lot and through the windows of a van. And then, his friend is a friend no more. Sorry, nerds stick together a bit better than all that.

The island scenes were only slightly less nonsensical. Hurley is put in charge of the storage of food found in a bomb shelter on the island, but Hurley is so overwhelmed by the responsibility that he attempts to blow up the storeroom before being talked out of it by Rose. Only then does he come to a better solution: a luau and free distribution of the food, which was too small to really help the castaways via rationing anyway.

Of course there are hints that Hurley is unstable—he did spend time in a mental hospital—but the drama of "Everybody Hates Hugo" struck a false note. Hurley was already established as a social shark and problem solver, even able to anticipate needs like the census and pleasures like the golf course. He may hate change, and that makes sense, as many nerds do tend to demonstrate signs of developmental delay (including love of the TV shows, toys, and books of their childhoods and adolescences), but I have to say that being stranded on a secret magic island with an invisible robot dinosaur is about as profound a change as one can possibly experience. Worrying about a potential tussle over potato chips and Australian candy bars just seems out of character.

"Dave" was in some ways better, and in other ways worse. Hurley's been hoarding food (because he's fat, see, and thus unable to share), and driven mad by his imaginary friend (no real confidants for Hurley anymore), even gets into a big fight. It's nerd fury, though, the kind of blinding rage that was played for laughs in the film *A Christmas Story*. And he finally gets a kiss too, but is it real or just another hallucination? This being *Lost*, we probably won't find out for another two years, and then it'll all be reversed a few times anyway.

The themes of growth and change are necessarily limited when it comes to nerd/fannish characters. Most science fiction or fantasy shows (*Lost* seems to straddle both genres; we can call it a program "of the uncanny") will offer up a heroic nerd, generally in the form

71

of a well-meaning bumbler who comes through in a pinch. Barkley in *Star Trek: The Next Generation*, Rom in *Deep Space Nine*, Andrew in the later days of *Buffy* (and Willow before him and before hip-lesbianism) are a few. Recent films have the same, including Mr. Universe in *Serenity*, Mouse in *The Matrix*, and any other characters of the same computer hacker/never-leaves-the-house/my-girlfriend-is-a-robot type. That's the homage to the hardcore fan, the tribute to the buyer of novelizations and the convention attendees. They are the end result of the snickering in the Green Room at the San Diego Comic-Con.

That's what they think of *you*.

Hurley is a bit of an improvement on the traditional model, thanks to the theme of self-discovery and rediscovery that runs throughout *Lost*, and thanks to actor Jorge Garcia's natural charisma. (Never has "dude!" sounded so natural.) But ultimately, Hurley is comic relief. When he's around, people plummet past office windows on their way to the pavement. When he gets slapped across the face by a woman, it's his mother, it's because of her traditional Catholic beliefs, and it's played for comic effect. Even the chicken shack he worked in was annihilated by a meteorite ("a meteor...well, a meteorite," says Hurley, a nerdish pedant); it's a funny improbability noteworthy because it sounds so science fictional.

Hurley's curse is also the curse of the scorch, the sad sack. It's his brother who lost his wife, not him, because a fat television loser cannot have a woman outside of the screaming-in-the-living-room model sitcoms. His grandfather died with all the gravitas and pathos of Bikini Girl #2 in a slasher flick. Hurley's first-season flashback episode, "Numbers," was among the funniest and best, and was certainly worth the wait, but dignity is still a ways in coming for the fannish character on fannish television.

Nick Mamatas is the author of the Lovecraftian Beat road novel *Move Under Ground* (Night Shade Books, 2004) and the Marxist Civil War ghost story *Northern Gothic* (Soft Skull Press, 2001), both of which were nominated for the Bram Stoker Award for dark fiction. He's published more than 200 articles and essays in the *Village Voice*, the men's magazine *Razor*, *In These Times*, *Clamor*, *Poets & Writers*, *Silicon Al-*

ley Reporter, *Artbytes*, the *UK Guardian*, five Disinformation Books anthologies, and many other venues and more than forty short stories and comic strips in magazines including *Razor*, *Strange Horizons*, *Chi-Zine*, *Polyphony*, and others. *Under My Roof: A Novel of Neighborhood Nuclear Superiority* (Soft Skull Press) will be released in late 2006.

Lost in Love

A Romance Writer Takes On the Love Stories in *Lost*

LANI DIANE RICH

Romance writers get so little respect in this world. Male chauvinists despise the romance novel because it's "women's literature"; feminists despise it because romances are built around a woman yearning for "the right man." But romance readers know the difference between a great love story and a mediocre one—and romance writers have to learn how to stay on the right side of that line. The good ones soon understand why some love stories intrigue us and others merely put us to sleep.

Let's face it. If love didn't interest us to the point of obsession, we not only wouldn't have an overpopulation problem, we wouldn't even know how to sell cars. And trapped on an island, constantly staring death in the face, you know people will still eye each other and make up their own hot/not-hot list and start rehearsing pickup lines. "Come here often?"

I MUST CONFESS: I'm not big on worst-case-scenario entertainment. Plane crashes, train wrecks, little boys floating in rafts with tigers…it's just not my thing. Watching people in high-stress situations makes *me* highly stressed, and it's just not my cup of tea.

Me, I like love stories. No, scratch that. I *love* love stories. Love stories feed the heart, mind, and soul, and for my money, there's no better storytelling around. And I'm not alone. It's hardly a fluke that every myth that has been passed down through the oral traditions of the ancients started with love—the Egyptians had Geb and Nutt, the Greeks had Zeus and Hera, the Romans had Venus and...well...everyone. (Go, Venus.) Love speaks to the very core of what makes us human, it's a need as real as food, clothing, or shelter, and without it, that core dries up and begins to crack.

Lucky for me, because love stories speak to such a core need, it's the one storytelling element that is truly ubiquitous. While I can think of plenty of stories that don't have horror elements, or comedy, or adventure, or science fiction, I can only think of a small handful that don't include some element of love. And I'm not just talking about romantic, wind-in-her-hair, sex-in-the-surf kind of love, although I'd say easily ninety percent of the entertainment out there includes some of those elements. I'm talking about love in all its incarnations, which, when done right, can completely tweak a character's personality until they either rise above or sink below, but one thing's for sure—they'll never be the same. Love for the family pet (*Old Yeller, ET: The Extra-Terrestrial*), love for a core group of friends (*Divine Secrets of the Ya-Ya Sisterhood, The Big Chill, St. Elmo's Fire*), love between a parent (or parental figure) and a child (*Annie*, any of the Harry Potter series)—they all have that one thing that will make one person put in the effort, take the leap, get totally stupid, and sacrifice everything they hold dear for the sake of the other person.

And, not surprisingly, 2004's biggest worst-case-scenario plane crash of a hit television show is no exception. By the second act of the *Lost* pilot, in the midst of the kind of terrifying event that keeps most of us up nights before boarding a plane, there's sparks flying between our two main heroes, Kate and Jack. She squicked at sewing his wound, he gently talked her through it, and there was the spark. Still, I wasn't sold. For me to be hooked on a television series, I have to love the characters and they have to love each other. Here we had two attractive leads in a new television series—*of course* there's going to be a spark; that couldn't be avoided even if the producers had wanted to. My jury was still out, though; if I was going to sit through the bloody aftermath of a plane crash, the creative team behind *Lost* was going to have to give me more.

And boy howdy, did they. By the end of the first season, love stories were popping up all over the beach. When Michael put everything he had into building a raft so his son, Walt, wouldn't have to grow up on an island, that was a love story. When Rose insisted that her husband Bernard was alive despite the fact that he was in the severed and (at the time) unrecovered tail section of the plane, that was a love story. Sun and Jin, separated from everyone else (and, as it turned out, each other) by a communication barrier, and yet, still having small tender moments between them—love story. Even in the tension between Boone and Shannon—speaking of squick, we'll get to that later—there was a love story. Mysteries and hatches and Others aside, I'm here to tell you that *Lost* is as much about love stories as anything else, and I would argue that Abrams, Lindelof, and Co. are very much aware of that fact. How does *Lost* do love? Let me count the ways....

Kate and Jack. Or, Kate and Sawyer. You Know. Whatever.

The thing that is so amazing about this story is how well something so obvious and overplayed on the surface can work. From the second Kate and Jack make eye contact, you know there's going to be something. They're good looking, they're stranded, both actors have a full-season commitment...instant love connection. Even for a love addict like myself, it was fairly yawn-worthy. Yes, there was chemistry, and the "five seconds of fear" thing in "Pilot (1-1)" worked, especially when Kate used it later after the monster gobbled up the pilot, but still, the Kate-Jack thing was painfully obvious from jump street. Then, later in the season when bad-boy Sawyer starts to spark with Kate, we got the grand poobah of all love-story clichés—the dreaded Love Triangle. For a while, it seemed like this storyline was Number One with a bullet on the Overplayed Parade.

And yet, somehow, it works. Jack manages to be the Hero, good and honorable, without being sanctimonious or annoying. Kate is the Girl with a Past who manages to be neither too self-pitying nor so tough that you no longer care. Sawyer is the Tough Guy Con Artist with no apparent redeeming characteristics aside from a cleft chin and an ability to make five-day stubble look really, *really* good. It's the love triangle you want to hate, but just can't. The reason for this is that a love triangle, in and of itself, is not a bad thing. The problem with love triangles is that traditionally writers sprinkle them over a sagging show like some sort of magical story elixir. No conflict? Add a love triangle. Poor ratings? Add a love triangle. It's Thursday? Add a love triangle. They're as cheap and easy as boxed macaroni and cheese, and when used without care, they're every bit as cardboard.

With Sawyer, Kate, and Jack, though, the love triangle actually serves to push character and story forward. Kate is a good-girl-gone-bad who has a chance to start fresh. She's definitely attracted to Jack, but she kinda got the last doctor she loved killed "Born to Run (1-22)," and she seems to feel pretty bad about that. She's also attracted to Sawyer, who seems like a good match for her. He's flawed to the very core of his being—bonus, she doesn't have to worry about not deserving him. And, deep, deep, *deep* down, he's got a tiny little shred of honor that occasionally bobs to the surface, which redeems him just enough to keep Kate—and us—from writing him off altogether.

For Jack, the love-triangle element plays astonishingly well. While most triangles exist to make people jealous, thus providing instant conflict, Jack defies the cliché. It's obvious he cares about Kate, but he doesn't let that overshadow the other, more important, things going on—like people getting kidnapped, giving birth, being hung from trees, and just generally getting themselves into oooh-I-need-me-a-doctor kinds of trouble. By not making a big deal out of the thing with Kate, the little moments become even more interesting.

Also refreshing is Sawyer's role in the love triangle. He's not overly jealous and angsty about Kate's relationship with Jack; mostly, it appears he's just ready to pounce when the opportunity to cop a feel arises "Confidence Man (1-8)." He's got enough bad in his past to give him some keen insight into Kate's soul, and he can typically be trusted to see through any pretense she might manage to put up. He also doesn't just allow her to see into his past; he willingly pushes it on her by making her read aloud, in one of the most painfully clunky scenes of the season, the letter he carries around in his back pocket in "Confidence Man." He doesn't romanticize her, as we see when he goes head to head with her for the spot on the raft in "Born to Run," and that's a good thing. Unlike Jack, Sawyer knows firsthand what's in Kate's soul. But also unlike Jack, he doesn't really care. And he's got that stubble thing going on, which makes it easier to understand why it's so hard for Kate to choose....

Michael and Walt

As far as love stories go, this one is about as heart-wrenching as any. Michael is the absentee father who loved his son enough to give him up. Then, when Walt's mother dies, Michael's suddenly saddled with a ten-year-old kid to raise and, instead of being thrilled, he's reasonably conflicted about it; he's moved on with his life, and he doesn't know how to fit Walt in. Still, when the choices are in front of him, he chooses to do right by his boy every time. When Walt sees the letters Michael had written, which his mother had kept from him, Michael refuses to play the innocent victim, telling Walt that his mother only did what she thought was best. Still, as the days on the island drag on, Michael lives with his conflict. As Hurley points out in the early days after the crash, Michael seems to hate being a dad. Still, he looks after Walt, and as the story progresses, we can see that everything he does is for Walt. He tries to protect him from danger (the polar bear), bad influences (Locke), and heartbreak, as he cares for Walt's dog, Vincent in "Special (1-14)." He decides to build a raft because he can't stand the thought of Walt growing up on the island, and does everything short of killing himself to get the raft launched. Everything he does, every choice he makes, shows his love for Walt, and when Walt confesses in "Born to Run" that he was the one who burned the original raft down, Michael's automatic, immediate forgiveness and understanding is as taut an illustration of love as we're ever likely to see. When the Others kidnap Walt in "Exodus Pt Two (1-24)," Michael's heartbreak and helplessness is thick and suffocating. Even with his internal conflict over not being sure he's ready to raise his son, Michael is the epitome of parental love, and the hope of his reunion with his son makes tuning in every week in season two an absolute must.

Rose and Bernard

Although for much of the series Rose and Bernard have been secondary characters, their love story is every bit as engaging and powerful as any. Unlike most romantic love stories, which follow through the exciting days when love first evolves, Rose and Bernard are representative of true, lasting love. As a middle-aged couple, they've already done the exciting early days of love, and they have kept their fire burning through the years. Early on, when Rose sat on the beach, stared into the surf, and claimed her faith that her husband was still alive in "Walkabout (1-4)," my heart broke for the poor, deluded woman. Later in the season, as her occasional appearances livened up the episodes she graced, I started to believe her. In season two, when Bernard showed up as one of the survivors of the tail section in "Everybody Hates Hugo (2-4)," I rejoiced and waited anxiously for the moment when her faith would pay off and she and Bernard would be reunited. When that moment finally happened in "Collision (2-8)," it was as joyous as I'd hoped it would be. The thing that makes Rose and Bernard's story work is the strength of their connection to each other. Rose's unshakable faith becomes believable even before we know about the other crash survivors. When we see Bernard, who was lost beyond hope but never beyond Rose's faith, we can share in his joy as he learns that his wife is alive. Very few love stories focus on the beauty of a love that has lasted, but this one does, and does it wonderfully.

Shannon and Boone

While the other love stories focus on the heartbreak and joy of love, Shannon and Boone focus on the dark, "Oh, no, they di-int," side of love. Okay. Sure. They're not *biologically* brother and sister, fine. But still. Raised from the age of ten as brother and sister has a comparable squick factor. Shannon is unlikable from the moment she neglects to help with the wreckage so she can give herself a manicure on the beach, and continues to become less likeable as the series progresses. When she uses the knowledge that Boone loves her to manipulate him into giving her money, it's bad. When she goes to his hotel and sleeps with him, knowing what that would do to him, and then insists they pretend it never happened, she's crossed the border into Supreme Bitchville. Sadly, too-stupid-to-live Boone still pines for her, still makes her wish his command. It's a shame that it takes a trip down Dead Shannon Lane sponsored by Locke's Hallucinogenic Paste in "Deus Ex Machina (1-19)" for Boone to finally strap on a sack and cut the incestuous apron strings. It's an even greater shame that Boone only has possession of said sack for about two episodes before he proves by crawling into a plane held over a cliff by two vines and a spiderweb that he is, literally, too stupid to live in "Do No Harm (1-20)." Ah, Boone. RIP.

Shannon and Sayid

With all due props being given to Abrams, Lindelof, and Co. during the course of this essay, I have to say that I'd like to know what kind of high-class Oahu crack these guys were smoking when they put this pairing together. Sayid is a fascinating character with integrity and strength and inner turmoil and a butt-load of angst, and they paired him with... Shannon? Sure, her dad died and her superbitch of a step-mom cut her out of the family fortune in "Abandoned (2-6)," but for all of us who have had to work for a living from day one I say, boo-frickin-hoo Shannon. She's too shallow to love anyone but herself, too dumb to be truly evil, too narcissistic to care about anything that doesn't directly affect her, and we're supposed to believe that Sayid could love her? I mean, sure, she's pretty. But pretty is just... pretty. And the fact that she takes care of Walt's dog does not mean she has a soul, it just means that the writers were desperate to soften her character. Right next to the "Love Triangle = Conflict" equation in the TV Writer's Handbook is "Dog Lover = Soul" and it's equally fallacious. Vincent's incredible luck of surviving Shannon's indifference does not make her worthy of Sayid. The last woman Sayid loved was a freedom fighter who risked her life for her principles in "Solitary (1-9)," and now he's hot for... Shannon? What? I could understand it if he was just a guy looking for sex—I mean, let's face it, forty days on a desert island and Shannon might start looking good to *me*—but... *love*? *Shannon*? What? Hello? The only thing redeeming this storyline is that Shannon bites it in season two in "Abandoned (2-6)." While Ana Lucia isn't much better, at least she's not...Shannon. Igh.

Sun and Jin

Following the squick and igh that are the romantic misadventures of Shannon Rutherford comes one of the greatest love stories ever to grace the small screen: the love between Sun and Jin. He loves her enough to brutally beat up politicians for her mob-boss father, and she loves him enough not to leave him even when it seems he'll never again be the man she fell in love with in "House of the Rising Sun (1-6)." The thing that's so great about their story is that you never see it coming. At first, it seems like your typical doormat-thug pairing. Nothing interesting to see here, folks. Then, we discover that Sun learned English, that she was going to leave him, that she almost did but when he held up a flower for her, she saw a glimpse of the man she loved, and she changed her mind. Jin, who is distant and unlikable through much of the first season, turns out to have a depth all his own. The fact that he could only have her if he worked for her father, and that he didn't understand entirely what he was getting into until it was too late, makes him sympathetic and tragic. As we learn more about him, see him apologize to his fisherman father for being ashamed of his roots in "...In Translation (1-17)," he only becomes more endearing. When Sun, believing Jin to be dead, loses her wedding rings, we share in her heartbreak in "...And Found (2-5)." And when Jin returns to the beach and they are reunited, it's truly a magical television moment coming from two characters who at first didn't seem like they had much to them in "Collision." They are two people for whom landing on the island was a great blessing—if you forget the monsters and the crazy French lady and the murderous Others. On this island, these two have the one thing they didn't have in the regular world—hope.

Lost is a lot of things. It's a mystery show, a worst-case-scenario show, a show that dissects themes of Science vs. Faith and Man vs. Nature, and a show that breaks new ground on a regular basis. But more than any of this, Lost is a collection of engaging love stories.

And I, for one, wouldn't have my Wednesday nights any other way.

Lani Diane Rich is an award-winning author from Central New York, and also an unapologetic television addict. You can find out more about her at www.lanidianerich.com and also through her group Web blog at www.literarychicks.com.

There Are No Coincidences

Making Meaning in *Lost*

LEIGH ADAMS
WRIGHT

Scientists who study the brain keep finding themselves bumping into the great philosophical issues. One of the greatest and most puzzling is causality. Philosophically speaking, it is impossible ever to be completely certain of cause and effect. Even though event B follows event A every time for a billion times, it doesn't necessarily mean that A causes B. And what brain scientists have found are some clear indications that our brains are predisposed to invent causality. Post hoc ergo propter hoc isn't a logical fallacy, it's a way of life.

I'M THE TYPE OF GIRL who always likes to be prepared. A quick inventory of my purse tells you everything you need to know: mixed in with the usual (wallet, checkbook, Chapstick) are a sewing kit, a bottle opener, and a bundle of twine—just in case.

So you can imagine me packing for my first post-*Lost* plane trip—even 9/11 didn't give me this much trouble, probably because death requires a lot less prep work than an extended stay on an island in the middle of God-only-knows-where. Clothes were selected for all-weather practicality; I added a lighter to my sewing kit for sterilization purposes; I threw in the whole economy-sized bottle of ibuprofen. So that if, by chance, my plane went down and I managed to survive, I'd be ready. (Being useful, in addition, pretty much ensures not being killed off for dramatic purposes. Though, really, all my forethought would have secured was the survival of my luggage.)

It didn't take long before it became clear that my concern (not to mention my packing) was unfounded—and not just because I only ever fly over the continental United States. Not because I don't have any deep dark secrets in my past, either, or because I get along with my parents just fine. Nobody is on this island by chance (except the extras). They're there for a reason.

It's not evident in the first handful of episodes. Initially, the show framed the crash as a tragedy like any other: random, pointless, pure chance. "Act of God" is perhaps the correct term—except not the master-plan type. More along the lines of the your-insurance-isn't-going-to-pay-for-this variety. The first episodes were about the struggle to survive: treating injuries, salvaging suitcases, searching out food and shelter. They were also about getting to know the characters, whether through flashback, through their on-island actions, or through the disparity between the two. But as the survivors settled into island life, and we settled into the rhythm of the show's flashback-centric pacing, something else began to creep in: a sense of connection between the passengers of Oceanic Flight 815, the feeling that neither their presence on the plane, nor the plane's crash landing on that particular island, was an accident.

It was subtle at first: eerie coincidences, bizarrely fortunate circumstances. But after a while the writers dropped the ambiguity. Technically, they kind of started hitting you over the head with it. By Episode 20, I admit, I actually started cringing a little bit whenever it was alluded to. "[I]t's not happenstance that you and Essam met at the mosque," terrorist cell member Hassad told Sayid in a flashback in "The Greater Good" (1-21). "Perhaps it is fate." (Though you could also pretty convincingly argue it was Australia's version of the CIA.) If I hadn't picked up on it before, I certainly would have by then.

What took me a little longer to realize was that it is this very notion—of fate—that makes the show so appealing, and so popular with an audience for which the last must-watch television hit was something along the lines of *Who Wants to Be a Millionaire?* or *Friends*.

There Are No Coincidences

Post-9/11 (and I know, everything these days is explained in terms of being "post 9/11," from legitimate changes in things like airline security to inexplicable ones like in the proverbial price of tea in China—but bear with me), America's taste in entertainment has taken a turn away from reality and into the waiting arms of the metaphoric and the mythic. A blatantly SF/fantasy show like *Lost*, no matter how well-written, well-cast, and well-plotted, never would have survived on a big-three network before the Twin Towers went down, much less become one of the most talked about (not to mention critically acclaimed) shows of the television season. (You could try to argue *Star Trek* with me, but I suspect you'd lose—the last two *Trek* offerings were relegated to third-tier network UPN, and even *Next Gen* never matched *Lost's* numbers. Besides, when is the last time you caught someone debating the *Enterprise's* latest scrape at the office watercooler?) The reason for this isn't, as a lot of people like to believe, that we're looking for escape. What we're looking for, in shows like *Lost*—and in books like the Harry Potter series and movies like the Lord of the Rings series—is *meaning*.

All narratives create meaning. The act of telling stories itself is the act of making meaning, from Tolstoy's *War and Peace* to an episode of *Survivor*: to tell a story is to organize events into a series of causes and effects. A story asserts reasons for actions by selecting the important (in other words, applicable) details and leaving out the extraneous ones—by distinguishing between the ones that *mean* something, and the ones that do not. But *Lost* is particularly explicit about doing so. The relentless way in which even the most menial, inconsequential details of the survivors' lives seem to interconnect—from Sawyer's late-night bar conversation with Jack's father to Hurley's lottery-winning appearance on a television screen in the house of the minister Jin was sent to kill—supercharges everything we see with importance, and lends the *Lost* characters' shared presence on the island an inevitability that speaks of something, some meaning, bigger than they are.

Even without these past connections as reinforcement, the number of last-minute boardings and unintentional bookings alone would have given us pause. Almost none of our heroes, it appears, would have been on that plane if they'd had any other choice. Jack's mother forced him to go to Australia in search of his father in the first place. Kate was arrested, and boarded against her will—in handcuffs. Locke was sent back earlier than planned when he wasn't allowed to attend the walkabout he'd registered for. Sayid's flight was chosen for him after he refused to leave his friend's body. Throw in a couple of mystical occurrences—Hurley's investigation into the numbers curse taking him to Australia, and Claire's psychic friend's insistence that she *must* be on that plane—and you can't help but get the sense that the universe had been somehow aligned against them. (Or maybe, in some cases, for them.)

And speaking of Hurley's numbers, their presence on the island—the continuity they provide for the viewer between the Real Life flashbacks and the God-Knows-What of the island "now"—is perhaps the most convincing, if also the most foreboding, evidence that there's something seriously, *seriously* weird going on.

We don't know what, exactly, that weird thing is. But really? It doesn't matter. The important part is not what the answer to the riddle is, but that there's an answer to find at all.

Lost is generally referred to as a supernatural thriller, but we won't really be able to say, with any certainty, what kind of show it is until the end—that is, the solution to *Lost's* mystery will be what provides us with the correct context in which to understand everything we've seen. In the absence of that resolution, however, we can look at what the show has given us so far, and the types of theories those hints suggest. Those theories, at least from what I've read online, tend to fall into one of two basic categories: fantasy and science fiction. The first season's events, especially, point us toward a mystical answer; between strange black smoke and the mysterious Others, Locke's miraculous recovery and a series of numbers that carry a curse, the idea that there's something super spooky going on isn't a hard one to believe.

Locke's recovery of the use of his legs, or rather the language he (and I) chose to describe it, also points to another answer to the mystery: a religious one. The show sets up (and, okay, hammers in a little bit at the end of the first season) a dichotomy between faith and science, between Locke and Jack, for good reason: faith, or rather the thing in which one places that faith, is a front runner for the Answer-to-the-Mystery crown. Locke's success in the first season—from his talent at survival to the way "listening to the island" always seemed to pay off (even if it exacted a price, like Boone's death, or resulted in unexpected consequences, as opening the hatch did)—is a strong indication that a religious explanation might not be a bad one to keep in mind. But a religious answer—they're in purgatory, God is playing with or testing them—is the same, for narrative purposes, as a fantastical one. Change *the* God to *a* god, and you've landed yourself squarely in fantasy territory. And either way, the force at work is *su-pernatural* and largely inexplicable, and the best way to find the answers you're seeking is to follow the signs you encounter, fulfill the tasks you're given and hope for the best—trusting that, even if the force at work isn't exactly benevolent, there is in fact intention behind its (or Its) actions.

In a science fiction explanation, in contrast, the force(s) at work are impersonal. Rather than through its intentions, an SF "force" and its "purpose" are discernable through their consistency—through experimentation and the analysis of that experimentation's results. (This is the real difference between Jack's and Locke's reactions to the "Doomsday Button": Locke's impulse is to follow the plan to its end to learn its purpose; Jack's, in effect, is to vary the plan and observe the results.) The revelations of the second season—the introduction of the outdated, but functional, technology inside the hatch, and even, cheesy as they may be, the scientists in lab coats in the Dharma Initiative training film—have encouraged a science fiction explanation, even if we don't yet understand exactly how that science works.

But the important part of both the fantasy and science fiction solution is that there is an explanation to the survivors' presence on the island, and that the explanation is *knowable*—though the ways in which one might come to know it differ. There is a reason for them being there, whether an incidental one in which these people have been inexplicably caught or a purposeful one for which these people were intentionally selected. Because where there is a reason, there is the possibility of negating that reason—of solving the puzzle, of sussing out its purpose, of assuaging the angry god. Where there is a reason, there is also hope. Because where there is a reason, there is the possibility of *control*.

Lost, in the end, is more comforting than it is frightening. What's really scary isn't the *Black Rock* or the Others; what's scary is the unknown, and that which is unknowable. What's scary is the idea of a threat that doesn't care who you are—that you cannot reason with, that has no intention you can ascertain. Lack of control, and lack of any hope of ever gaining any. That's what keeps us up at night, worrying over what to pack. We attempt to exert some sort of control with sewing kits and ibuprofen, handguns and herb gardens, over things that cannot be controlled, things like plane crashes that come upon us unawares, and about which there is nothing we can do.

Whatever the mystery eventually turns out to be, the island has intent. Or the numbers do. Or God, or the devil, or whatever it was those Dharma Initiative scientists were studying. Maybe the scientists themselves. The point is, there's a *plan*. And no matter what that plan ends up being, that one exists at all is an inalienable comfort in a world that often seems random, senseless, and unnecessarily cruel.

Pop-culture devotee Leigh Adams Wright is often teased about the size of her purse but, curiously, no one ever complains when they need a Band-Aid or a nail file. See her previous work in the other Smart Pop anthologies *Finding Serenity*, *Alias Assumed*, and *Totally Charmed*.

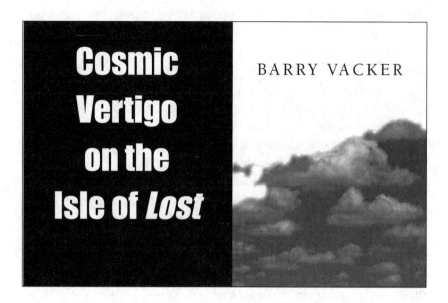

Cosmic Vertigo on the Isle of *Lost*

BARRY VACKER

My wife hates islands. They're so small. When it took us only an hour or so to drive around Oahu, she started getting antsy to go home to the continent, where you can drive and drive and drive and still be in Texas.

But islands still intrigue us. When I stand on a shoreline and see a tiny outcropping of rock, I find myself trying to figure out a way to get onto it without drowning or getting pounded to death by surf against stone. Tom Sawyer and his gang couldn't resist that muddy island in the Missizip. Cartoonists have been sticking people on that same tiny island with a single palm tree for more years than I've been alive. Islands are tiny universes; we can look around and see everything. Islands are the end of the world.

> The terror was so crazy, so real, and I knew I had to deal with it.
> —Jack

Lost Amidst the Seas or Stars?
The show is about lost people on a lost island.
—J. J. Abrams and Damon Lindelof (co-creators of *Lost*)

GETTING LOST

SO, HERE WE ARE, humanity having survived six years beyond the three zeros of the new millennium, six years beyond 2000. Are we lost?

Is being lost the condition symbolized by Jack's compass-like tattoo at the top of his left arm, a tattoo which is on vivid display in the first minutes of the pilot episode of *Lost*? The tattoo is not a complete compass, only a partial compass, perhaps suggesting a compass broken or rendered inoperable. Such meaning seems likely, especially considering the tattoo of spirals and flaming stars, which lie almost completely hidden, tucked on the inside of Jack's left bicep and elbow? Shirtless, Jack may be a sexy guy, but is he bearing the mark of a human compass no longer able to navigate the seas and stars?

Lost. It's a great story, one for the ages.

Swept by fate to an island amidst a vast ocean, a solitary island filled with mysterious wonders, generating awe and fear, the ugly and the beautiful, the ridiculous and the sublime. As the survivors tell us the stories of the island, we realize they are actually talking about our world, the modern world situated across the seas, far removed from the island paradise. In these stories, we see the mythos of modernity, the destiny of its future that is past. It's a great story, one for the ages—it is called *New Atlantis* and it was written in 1629 by Francis Bacon.[1] *New Atlantis* is perhaps one of the most influential and prophetic fictional futures ever penned, because the story theorized a technological future that has been realized over the subsequent centuries.

So, what could a short story written four centuries ago have to do with decoding *Lost*, a hit television show in 2006? At first glance, *Lost* reveals a televised synthesis of *Lost World* and *Lord of the Flies*, offering a metaphorical tale of human survival and human civilization. While accurate, there is another theme, perhaps deeper and more disturbing. *Lost* indeed depicts a "lost world," yet the show illustrates the paradox of a "new world" fast becoming a "lost world," the very conditions humanity faces entering the new millennium. The modern world was once the new world, yet it is now entropic, leaving the emerging postmodern to confront the reemerging pre-modern. Yes,

---

[1] Francis Bacon, "New Atlantis," in *Ideal Commonwealths* (New York: Dedalus/Hippocrene, [1629] 1988): 103–37.

Lost is fun and strange, but it is also loaded with heavy meanings, very heavy, so heavy they cause things to crash.

The heaviest meanings in *Lost* can be found by situating the island-based show on a trajectory shared with two other island myths, each of which points toward the cultural and technological conditions of humanity, past and future. Plato's Atlantis foresaw the human condition in the tale of the ideal society for pre-modern conditions, Bacon's *New Atlantis* prophesied the modern technological ambition, and *Lost* projected the postmodern technological vertigo. From Atlantis to *New Atlantis* to *Lost*, we see the trajectory and vertigo of human possibility, manifest in plane crashes and mysterious islands, symbolizing humanity's relations with technology and nature. Yes, the trajectory of human culture is televised as if a disaster movie!

93

Visions of Vertigo
My head is a little dizzy right now.
—The Pilot

In the pilot episode of *Lost*, the first scene shows an extreme close-up of a human eye, dilated and then coming into focus. The eye belongs to Jack, the doctor, the man of science, lying on his back in the jungle, looking upward, toward the skies, which lie mostly hidden beyond the forest of bamboo towering above him. After Jack struggles to his feet and dashes through the bamboo toward the beach, his eyes soon survey a most extreme condition. A jetliner has crashed on the beach of an island, flames still burning, debris everywhere, people dead or dying, and the survivors staggering around in utter shock. The first few minutes of the pilot episode set the technological trajectory for the first season—crashed airliners, the cockpit landing in a tree, a passenger sucked into a jet engine, the fuselage of the plane used as a funeral pyre, cell phones with no connections, mysterious radio transmissions, wires buried beneath the beach, useless laptops pillaged for batteries, sailing ships filled with skeletons stranded high up on the island, and glowing hatches leading to the depths.

Of course, Jack's eyes are our eyes, and through Jack's eyes we are seeing some kind of vision, a cinematic technique employed in any number of science fiction films, from *2001: A Space Odyssey* to *Blade*

Runner to *The Terminator*. Through Jack's eyes in those first few moments we surveyed a certain human condition, a cultural condition illustrated across the first season, the postmodern condition of technological and cosmic vertigo.

Since the arrival of the Bomb, urban decay, energy crises, blackouts, widespread pollution, and all the other unintended and unexpected consequences of industrialization, the once-soaring confidence in modern technology has not only been shaken, but also symbolically brought down to Earth. This vertiginous condition is illustrated by the proliferation of apocalyptic films and "disaster movies" involving technology—*Dr. Strangelove, Fail-Safe, Planet of the Apes, Soylent Green, The Poseidon Adventure, Airport, Westworld, The Towering Inferno,* the *Mad Max* trilogy, *The Matrix* trilogy, and many others. Regarding disaster movies, *Lost* co-creator J. J. Abrams exclaimed: "I love those movies!" Co-creator Damon Lindelof added: "Me, too. *The Towering Inferno* is like the greatest movie, ever." The cinematic milieu of disaster movies informed the creation of *Lost*, as explained by Abrams:

> *I grew up on movies like* Earthquake, The Poseidon Adventure, *the* Airport *movies.... The approach was not to consciously avoid any clichés or stylistically borrow from some other genre, but to take a storyline that might easily fit into the classic 1970s disaster movies and then tell it in a way that felt committed and real and scary and unique.*[2]

In apocalyptic and disaster movies, something is always falling, literally and figuratively—bombs dropping, skyscrapers collapsing, jets crashing, ships sinking, civilization collapsing, and of, course, people falling from buildings, falling from planes, drowning in the ocean, and so on. *Lost* continues this vertiginous trajectory, with a jetliner crashing on a mysterious island, bringing survivors down to Earth to confront life without the infrastructure of modernity, without a compass for the stars.

94

[2] Mark Cotta Vaz, *The Lost Chronicles* (New York: Hyperion, 2005): 79.

Cosmic Vertigo on the Isle of *Lost*

Launched on the Isle of *New Atlantis*
Everyone gets a new life on this island.
—Locke

Locke's observation about everyone getting a "new life" was implied by the title of the first episode (following the two-part pilot), called "Tabula Rasa (1-3)." By crashing on the island, everyone was given a blank slate, and a new start, a new future, a new tomorrow. Of course, the condition of "tabula rasa" has a double meaning. Not only is everyone given a personal clean slate, but the life they would live would be new, at least in contrast to their lifestyles in the modern world they previously navigated, with all the technological and cultural compasses. Though mostly forgotten now, one of the central promises of modernity was a "new life" in a "new world," where science and technology would guide humanity out of the poverty and ignorance that had dominated most of human existence.

In *Lost*, a jetliner encounters turbulence over the ocean and eventually crashes, partially on the island and partially in the sea. The survivors are those from the fuselage section that tumbled down on the island. In Bacon's *New Atlantis*, the vessel is a sailing ship, which encounters the turbulence of a massive hurricane. In the televised terms of the Weather Channel, this hurricane was likely a "Cat 5" (Category Five, the most powerful hurricane). As with the passengers in *Lost*, the surviving sailors are hurled beyond the space-time coordinates of the known world. A few sailors managed to survive in a life raft but are without a compass, adrift for many days in the vast ocean. Eventually, the sailors encounter a very mysterious island. Most strange is that this island, previously unknown to the world, is home to a functioning utopia, the first model of the modern technological society.

The apocalyptic hurricane transported the sailors beyond the old world, cleansing their vision, enabling them to arrive in the new world, a blank slate written anew. The world that Bacon theorized was a post-medieval world, a modern world ordered via science and technology. In *New Atlantis*, the scientist and technologist would assume equal status with the politician and theologian, with the planners of the utopia using scientific procedure and empirical knowledge to establish the technological sovereignty of humans over nature. This philosophy was expressed in the guiding principle of the island civilization: "The end of our foundation is the knowledge of causes, and secret motions of things, and the enlarging of the bounds of human empire, the effecting of all things possible."[3]

Four centuries later, it is easy to dismiss this principle as utopian hyperbole, especially after seeing the industrial consequences of "the effecting of all things possible." However, it is impossible not to see that many of the technological themes in *New Atlantis* have been realized in building the modern world, where we now inhabit a technological mode of existence. To display these themes, the island was structured much like a World's Fair or theme park, with palace-like "houses" for modeling nature, conducting experiments, and demonstrating technological possibilities.

Though Bacon was speaking in general terms, the following examples offer a striking anticipation of specific technologies of the modern world: 1) machines for generating varieties of heat, including heat from the sun and heat from motion; 2) houses of metallurgy, for creating all kinds of precious minerals and re-creating precious gems; 3) "engine-houses" for machines generating all kinds of motion, natural and mechanical, including rapid acceleration and perpetual motion; 4) artificial wells and fountains filled with water; 5) towers one-half mile high, used for all kinds of meteorological observations; 6) "perspective-houses" for conducting all kinds of experiments with light, including "multiplications of light" which they transmit to great distances, and which they receive from afar; 7) the "interknowledge" of other nations via "magicians" of land and air; 8) "sound-houses" for re-creating all kinds of harmonies—natural, artificial, and musical; the human voice is also amplified over great distances; 9) gardens and orchards for manipulating every kind of agricultural production—increasing the variety of foods and making them "greater than their nature"; 10) parks for breeding and re-designing all kinds of animals—altering size, shape, and color; 11) houses for simulating various weather phenomena—rain, storms, lightning, and so on; 12) the greatest inventions are housed in galleries, along with statues of the greatest inventors.[4]

---

[3] Francis Bacon, *New Atlantis*, 129.
[4] Francis Bacon, *New Atlantis*, 113–114, 129–37.

Bacon's vision is remarkable, considering he was writing in 1626, before Newton and before the steam engine, electricity, and electronic media. Examples 1–5 point toward the foundations of the modern metropolis: electricity, industrialization, mechanization, motorized transportation, indoor plumbing, human control of water resources, and skyscraper-like towers. Examples 6–8 point toward the foundations of the information age: electric light and mass media, including photography, sound recording, radio, and television. Some might go so far as to suggest the multiplications of light and sound across great distances is what makes possible the Internet—the "interknowledge" among nations. Examples 9 and 10 point toward advanced agricultural technologies, breeding of animals, and perhaps even genetic manipulation. Though humans have not learned to control the weather (yet), it is certainly being simulated and modeled on the Weather Channel. The final example illustrates the reverence for the great inventors and inventions, not unlike how scientists, innovators, and industrialists are viewed in the modern world, from Newton to Einstein to Hawking, Henry Ford to Steve Jobs to Bill Gates.

Francis Bacon's *New Atlantis* remains one of the most visionary and influential utopian models ever imagined, for launched on the mythical island was the all-too-real trajectory of the modern world. Abandoning cave and castle for city, we now inhabit electrified metropolises with towering skyscrapers and sprawling suburbs. There are malls and stores brimming with goods and foods, cars and planes crossing continents, satellites and space shuttles orbiting the world, cyberspace and the Internet circling the world. Launched from *New Atlantis*, the modern world has indeed rocketed across the skies and into the stars, from planes to satellites to rockets. From *tabula rasa* to total technology, the blank slate is no more.

So why, at the pinnacle of building this world, has there been such a proliferation of apocalyptic films and disaster movies, all suggesting the crash of the modern world? And why is there *Lost*, a hit show inspired by such films, in which there are lost people having crashed on a lost island? To fully answer this question, we must return to the birth of all lost-world mythologies, the island of Plato's Atlantis. Yeah, more heavy meanings are coming, but it takes heavy stuff to crash things down to Earth, be it gravity or vertigo.

Vertigo on the Isle of Atlantis

You guys... is this normal? Kind of day turning into night... you know ... end-of-the-world kind of weather.
—Charlie

Early in the pilot episode of *Lost*, Charlie joined Jack and Kate in a quest to find the cockpit of the crashed plane, which they think may have landed on the island. As they walk through the jungle-like growth on the island, the searchers are drenched by monsoon-like rains, prompting Charlie to wonder aloud if they were facing "end-of-the-world kind of weather." Perhaps Charlie's predicament is not merely a dependency on drugs and being a rock star. After all, his band's name was "DriveSHAFT," surely a technology central to modern mechanization and transportation. Has modernity driven so far it has crashed on the island? And DriveSHAFT's most famous song was "You All Everybody," the phrase Charlie sang to Kate and Jack when she mentioned that he seemed vaguely familiar. If Jack and Kate are "everybody," then is their fate our condition?

Like the disaster movies cherished by the creators of *Lost*, Charlie's end-of-the-world paranoia taps into a long trajectory of apocalyptic mythologies, where the human world is destroyed by hubris, arrogance, greed, ideology, or technology run amok. Here, one might immediately think of the biblical prophesies of Revelation, where the end of the world was greeted by all kinds of turbulent weather phenomena. If the Revelation version of The End occurs anytime soon, it will surely be hyped 24/7 on the Weather Channel. After all, the Weather Channel has created an apocalyptic new series called *It Could Happen Tomorrow*, and the first three episodes featured a hurricane drowning the Big Apple, a tornado destroying Big D (Dallas), and a volcano making a big mess with Seattle. Despite the cool special effects prophesied in Revelation, we must go back further in history to find the origin of the apocalyptic fears and fantasies about lost worlds.

If the trajectory of the modern world rises from Bacon's *New Atlantis*, then the trajectory of the "lost world" reaches back to Plato's *Atlantis*, where a new world became a lost world. Here is the origin for the vertigo that faces every culture at its height—in the power to create a new world we can also destroy the world.

Plato's Atlantis was an island utopia, the first utopia in Western culture, the first utopia to disappear in an apocalypse and the first science fiction utopia to project a technological future where humans lived with nature by conquering nature. Born in the dialogues of *Timaeus* and *Critias*, the myth of Atlantis was described by Plato with such poetic detail that is seemed like a civilization that surely could have existed. The story was told by Critias in response to Socrates's question about whether an ideal society had ever existed.[5] The story of Atlantis went as follows.

Nine thousand years earlier, Atlantis existed as a great civilization situated on a magnificent island, somewhere in the oceans beyond the known world. Three sides of the island contained cliffs and mountains, while one side was open to the seas. Between the mountains was a rectangular plain, a fertile agricultural area irrigated with a grid of canals and channels, which carried river water flowing from the mountains. The island was also populated by many kinds of animals, along with exotic plants and fruits. There was an abundant supply of precious metals and food, so much that Atlanteans wanted for nothing in this paradise on Earth. Possessing great wealth, the power of Atlantis extended around the world.

The capital of Atlantis was situated on the open side of the island, between the plain and the seas. The city was structured as a series of concentric circles—alternate rings of land and water. Connected by bridges, the rings of land contained places to appreciate art and nature, gardens and fountains, places for exercise and contemplation. At the center of the city was the palace of the gods, surrounded by walls of gold and statuary. Ruling over Atlantis was a benevolent royalty, and the island utopia was protected by a powerful military. Despite the wealth and luxury, the Atlanteans were not intoxicated by the abundance and dedicated themselves to pursuing knowledge and living in harmony.

Eventually hubris and power-lust emerged on the island civilization, and the Atlanteans began enslaving other cultures around the world. However, the regime of Atlantis soon met its fate, for Athens dealt the Atlanteans a crushing military defeat, ending the civiliza-

---

[5] Plato, *Timaeus and Critias*, trans. Desmond Lee (New York: Penguin Classics, 1971): 109–21.

tion that went from utopia to dystopia. The cosmic forces turned against Atlantis, for it was soon destroyed in an apocalypse of earthquakes and hurricanes, causing the island to disappear forever beneath the ocean. For Atlantis, which had risen to such heights, it was the end of the world, exactly what Charlie feared in *Lost*.

Over the millennia, Plato's Atlantis exerted a lasting influence. Atlantis was the first utopia where nature and technology existed in harmony, with agriculture and irrigation amplifying the bounty of nature. Atlantis was the first model of the urban plan, where the city is ordered through geometric forms. Circles, spheres, and grids dominated virtually all subsequent utopian models, up through the twentieth century, from Le Corbusier and the modern metropolis to Walt Disney and the postmodern theme park. Perhaps most important, Atlantis originated two key utopian concepts that have spanned the millennia—the "new world" and the "lost world." It is these two concepts that inform the technological trajectory illustrated in *Lost*.

Atlantis was the first model of a utopian "new world," a human-created world that overcame the constraints of pure nature through the deployment of technology. In other words, Atlantis was the first example of the machine that transformed the garden. Since Atlantis deployed technology and planning, it was the genetic origin for the succession of rationalized utopian models, all oriented toward the future—the new world, the march of science, technological paradise, land of progress, metropolis, global village, information age, network society, and so on. Since Atlantis was destroyed in an apocalypse, it was also the first model of a "lost world," a world or civilization that was destroyed or had disappeared. Atlantis is the genetic origin for an endless variety of nostalgic utopian models, all looking toward the past—the lost world, return to nature, garden paradise, promised land, small towns, local village, golden age, Gaia hypothesis, and so on.

Proponents of either utopian model (lost world or new world) believe that their vision will enable humanity to live more peacefully and harmoniously, with nature and/or with each other. Proponents of "lost world" utopias view the current cultural and/or natural worlds as degenerating toward doom and destruction, and thus assert that we need to preserve a world being lost, a world that existed in a more perfect yesterday.

Proponents of "new world" utopias also view the cultural world as entropic or chaotic, but assert that we can technologically improve this world, a world that will exist in a better tomorrow. Proponents of new world utopias often view the lost world utopias as simplistic and sentimental, antiquated, and outdated.

In the end, Atlantis poses the great paradox for humanity—we possess the power to improve the world or destroy it. We can ascend the heights to create a new world, or come crashing down to create a lost world. In the technological heavens, we have experienced the vertigo, the fear of the great fall. This vertigo is perfectly illustrated on another lost island, where the survivors have experienced the great fall in the crash of a jetliner.

Crashing on the Isle of Lost
Don't worry, it's gonna be over.
—Jack (to a passenger while on the plane
during the turbulence that caused the crash)

So, here we are, six years into the millennium. Are we lost? As suggested by Jack's tattoos, are we now navigating with a broken compass, lost amidst the seas and stars?

Well, it is not enough to merely say that the trajectory of modernity has encircled the planet with all its technologies. Since World War II, the atom has been split, the gene mapped, sheep cloned, crops modified, organs transplanted, breasts implanted, penises inflated, ozone depleted, planet polluted, wars waged, bombs dropped, privacy ended, malls filled, wealth created, capital virtualized, space-time relativized, black holes verified, chaos theorized, reality televised, and the village globalized. *Apollo* landed on the moon, *Voyager* left the solar system, and Hubble gazes from outer space across the universe of the Big Bang.

Sending astronauts to the moon and media throughout the solar system, the space age and information age reflect the heights of modernity, the pinnacles of technological achievement in the stars of outer space and cyberspace. Surely, jetliners are another triumph of modern technology, propelling people around the planet, just like the information circulating throughout the global village. In the first ten minutes of the pilot episode, the creators of *Lost* crafted a brilliant synthesis of the technological vertigo that underlies the disaster movies. They also captured a certain cosmic vertigo.

The first scene shows a close-up of Jack's eye, dilated and then coming into focus. As Jack focuses his eyes and directs his awareness, he is staring up toward the sky, largely hidden beyond the vanishing point created by the bamboo rising above him.

Anxious and uncertain, Jack experiences shortness of breath. Jack struggles to get up, and then begins running, passing a shoe dangling from a bamboo shoot. Someone has fallen back to Earth. After the mad dash through the bamboo forest, Jack finds himself surveying the shoreline. To his right is a pristine beach, untouched by humanity, with nothing but nature. As Jack scans to the left, we hear screams in the distance, becoming louder as Jack steps farther from the foliage to see debris of a jetliner, having crashed in part on the beach. The patterns of Jack's eyes are revealing, going from dilation to focus, from pristine nature to technological carnage.

Jack instinctively runs toward the crash site and then begins to scramble and stumble through the wreckage. Surviving passengers are staggering around, stunned or screaming. Some are shouting for family members, while others are trapped beneath parts of the plane. As Jack helps Claire, who is eight months pregnant, another man is sucked into a jet engine. The engine is lying on the beach but still connected to one wing and apparently receiving some power. Immediately upon sucking in the man, the engine explodes with an apocalyptic blast, knocking Jack and some others to the ground. Should we wonder: to what are we giving birth with our technology, a new world or our demise? In the context of *Lost*, it would be easy to conclude the technology we created is sucking us up, destined for an apocalypse, the technological vertigo of modernity.

Jack pauses his scramble, seeming to get his bearings, trying to get his mind around what has happened. As he is doing this, he glances upward, toward the sky. Towering above him is a wing of the plane, spewing fuel and still attached to the remaining fuselage, smoldering upside down on the beach. The jet engine is missing from the wing. In the background, we hear screams: "Help! Help!" We then see a shot of Jack, standing amidst the debris, staring up at the wing, extending from the fuselage toward the skies, at a forty-five-degree angle. It is a very striking image. Soon after, the wing comes crashing down, triggering a massive explosion that knocks down Jack and Claire.

When Jack's eyes first open while lying beneath the bamboo, we see his tie, lying across his heart as he comes to consciousness. The tie has a repetitive pattern on a dark fabric. Crossing the tie at forty-five-degree angles is a series of propellers. When Jack, Kate, and Charlie discovered the portion of the plane with the cockpit, it was leaning against a large tree at a forty-five-degree angle. This portion of the plane soon crashed to the ground.

Jet engine or propeller power, technology has crashed, apparently returning to Earth at a forty-five-degree angle. Strangely the jetliner in *Lost* met the same geometric fate as the Space Needle in *Fight Club*. The Space Needle was designed to symbolize the space age, one of the themes celebrated at the 1962 Seattle World's Fair. In the following passage from the novel *Fight Club*, Tyler Durden described his vision of utopia:

> "You'll hunt elk through the damp canyon forests around the ruins of Rockefeller Center, and dig clams next to the skeleton of the Space Needle leaning at a forty-five degree angle.... You'll wear leather clothes that will last you the rest of your life, and you'll climb the wrist-thick kudzu vines that wrap the Sears Tower. Jack and the beanstalk, you'll climb up through the dripping forest canopy and the air will be so clean you'll see tiny figures pounding corn and laying strips of venison to dry in the empty car pool lane of an abandoned superhighway stretching eight-lanes-wide and August-hot for a thousand miles. This was the goal of Project Mayhem, Tyler said, the complete and utter destruction of civilization."[6]

In Tyler Durden's ideal future, civilization is destroyed and the survivors become hunter-gatherers wandering amidst the cultural debris. A similar fate awaits the survivors on *Lost*, beginning a hunter-gatherer existence amidst the debris of a plane crash.

So, why are things crashing at forty-five-degree angles? Since a

---

[6] Chuck Palahniuk, *Fight Club* (New York: Henry Holt and Company, 1996): 116.

103

forty-five-degree angle is an "acute" angle, perhaps this means *Lost* and *Fight Club* are perceptive in suggesting civilization has reached a critical stage, a severe crisis. In the *Fight Club* future, the modern world becomes the lost world. In *Lost*, the modern world is now a lost world, lost to those survivors, stuck on a lost world that is their new world, their new life, their *tabula rasa*.

In the opening minutes of the pilot episode, we also see the end of the first day, with the sun setting beyond the ocean horizon. Humans have built fires, perhaps to stay warm or to signal to passing planes. Boone is dialing his cell phone but unable to receive a signal. As Boone is trying to make an electronic connection, he walks past Sayid tossing logs on a fire. In these few scenes it is clear—the global village is now a local village.

The forty-five-degree angle was also present in Jack's compass tattoo. The left part of the tattoo looks like the lines on a compass, which extend around like numbers on a clock. At the left-center of the tattoo is the number "5," leaning to the right at a forty-five-degree angle. The number 5 refers to how Jack confronts his fears, his own vertigo. As Kate sews up a laceration on Jack's left side, across from the tattoo of stars, Jack relates how he dealt with his fears during a surgery that seemed to be going awry:

> *"The terror was so crazy, so real, and I knew I had to deal with it. So I just made a choice. I'd let the fear in, let it take over, let it do its thing. But only for five seconds. That was all I was going to give it. So I started to count: 1...2...3...4...5. And then it was done. I went back to work and sewed her up and she was fine."*

For Jack, the five seconds of fear functions like a compass, enabling him to navigate the existential conditions of his life and career.

Atop the leaning "5" are three lines that form the shape of an arrow, which comprise the upper right half of the tattoo. The arrow points at a forty-five-degree angle, up and away from the stars tattooed on the inside of Jack's arm. Perhaps the stars are suggestive of a more radical condition than being lost on an island. There are seven stars discernable in the tattoo. The largest stars are clustered close to a swirling red flame while the smaller stars are located farther away from the center—is this tattoo a microcosm of the Big Bang and the fate of the universe?

In a cosmic sense, perhaps we have become lost, precisely as we discovered our location in the universe. We no longer reside on a world at the center of the cosmos. Earth is spinning around the sun, in a solar system located in a remote region of the Milky Way, a spiral galaxy spinning in an isolated region of the ever-expanding universe. Our blue planet orbits one of 200 billion stars in the Milky Way, which is one of 200 billion galaxies, all filled with billions of stars. Despite the number of galaxies, the Milky Way is destined to become ever more secluded as the void-like nothingnesses expand to push the galaxies away in all directions. In that sense, no computer knows precisely where we are, other than to say we are spiraling around the super-massive black hole at the center of the Milky Way, and the entire galaxy is hurtling through the universe. Since the Big Bang occurred fifteen billion years ago, this universe has been expanding in all directions. Moving apart at ever greater speeds, the galaxies are destined to move farther away from each other, until each one seems ever smaller as it disappears beyond the horizons of all the other galaxies. All of the universe is receding from view in all directions.[7]

And we should not forget that it was electronic media (radio telescopes and satellites) that confirmed the Big Bang after it was first theorized by Edwin Hubble, using images gathered via telescopes and captured on photographic plates. This seems a strange fate—to be lost amidst a cosmos we know ever better.

Perhaps this fate is why Jack's tattoo is a compass disconnected from the stars. The electronic transceiver recovered from the plane is almost broken and low on battery juice, thus making it risky to send out any signals that may not be received. According to the pilot, the jetliner had a broken radio and no ability to be tracked by radar. The pilot and crew had turned the plane in the direction of Fiji, so the plane was one thousand miles off course before crashing. So, no one knows where the survivors are, including the survivors and any possible search teams. Disconnected from the global networks of elec-

---

[7] Brian Greene, *The Fabric of the Cosmos* (New York: Vintage, 2004): 272–303.

tronic media, the hopes for rescue seem slim. In terms of both space and time, the survivors are lost. They do not know where they are or when they are. The absence of modern technologies is propelling the survivors further back across the millennia, to living as hunter-gatherers and cave people in a lost world. In an expanding universe, their world has collapsed into an island cosmos, which they navigate with their hand-made compasses. In this sense, *Lost* is in *The Twilight Zone.*

In splitting the atom, we can power the world or destroy the world. In the Hubble telescope we can discover our place in the cosmos precisely as we realize we are lost in space. In our most powerful technologies, we face a Möbius condition—the flip side of atomic power is total destruction, the flip side of electronic telescopes is discovering that our place in the universe is no "place," as in not any place other than in perpetual motion amidst the vast voids. Entering the millennium, we face an ironic paradox of technological accomplishment, for our technologies threaten to destroy the world while our telescopes reveal a disappearing universe.

If that is not heavy enough to provide a bit of cosmic vertigo, then nothing will, not even crashing on the isle of *Lost*. Perhaps we will always seem a bit lost, especially if we do not choose to confront our cosmic vertigo, to accept the fate of our universe, to let it expand around us and all through us, even if for only five seconds.

Barry Vacker is a professor of media theory at Temple University in Philadelphia. His writings explore the models of utopia and dystopia that are shaping the postmodern world; influenced by Sartre, McLuhan, and Baudrillard, he recently completed the book manuscripts *Utopia and Nothingness* and *Media and Nothingness*. Vacker's writings have critiqued the utopian and dystopian themes represented in the Big Bang, the Millennium Dome, the Twin Towers, the Gaia hypothesis, the Guggenheim-Bilbao, Burning Man, *Fight Club*, Las Vegas, Death Valley, *Fahrenheit 9/11*, New Orleans, Coke Zero, chaos theory, cyberspace, and many others (www.barryvacker.net). Not limited to writing, Vacker co-organized a symposium that was one of the earliest telecasts on the Internet in 1996; he questioned the meaning of *The Matrix* with Anderson Cooper on CNN in 2003; and he wrote and directed the experimental film *Space Times Square*, which will be released in fall 2006. Vacker earned his Ph.D. from the University of Texas at Austin in 1995.

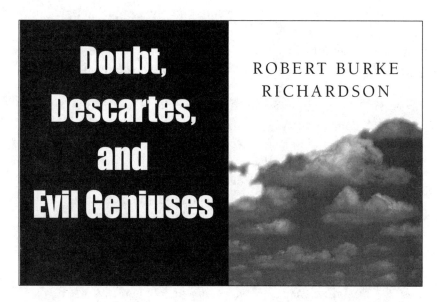

Doubt, Descartes, and Evil Geniuses

ROBERT BURKE RICHARDSON

I'm basically a decent guy, but I have one obsessive vice. My legs, from toe to knee, are exactly the right height that I can sit at most dining tables and, without any visible effort, raise up the table, slowly and imperceptibly, and then make it move very slightly from side to side. As long as no one was leaning on the table, they don't notice I'm doing it. But their peripheral vision picks up the motion of the table and some of them, at least, become slightly uncomfortable; some even get hit by a bit of motion sickness. And then, just as they're about to comment on it, I stop, having fiddled with other people's reality and made their world just a little more strange.

Trust me, this has everything to do with the essay you're about to read.

IN THE FIFTEENTH CENTURY, the French philosopher René Descartes formulated his most famous dictum, *cogito ergo sum* (I think, therefore I am), while meditating by the fire. Some of my own best thinking occurs in a similar setting, only instead of a flickering fire, I stare at a flickering television screen. The times when my mind is most engaged and my need to know at its most pronounced, I am usually watching

Lost. A show like *Lost*, I will argue, that is popular with both a mass audience as well as a cult audience, with a more pronounced interest, can be considered an ongoing group meditation, the insights gleaned from which will be of particular relevance to that audience.

In his meditation, Descartes sets out—solely by thinking while gazing upon the fire, mind you (the work in question is called *Meditations on First Philosophy*)—to prove that everything he already believes to be true, really is true (the basic beliefs most people take for granted, such as that he himself exists, that the world around him exists, and that God exists). Moreover, he hopes to prove that it is impossible for these basic beliefs to be false, and to thereby establish an unshakable ground upon which to base all future science and philosophy (and upon which, it could be argued, the modern world—or at least a certain modern sensibility—has been built). The method by which Descartes hopes to accomplish this task is by exercising extreme skepticism; essentially, he doubts everything it is even remotely possible to doubt, then concentrates on anything that survives the process, reasoning that these surviving beliefs will not just be true, but true *undoubtedly*. Descartes's doubt, then, is of a special kind: it is doubt with a purpose, a temporary loss of certainty with an implied promise of future revelation that will make the period of uncertainty worthwhile. This sort of doubt is what, in *Lost*, we call mystery.

Already there is a fundamental difference in the purposes of Descartes's doubt and *Lost*'s mystery: as viewers of *Lost*, we absolutely do not want to find out everything is just as it seems to be. If the island turns out to be just a plain old humdrum island, with nothing mysterious going on whatsoever, we as viewers will be sorely disappointed, to say the least. We know one thing with some certainty, then: we expect something—something new, thrilling, or entertaining—to be revealed as the series progresses. We'll explore the nature of this revelatory "something" in the second half of this meditation; let us use this first section to examine *Lost* in light of Descartes's methods, and see if we can get the island to divulge some of her secrets.

The initial mysteries on *Lost* are rooted firmly in the mundane: Who are these people? Why did their plane crash? Where are they? Why has no one come to rescue them? There is a seemingly very large creature on the island, but it need not be supernatural in origin—it might have turned out to be an elephant, for example (before it was revealed to be—apparently—some sort of smoke monster). One of the first things to strongly suggest that something extraordinary may be going on is the visions had by some of the characters: Jack sees and interacts with his dead father, and Locke has a similar experience with a vision of his mother. These visions could be mere hallucinations—the result, perhaps, of snacking on the local mushrooms—but each is revelatory in nature: Jack's father points the way to both his coffin and a desperately needed fresh-water supply, and Locke's mother leads her son to the plane in the tree, which could potentially help him get inside the mysterious hatch.

Descartes, too, begins his journey by focusing on what he can see, but soon discards all information derived through his five senses because they have fooled him before, and therefore cannot be trusted: distant things look smaller, for instance, even though an elementary understanding of perspective reveals that they really aren't. Still, Descartes's extreme skepticism demands that anything that cannot be absolutely trusted must be eliminated as a source of information. Descartes even goes so far as to doubt whether or not he sits beside his fire at all, reasoning that he could merely be dreaming, when really he is home asleep in bed. As viewers of *Lost*, we know the characters aren't simply dreaming; there are a lot of focal characters, for one thing, each of whom seems to have a life that stretches off into the past and to exist largely independently of the other characters. Ultimately, though, we know the characters aren't simply dreaming—or in some sort of limbo or purgatory, working away their sins—because the show's creators have come out and told us as much.

Descartes appeals also to his creator as a means of restoring credit to his senses (a benevolent God wouldn't let one of his creations be so deceived as Descartes fears he is, would he?)—but this gets him nowhere. As soon as Descartes brings God into the equation, he must also posit the opposite situation, an Evil Genius (by which he means an evil genie or spirit) who, simply being true to its own malevolent nature, uses its limitless power to deceive. In this way Descartes loses the certainty of even the most basic, abstract facts, including mathematical equations such as $2 + 2 = 4$. Even reason can't be trusted in a universe run by a malevolent God!

The *Lost* viewer finds himself/herself in a similar bind. That there are gods (all-powerful beings, at least in terms of how they can effect the show) behind *Lost* is a given: *Lost* is a fictional story made up by writers, enacted by actors, directed by directors, and otherwise enabled by a host of people from the production crew to the executives at the network. But are the creators and writers behind *Lost* gods (benevolent and fair), or are they Evil Geniuses (malevolent masters of misdirection)? Like Descartes, we have no real way of knowing. (The writers of *Lost* appear to be both benevolent gods and Evil Geniuses simultaneously, often seeming to take great joy in misdirecting us, but usually playing fair in terms of story logic and viewer satisfaction; in other words, they fool us, but we like it.)

The hatch, and the computer that needs to be fed the code lest some unspecified (but potentially deadly and explosive) disaster occur, is very Cartesian in flavor. The flickering, jump-cutting orientation filmstrip left by the Dharma Initiative doesn't go out of its way to either inform or reassure, and it seems just as likely that nothing will happen if the button is not pushed—that the Dharma Initiative is simply a bad joke, or psychological test designed to fool those unlucky enough to fall into its clutches—as that the world will end, or the island blow up. Just as Descartes must contend with the sneaking suspicion that he is being toyed with by a supernatural Evil Genius, the characters on *Lost* must deal with similar reservations (voiced most often by Jack, the show's resident rational skeptic), and we as viewers are left to squirm as we ponder the minds of Evil Geniuses of an entirely different sort.

While Descartes sits by his fire, and we by our TVs, the characters on *Lost* confront the island itself. The island can throw one's sense of self into doubt, as it does initially with Jin, leading to his estrangement from Sun when he discovers she has learned to speak English—but it can also clarify and bestow purpose, as it does with Locke, who seemed rather lost in his previous incarnation as regional manager of a box company. None of the characters have a handle on the island's mysteries, or know what will happen next, or where they are all headed, but self-doubt doesn't seem to be a necessary effect of being placed in this position. So too it is with Descartes: he can doubt the existence of the fire, of his physical body, even of reason itself, but he can not doubt that he, himself—whatever his ultimate nature and status in the world—is thinking. If there is a benevolent god vouchsafing his experience, then Descartes is where he appears to be, before the fire, thinking. If, on the other hand, he is in the clutches of the Evil Genius, deceived into thinking he sits before the fire, he is *still* thinking. Either way, he thinks, and, therefore, he is.

Ingenious though it is, Descartes's self-affirming statement isn't necessarily enough to convince a modern reader. Descartes says, in essence, it is either the case that I am being deceived by an Evil Genius, or it isn't. In either case, I am thinking, he reasons: therefore, in any conceivable case, I exist. Many thinkers, including Friedrich Nietzsche, have doubted the *I* in Descartes's equation. Does thought absolutely have to be attached to a thinker? Stripped of the assumption that thought must be rooted in an existing consciousness, Descartes's formulation only proves that thought itself exists. Put another way—in light of our Evil Genius—perhaps all he proves is that deception exists. There is a long tradition in Indian thought holding that the self is mere illusion—and these are the folks who originated the concept of *Dharma* (as in the Dharma Initiative, the people who built the hatch), which refers both to the work one must do (carry on the Buddha's teachings) and also to the most basic unit of reality.

In the end, Descartes probably doesn't end up establishing a convincingly unflinching philosophical ground upon which to base all future science and philosophy. Likewise, I don't think it is possible to say anything with absolute certainty about either the show *Lost* or the island (beyond that there is something wildly entertaining and intellectually intriguing about both). What our investigation has done, however, is set us on the path to begin nailing down just what the "something" is that we hope *Lost* will deliver. The way to do this, I think, is to reverse our lens (looking at *Lost* via Descartes), and instead examine Descartes in light of *Lost*. I believe *Lost* can help explain why Descartes's *Meditations on First Philosophy* remains such an enduringly popular work by helping us see that Descartes's meditational journey serves as a model for how one can engage with—and ultimately come to terms with—doubt.

Meditations on First Philosophy works not only as philosophy, but also as a kind of story—the *Lost* of its day, a firsthand account of one man's engagement with doubt and the road he takes out of it. The story Descartes presents in *Meditations*, and kindred stories from *Lost*, follow a specific pattern: a common motif in mythic literature called the journey to the underworld. In journeys of this sort, a hero travels to the underworld—literally, as in the Greek myth of Persephone, or metaphorically, as in Luke Skywalker's descent into the bowels of the Death Star or to the misty swamps of Dagobah—and emerges with something new, a power, weapon, or previously unknown bit of knowledge, enduring truth, or way of life.

It is because Descartes's meditation provided an all-new version of this archetypal journey—a scientific myth that satisfies basic storytelling needs while seemingly breaking with all that had gone before it—that it has remained so popular, and it is for similar reasons that I think *Lost* is able to hold such a formidable chunk of our collective attention today. Modern television provides a means for communication on a mass level, and *Lost* is the focal point of a mass meditation that spills out past the edges of the television and into coffee shops and office lunchrooms, onto Web blogs and message boards, and books like the one you hold in your hands. It fulfills our desire for the journey to the underworld motif, but filters it through the sort of personal, structured, scientific values one associates with Descartes.

Some of the same aspects that make *Lost* so fun to watch also provide a framework for our group meditation. *Lost* is serialized, with each individual episode telling a piece (most often a dramatically satisfying piece, with its own beginning, middle, and end) of a much larger story. The events of previous episodes—and by extension, the past actions of the characters, stretching back beyond the beginnings of the show—affect later episodes, so the characters' pasts have a way of catching up with them. Contrast this with a more episodic television show like *The Simpsons*, where the status quo is re-established at the end of every episode; lasting change is difficult to effect in the world of *The Simpsons*, but it is a very real, often terrifying possibility for the characters on *Lost*.

The structural framework of the show, then, provides the enabling boundaries of our group meditation. The past matters, choices, and actions have weight, and the consequences of said choices are very, very real. Each character on *Lost* deals with these issues, but let us focus on the character of Sayid and how he lives with the choices he makes. When Shannon has an asthma attack, and Jack believes Sawyer has the medicine that will help her breathe, Sayid decides to torture Sawyer, reviving memories of his past with the Republican Guard in Iraq. Sayid doesn't hide from his choice, or argue that he did what was required in difficult circumstances—instead, he leaves the encampment, nominally to map the shoreline, but also because he needs some time to be alone. It is on this journey that Sayid meets Rousseau, the probably deranged French woman with knowledge of the Others (a metaphorical journey to the underworld in which Sayid comes away with knowledge both of himself and of the island).

Accepting and dealing with his choice to torture Sawyer rather than wiping the act away with an easy rationalization leads Sayid to his budding romantic relationship with Shannon, the girl he fought to save. Shannon is later shot by Ana Lucia, and in the aftermath, Sayid's experiences in Iraq and with Sawyer help Ana Lucia come to terms with shooting Shannon, as well as the troubled past in which she killed the criminal who had previously shot her, terminating her pregnancy. (Following threads on *Lost* can be a twisting, unpredictable road, but that, of course, is one of the things we love about it.)

Confronting inner demons seems to be the only way to penetrate the external mysteries of the island. Jack finds the fresh water source only after confronting his conflicted feelings for his recently deceased father; Locke discovers the hatch only after wrestling with his own complex and endearingly pathetic past. The hatch itself, as discussed earlier, is very much in tune with Descartes's conception of a world ruled by an Evil Genius, and it is also a literal journey to the underworld. The hatch places characters in an extremely conflicted state—when Jack asks Desmond if he has ever considered that pushing the button may merely be a psychological test, Desmond replies, "Every waking minute"—but the hatch also rewards with information (which on *Lost* is almost always accompanied by more questions).

I think television has taken up some of the role once played by philosophy in Western culture, particularly shows that inspire a cult following while simultaneously appealing to a mass audience. Viewed in this light, *Twin Peaks* might be considered a thought not given the opportunity to complete itself, while *The X-Files* might be an example of a thought forced to go on so long that it loses coherency. At the time I am writing this, *Lost* is only a handful of episodes into its second season, but it looks able to weather being either cut short or going on too long; it is popular enough that its future is assured, at least for the time being, and its pace is leisurely enough and mysteries rich enough to support years of storytelling. As a coherent story—as a single, structured thought—*Lost* has the potential to take us places no show before it has gone. (It is interesting to note, as an aside, that, if my theory of popular entertainment now carrying some of the weight of philosophy is true, it means that philosophical inquiry is now determined at least in part by the same vagaries that determine which TV shows stay on the air; a disturbing thought, though one that seems somehow fitting with the modern world.)

If *Lost* is a group meditation of specific relevance to the culture that birthed it, what is it trying to say? The cast of *Lost* seems to have been consciously constructed to function as a microcosm of current American society, and to reflect those things of specific interest to America at the moment: thus we have both an Iraqi (Sayid) and a redneck (Sawyer), a man of science (Jack) and a man of faith (Locke); there are immigrants (Sun and Jin), mothers (Claire), fathers and sons (Michael and Walt), outlaws (Kate and Sawyer), cops (Ana Lucia), brothers and sisters (Shannon and Boone), husbands and wives (Rose and Bernard), and celebrities (Charlie); even the rich are represented by the unlikely lottery winner, Hurley. These characters are, effectively, average Americans, taken from the lives they knew and deposited somewhere strange and filled with doubt. How do they make their way back to certainty? (Or do they at all?)

Corruption in big business, governments, and religious institutions are regular stories in the news, and opinions as to who to trust and what to believe in differ strongly from person to person. The new millennium has been characterized by a general erosion of trust in authority, and this condition has been developing throughout the modern era—to as far back as Descartes, at least. In such a climate, it's easy to see how the story of folks more or less like ourselves—trapped in a place where they don't know who to trust or what to believe in, and where opinions as to how to proceed differ strongly amongst strong personalities—could so capture our imaginations.

Lost doesn't offer specific answers, even metaphorically, that we can then apply to the real world; what it points to, instead, is a link between the inner world we construct and the outer world we inhabit.

Lost is a thought that has only just begun, and there are many directions it could grow along. Given the focus on character and the importance of facing guilt and pain, it's tempting to link *Lost* with the first noble truth of the Buddha's teaching (the *Dharma*): life is suffering. Really, though, it's too early to put forth anything that definite (besides which, the whole Dharma Initiative may turn out to be nothing but a red herring). *Lost* shows us that you've got to make do with what you've got (there's no way off the island), and that the only way to make the world better is to become a better person. All things considered, I think that's a wonderful place for a thought to begin.

Robert Burke Richardson collects undergrad degrees in Edmonton, Alberta. He is the author of "Egg Drop Soup" in *Star Trek: Strange New Worlds 8*, "Negation Elimination" in *All-Star Zeppelin Adventure Stories*, and "The Coming Years of Good" in *On Spec*. Find out more about his fiction, comics, and his crazy theories about *Lost* by visiting his Web blog at http://elf-help.blogspot.com.

Oops

A Review of Survivability of Passengers in the Plane Crash, First Episode of the Television Series *Lost*

CLAYTON DAVIS

One word: Spoilsport.
Oops. I guess technically that was three words.
Now eleven.
I mean sixteen.

IN THE OPENING SCENE the hero is in pain lying flat on his back. Regaining consciousness, he is aware of the burning sun. In terrible pain he hears screams and sees a bamboo forest. He is overwhelmed with the realization the plane has been torn into large pieces in midair, and it has crashed on a Pacific island. He is a doctor and people need his help.

I am a professional aviator with Flight Instructor and Airline Transport Ratings with forty years experience in everything from gliders to jets. I find the crash premise totally bereft of logic. First, they hit an air pocket, and just before the disaster the scene shows oxygen masks dropping down for passenger use. They probably flew near or into the Jet Stream and encountered Clear Air Turbulence.

Conversation amongst the survivors indicates they were flying at 40,000 feet. If a plane hit turbulence at that altitude it would not be ripped into large chunks of falling parts. Moreover, should that have happened, the chunks would have splattered like rotten eggs when they hit the ground.

If the fuselage cabin had been splintered and ripped open there would not have been any living souls on board before the unplanned descent started. There is not enough oxygen sufficient for human life at that altitude. The temperature at 40,000 feet is minus seventy degrees Fahrenheit. Everyone would have been frozen solid.

Clear Air Turbulence at high altitudes is usually the result of disrupted air around the Jet Stream. This river of air is similar to a fire hose pouring a vicious stream of water high up in the Earth's atmosphere. It flows from west to east. All airline pilots know about it and recognize the onset of turbulence near the Jet Stream.

Pilots are taught to throttle back to Maneuvering Speed upon encountering turbulence. Maneuvering Speed is sometimes called Rough Air Speed. That is a slow speed in which abrupt full-control movement will not overstress the airplane. Turbulence requires control movement to keep the airplane on an even keel. At cruise speed, abrupt full-control movement would break off the airplane's wings. Or at least this would leave deep dents and wrinkles in the airplane's skin. There would also be unseen cracks and stresses within the aircraft structure.

Therefore, it is my belief that the pilots in this episode would never have allowed their airplane to suffer destruction from turbulence and air pockets.

Turbulence cannot break an airplane into large chunks that provide a ride for passengers falling to Earth. The most likely thing would be for a wing to separate and leave the fuselage to plummet intact to Earth.

From 40,000 feet the passengers would immediately be frozen to death or suffocate from lack of oxygen. In the opening scene of this television series when the big chunks of airplane smote the planet Earth they would have broken and splattered like rotten eggs.

Dialog among the survivors indicated they thought they would be located very soon because the aircraft was equipped with a Black Box. More likely, an Emergency Locating Transmitter would send a tone for search parties to locate the wreckage.

Having one of the engines still spooling in idle as the wreckage lay on the ground was not possible. The impact would have stopped the engine if fuel starvation did not do the trick.

Oops

"We smell gas," was heard from one of the passengers. Jet airplanes are fueled with kerosene or diesel fuel, something called Jet-A. It will burn but not blow up. And it smells very different from gasoline.

After considering the question of survival from such an airplane mishap alluded to in the first episode of the television series *Lost*, I ponder the shock value of using airplanes to introduce a television program. Television viewers and media consumers, in general, are fascinated by big loud machines that transport hundreds of passengers in a confined space high above Earth. This fascination is not related, in any realistic way, to the risks and realities of airplane disasters.

Bad Pilot

But what if the pilot was incompetent or poorly trained? Does this make the events somewhat more likely? The answer is no.

The Federal Aviation Agency (FAA) is the government agency that makes sure all pilots are qualified. Pilot certification is based on accumulated experience. The FAA issues certificates which authorize people to conduct operations in airplanes, helicopters, gliders, balloons, and probably anything else that will fly. Listed under the requirements are a certain number of hours. All the hours are cumulative, starting from the first lesson. For example, the requirement of ten night takeoffs and landings to qualify for the Commercial Certificate would be satisfied when you completed them for the Private Pilot requirements.

Here are the rules for different pilots: a student pilot must be sixteen years old to fly solo and have a Third-Class medical certificate. No, that doesn't mean the pilot is less healthy than everyone else. It means the medical certificate need not be renewed as often as Second Class and First Class.

A Private Pilot must be seventeen years old, have a Third-Class medical certificate, plus forty hours' flying experience.

Next is the Commercial Pilot certificate. It is for people who can and may be the co-pilot in the right front cockpit seat of a commercial airliner. That person must be eighteen years old and have a Second-Class medical certificate. 200 hours of flying experience is the minimum requirement to be a Commercial Pilot, and that pilot can also be rated as a Flight Instructor to give flying lessons.

You may want to know what kind of pilot the captain in front of the airliner is. He/she is an Airline Transport Pilot who is at least twenty-three years old with a First-Class medical certificate and 1,500 hours flying experience.

Would any of these minimally qualified pilots be flying a commercial airplane? Not likely. Ask any pilot you meet and the answer is the same. It is a long, hard process to land a job with an airline company.

Each and every pilot is given a flight check by an instructor every two years. It is called the Biennial Flight Review. This mandatory flight review is about as welcome as income taxes or a dental appointment. Sure, you can fly without it. There are some drawbacks, however. Your insurance policy will no longer be any good. Plus, one other thing, the Federal Aviation Administration will probably put you on their list of Most Watched Pilots. Make that agency mad and you're in a heap-o-trouble. Like dental appointments and taxes, Biennial Flight Reviews come due.

There are two quick ways to accomplish the Biennial Flight Review. Fly with an instructor or find an instructor willing to sign your flight log over a cup of coffee without flying with you. It all depends on how well he knows you. That "coffee shop sign-off" is highly illegal and frowned upon by the FAA.

The long, hard way is to train for another rating, perhaps the Commercial Pilot certificate. You'd be good for another two years. Even Airline Transport Pilots get a Biennial Flight Review.

The bottom line is that the pilots flying that ill-fated airliner in the television series *Lost* were unlikely to allow total destruction of their flying machine.

In my informed opinion, the script writers would have been more believable using a yacht and running it aground. *Gilligan's Island* already did that. Okay, let's make the airplane disaster a little more realistic. Have it run out of fuel and land it on a wide, sandy beach.

Running out of fuel can conceivably occur under conditions where the crew might be lost and off course. That would be more accurate than having large chunks of airframe find an island and conveniently plunk down right on the beach at the edge of the jungle.

Lost is a very entertaining series, with many fantastic and hard-to-explain events, from polar bears on a tropical island to bad-luck lottery numbers. But perhaps the most fantastic event was the crash itself. I'm looking forward to the explanation.

Clayton Davis lives with his wife in Severna Park, Maryland. He holds the Airline Transport Pilot and Flight Instructor ratings with more than 10,000 hours logged in everything from gliders to jets. He has published flying stories in aviation magazines and many short stories elsewhere. He served in the USAF as a codebreaker and Russian linguist. He was awarded the Saint Ignatius Gold Medal by the Azov Academy, Russia. After retirement from military service he was a high-school mathematics teacher. Clayton Davis graduated from Syracuse University, B.A. '67, and is listed in Marquis Who's Who in America.

Lost Connections

G. O. LIKESKILL

Some people need to have their subscriptions to the Internet Movie Database revoked.

But not G. O. Likeskill. In this essay, Likeskill takes the Kevin Bacon game to delightful extremes. Imagine if you were at a party where somebody got on a roll like this. Most of us, at least, would be completely in awe. Also a little scared.

Besides, anything that can wean you from FreeCell is a Good Thing.

Journal Entry, Day 1

After a number of false starts (wood sculpture in my cubicle proved unwieldy, as well as distracting to my coworkers, and my experiments with Electronic Voice Phenomena may have caused the blackout that afflicted the office for two days—fortunately, no one but me seems to suspect this), I believe I have come up with the perfect activity to occupy my lunch hour—personally diverting, yet unlikely to cause consternation or even notice with others in the office.

I find myself intrigued by the connections between the characters on the television series *Lost*, particularly by the suggestions that seemingly random interactions between the characters—Sawyer's fateful encounter with Jack's father, the appearance on television of Hugo in the background talking about his lottery win, etc., etc.—will prove to have much larger significance as more is revealed.

I have therefore become curious as to whether there are any connections between the actors who play the characters. Perhaps some pattern will emerge that may enlighten me about the workings of Hollywood casting, or even hint at something larger (though I admit this is unlikely). Investigating this via my computer on the Internet Movie Database (IMDb) should at worst prove harmless and will surely not take long—I foresee more lunch hours filled with games of FreeCell before the week is out.

Day 2

It should have occurred to me at the outset that some of the more prolific actors had directly worked together. Matthew Fox (*Lost*'s Dr. Jack Shephard) starred in *Party of Five*, which ran for six seasons, 1994–2000, on the Fox network. In six years on a relatively high-profile drama, it is perhaps surprising that he worked with only one future *Lost* regular, Daniel Dae Kim (Jin), who appeared in the 1998 *Party* episode "Opposites Distract." Further, Harold Perrineau (Michael) and Adewale Akinnuoye-Agbaje (pronounced, so I am told, "Ad-eh-wall-AY A-kin-OY-yay Ag-bah-JAY"—he plays Mr. Eko, pronounced "MISS-ter EK-oh") both spent years together as series regulars on HBO's prison drama *Oz*. While this is worth noting, for the purposes of the initial research, I am not at present investigating further connections between Akinnuoye-Agbaje or the other actors playing the "tailies" and the season one main cast, as—this is probably irrational, I know—I have a vague apprehension that combining the two groups of survivors may somehow skew my initial results, though no doubt I shall look into it later.

It initially appeared that there was a direct connection between Emilie de Ravin (Claire) and Terry O'Quinn (Locke), as he made a guest appearance on the WB series *Roswell*, where de Ravin had a role as a humanoid extraterrestrial. However, it turns out that de Ravin's Tess Harding was a regular in only the 2000–2001 second season, and O'Quinn's episode, "Michael, the Guys and the Great Snapple Caper," was the second episode of the third season. In other words, de Ravin and O'Quinn just missed one another, though of course they are connected by the show's theme and by working with the other regular actors.

I wonder, is it more significant that Fox and Kim did work together, or that de Ravin and O'Quinn almost worked together? And does the fact that de Ravin portrayed an alien mean anything? It surely cannot signify anything about the birth of Claire's baby—they're two separate series, different creative personnel, different networks, and practically different eras in television terms. And even if it *did* signify, how can it relate to the fact that she and O'Quinn came close but did not cross paths in their *Roswell* tenure?

Day 5

Colleagues have noticed and commented on my furrowed brow as I delve deeper into the interconnectedness of the *Lost* cast. I have variously explained away my concentration as preoccupation with a badly notated invoice (we have an abundance of these, if truth be told), a mild headache, or trying to figure out whether I know, should it become a life-or-death matter, the velocity of an unladen swallow. I cannot tell if anyone actually believes me, but they are leaving me to my work—in fact, they seem to be steering clear of me—which is all to the good.

My research has turned up a number of other near misses among the *Lost* cast, two more of which involve de Ravin. She was on *CSI: Miami* in the 2004 episode "Legal"; Maggie Grace (the lamented Shannon) was in the 2003 episode "Spring Break." They worked with the series' main cast, but not with one another, and neither worked with Ian Somerhalder (Shannon's likewise lamented brother Boone), who was in the 2003 episode "The Best Defense." Likewise, de Ravin was in the 2003 *NCIS* episode "Sea Dog"; Josh Holloway was in the 2004 *NCIS* episode "My Other Left Foot."

Holloway and Grace appeared in separate episodes of the short-lived 2003 legal series *The Lyon's Den*, starring Rob Lowe as an ambitious attorney. Grace was in "The Beach House" and Holloway was in (the apparently unaired) "Separation Anxiety."

But these are not the only connections of this sort. Daniel Dae Kim and Harold Perrineau have both been on *Law and Order*—Kim in the 1994 episode "Golden Years" and Perrineau in 1990's "Out of the Half-Light" and in 1993's "Virus" (as two different characters) and have *also* both been on *ER*: Kim did four episodes as a helpful social worker in 2003–2004; Perrineau appeared in *ER*'s 1997 episode "Freak Show." Is there a pattern here that foreshadows anything on *Lost*—a separation between the men, yet a strong commonality? Further, while the *ER* appearances by the two actors are years apart, Laura Innes, who plays Dr. Kerry Weaver, has been in residence on the series since 1995 and provides a connection for both men to Matthew Fox, as Innes made a guest appearance on *Party of Five* in that show's 1994 first season.

128 As for Daniel Dae Kim and Josh Holloway, they have a whopping *three* series in common, though they never worked together directly in any of them. Holloway appeared briefly as a character described as "Good-Looking Guy/Vampire" in the premiere episode of *Angel*, "City Of...," while Kim had a recurring role in *Angel*'s third and fourth seasons as smarmy lawyer Gavin Park, who ultimately was killed and then briefly resurrected as a zombie. Could the Others on *Lost* be zombies, I wonder? I digress. Both Holloway and Kim appeared on *CSI: Crime Scene Investigation*, Holloway in 2003's "Assume Nothing" and Kim in 2001's "Ellie," and both were in *Walker: Texas Ranger*, Kim in 1999's "The Lynn Sisters" and Holloway in 2001's "Medieval Crimes." Is there anything to be gleaned here? We have certainly seen law enforcement and law enforcers in action on *Lost*—but will there be forensic scrutiny, vampires, roundhouse butt-kicking, or, God forbid, lawyers? No, I am confusing the actors' careers with their characters' adventures. Must concentrate on more important things—such as, do actors who do guest appearances on *CSI: Miami* stand a fifty percent greater chance of having their characters killed off if they are later regulars on a different hit series? And if so, why?

And why can I not connect Yunjin Kim to anyone?

Day 9

Lord of the Rings may be the three-film metaphorical equivalent of Rome: all roads seem to lead to it. It therefore has not been difficult to connect Dominic Monaghan, famous for playing the hobbit Merry before becoming recovering drug-addict/aspiring surrogate father Charlie Pace on *Lost*, with virtually all of his castmates on *Lost* by means of the extensive *LotR* cast.

To wit:

Ian McKellen, *LotR*'s Gandalf, connects Monaghan through the *X-Men* films to James Marsden (McKellen is Magneto, Marsden is Cyclops), who guest-starred on *Party of Five* with Matthew Fox. McKellen also worked in *X-Men* with Bruce Davison, who went on to star in the short-lived Stephen King series *Kingdom Hospital*, which guest-starred Evangeline Lilly. In 1998's *Gods and Monsters*, McKellen starred as *Frankenstein* director James Whale opposite Brendan Fraser, who then worked in 2005's *Crash* with Daniel Dae Kim. Fraser also worked with Heather Locklear in 2003's *Looney Tunes: Back in Action*; in 2001, Locklear had been a regular on *Spin City* when Jorge Garcia guest-starred in the 2001 episode "The Arrival."

Viggo Mortensen, the kingly Aragorn in *LotR*, was in the controversial 1998 remake of *Psycho*, which also starred William H. Macy, who was in the 2004 submarine drama *In Enemy Hands* with Ian Somerhalder; Mortensen also worked in the 2000 alcoholism recovery drama *28 Days* with Sandra Bullock, who provides another Monaghan/Daniel Dae Kim connection, as she appeared in *Crash*—as Brendan Fraser's wife. If the actors are connected at a one-step remove by two other actors who play husband and wife, does that increase either actor's chance of playing a drug addict? I know contemplating the question is making me think *I* may need something medicinal soon.

I do not know what to make of the fact that Monaghan can be connected to all of the above-mentioned *Lost* actors using *LotR* actors other than Mortensen. Elijah Wood aka Frodo appeared as an American who joins an English "firm" of brawlers in 2005's *Green Street Hooligans*, which also stars Charlie Hunnam, who back in 2000 had a guest arc in the short-lived series *Young Americans*, which featured Ian Somerhalder as a regular. Orlando Bloom, *LotR*'s elf Legolas, starred in *Elizabethtown* with Kirsten Dunst, who provides yet another connection to Daniel Dae Kim, as both appeared in *Spider-Man 2*.

Hugo Weaving, known to *LotR* fans as the elf lord Elrond, is perhaps even more familiar via the *Matrix* trilogy as Agent Smith—

Harold Perrineau played Link in *Matrix: Reloaded* and *The Matrix: Revolutions*. Weaving also connects through the *Matrix* films to Harry J. Lennix, who played Lock in that trilogy and appeared in the well-reviewed but quickly canceled series *The Handler* with guest Emilie de Ravin. De Ravin connects to Monaghan with the same number of steps via her appearance in the 2002 telefilm remake of *Carrie* with Patricia Clarkson, who in 2000 worked in the character drama *Joe Gould's Secret* with Ian Holm, *LotR*'s Bilbo Baggins.

Sean Bean, Boromir in *LotR*, was in the futuristic 2002 actioner *Equilibrium* with Angus McFadyen, who was a series regular in the 2003 ABC supernatural series *Miracles*, which featured both Maggie Grace and Sam Anderson (*Lost* tailie Bernard) in the "Mother's Daughter" episode. He also provides an alternate link to Matthew Fox by having worked in the 2002 thriller *Don't Say a Word* with Brittany Murphy, who appeared on Fox's *Party of Five*.

Two *LotR* actors connect Monaghan directly to *Lost* regulars: John Rhys-Davies, the dwarf Gimli, starred in the 2002 horror film *Sabretooth* with Josh Holloway (who can likewise be linked to Fox via the Sean Bean/Brittany Murphy route and to Grace by the Bean/Angus McFadyen route), and Brad Dourif, *LotR*'s grimy Wormtongue, was in 1982's famously financially catastrophic Western *Heaven's Gate* with Terry O'Quinn.

There are also connections between *LotR* actors and Naveen Andrews, who was in the 1996 Oscar winner *The English Patient* with Ralph Fiennes, who then starred in *Oscar and Lucinda* opposite Cate Blanchett, *LotR*'s Galadriel. Andrews is also connected, more directly albeit through less high-profile projects, by working with both Miranda Otto (*LotR*'s Eowyn) and Hugo Weaving in 1997's *True Love and Chaos* and appearing with Dourif in 1991's *London Kills Me*.

However, possibly the most intriguing link between Monaghan and Andrews is a Britain-based actor with the unforgettable name of Badi Uzzaman. Mr. Uzzaman appeared in both *The Buddha of Suburbia*, a 1993 British miniseries starring Andrews, and in *Hetty Wainthrop Investigates*, a 1996 British mystery series that costarred Monaghan as the heroine's loyal assistant Geoffrey Shawcross. Badi Uzzaman . . . is the *name* a clue? Will Sayid and Charlie view each other as baddies? Will one of them desperately try to convey information about some "other man" while drunk, thereby slurring it into "Uzzaman"? Will some uzzaman connect the rest of the *Lost* cast for me? Or is it pronounced "Yoo-za-man?" If so, is it advice to "use a man," indicating that perhaps Charlie and Sayid, after Claire's cold shoulder and Shannon's death, may turn to one another romantically? Or should it be interpreted as "You za man!," meaning that Danielle (Mira Furlan) will reappear and affirm Sayid in her French accent? Or could it simply be the actor's name? So many questions....

Day 11

I was afraid that, as Evangeline Lilly's acting career is relatively recent and her list of on-camera credits on the IMDb only encompasses seven projects at present (including *Lost*), it might take many steps to find connections to her colleagues. However, I am relieved to find that I can link her, in no more than four steps, to most of the *Lost* cast members via only three projects: *Smallville*, in which Lilly appeared in the 2002 episode "Kinetic" as Wade's girlfriend, the 2003 HBO comedy film *Stealing Sinatra*, in which she played a model in a TV commercial, and *Kingdom Hospital*, the 2004 Stephen King miniseries, in which she played Benson's girlfriend.

Ian Somerhalder was in six 2002 episodes of *Smallville* (albeit none with Lilly) as Adam Knight. Although John Glover was not in Lilly's *Smallville* episode, he is a series regular (he plays Lionel Luthor) on the show and therefore worked with the regulars who *did* work with Lilly. Glover also worked with Harold Perrineau in two Shakespeare-based projects, the 1998 telefilm *The Tempest*, with Perrineau as Ariel, and the 1999 movie *Macbeth in Manhattan*, with Perrineau as the Chorus. Furthermore, Glover worked with Stephanie Romanov in the 2004 film *Tricks*; Romanov played Daniel Dae Kim's professional nemesis on *Angel* throughout his 2001–2003 tenure there.

Kingdom Hospital was originally a European miniseries created by Lars Von Trier (*Breaking the Waves*, *Dogville*) that was adapted as an ABC miniseries in 2004 by Stephen King (no explanation necessary). King often makes cameo appearances in filmed versions of his writings, and *Kingdom* was no exception. He also turned up in the 1990 miniseries *The Stand* with Rob Lowe, who starred in *The Lyon's Den*, which as noted before had Josh Holloway and Maggie Grace guesting in separate episodes. There are two more immediate connections between Lilly and Grace, however—*Kingdom* star Andrew McCarthy appeared with Grace in her episode of *Law and Order: SVU* and *Kingdom*'s Diane Ladd guested with Grace in the *Cold Case* episode "Volunteers."

Ladd also connects directly to Terry O'Quinn: both were in the 1996 drama *Ghosts of Mississippi*, along with *Sinatra*'s William H. Macy.

Bruce Davison, another star of *Kingdom*, worked with Marianne Jean-Baptiste in the pilot for CBS's *Without a Trace*; as mentioned earlier, she was in 1991's *London Kills Me* with Naveen Andrews. Davison also played the bigoted senator who is later impersonated by Mystique in the *X-Men* films with Ian McKellen, providing a connection to Dominic Monaghan.

Stealing Sinatra starred David Arquette, who was in all three *Scream* movies (1996, 1997, and 2000) with Neve Campbell, meaning she worked with him over a period of four years, two-thirds as long as she spent playing Matthew Fox's sister on *Party of Five*.

Thomas Ian Nicholas, another star of *Stealing Sinatra*, was in 2002's *Rules of Attraction* with Ian Somerhalder.

Lilly's other connections from *Stealing Sinatra* are all through another of its stars, the aforementioned William H. Macy, who in 2002 was in the caper movie *Welcome to Collinwood* with Patricia Clarkson, who also appeared that year in the TV remake of *Carrie* with Emilie de Ravin. In 1998, Macy was in the film *Jerry and Tom* with Ted Danson, who went on to play the title role in the sitcom *Becker*, with Jorge Garcia as a regular in its final year; in 2004, Macy was in the thriller *Spartan* with Derek Luke, who played Malcolm David Kelley's grown-up title character self in *Antwone Fisher*.

Speaking of *Antwone Fisher*, based on the life of the real Fisher, who wrote the screenplay, the 2002 film was directed by and co-starred Denzel Washington, who can be connected within a few steps to virtually everyone in the film industry.

Therefore, through Washington, Kelley can be connected to the following:

Naveen Andrews, who appeared with Sarita Choudhury in the

films *Wild West* (1992) and *Kama Sutra* (1996) and starred in the British television miniseries *The Buddha of Suburbia* with Roshan Seth in 1993. Both Choudhury and Seth were in *Mississippi Masala* with Washington in 1991.

Josh Holloway, whose *NCIS* episode also featured Bonnie Bartlett, who had been a series regular with Washington in the long-running (1982–1988) hospital drama *St. Elsewhere.*

Matthew Fox, via *Party of Five*—Vicellous Reon Shannon guest-starred in the episode "Have No Fear" in 1995, then costarred with Washington in 1999's fact-based prison/courtroom drama *The Hurricane. The Hurricane* and the Washington/Shannon link there also connect Kelley to Terry O'Quinn, who worked with Shannon in the 2001 telefilm about the Marines, *Semper Fi.*

Ian Somerhalder, who worked with Kip Pardue and Kate Bosworth in the 2002 sex drama *Rules of Attraction*; Pardue and Bosworth both worked with Washington in the 2000 high-school football film *Remember the Titans.* (Do actors who are linked to other actors by a pair of performers stand a statistically higher chance of having their characters killed off... ? Note to self: look into this....)

In the 1995 nuclear sub thriller *Crimson Tide*, Washington worked with Viggo Mortensen, who was in the *Lord of the Rings* trilogy with Dominic Monaghan.

A 2003 thriller called *Out of Time*, with Washington as a small-town Florida sheriff up to his neck in femme fatale trouble, connects Kelley via Washington's co-stars to two different *Lost* actors. Sanaa Lathan (the aforementioned dangerous beauty) was in 1999's romantic comedy *The Best Man*, with Kelley's onscreen *Lost* father, Harold Perrineau, and John Billingsley, who plays Washington's buddy, was a series regular on *Star Trek: Enterprise* that had Daniel Dae Kim as the recurring character Corporal Chang in its third season.

A little more investigation provides a more direct link between Kelley and Kim, also courtesy of *Antwone Fisher*—supporting actress Joy Bryant worked in that film with Kelley and in 2004's *Spider-Man 2* with Kim, who played an assistant to Alfred Molina's Doc Ock. A bit more digging, and we find that Bryant and Kim had worked together *before*, in the *ER* episode "Missing." So if Somerhalder's character is killed because he worked with two people who worked with each other and aren't on the show, perhaps there's a connection between the fact that Walt has disappeared and the fact that he is linked to Kim by Bryant, who has been in two projects with him?

So that's everyone…except Yunjin Kim. Maybe I can cheat and connect her by surname to Daniel Dae Kim? But if this exercise is meant to see if there is any significance in the connections between the cast members, won't that skew the results? Sun is not cut off from the other characters—there must be a solution….

Day 12

The Internet Movie Database lists eleven projects that Yunjin (they spell it "Yoon-jin") Kim has been in—all except *Lost* made in Asia, with costars whose names I do not believe I have seen before. Help.

Day 13

Taking a break from Yunjin Kim, I research Terry O'Quinn, who has at present ninety-seven listings on the IMDb and can probably be connected within a few steps to every actor now living and most who aren't—though I will limit myself to his *Lost* colleagues. I've already found the links to Kelley, Lilly, and Monaghan; it turns out that O'Quinn is only separated by one degree from most of the others.

O'Quinn was in *Hometown Legend* in 2002 with Lacey Chabert, who played Matthew Fox's youngest sister in *Party of Five*; another link to Fox is Donald Sutherland, who worked with him in *Behind the Mask* and with O'Quinn in 1997's thriller *Shadow Conspiracy*.

In 2002, O'Quinn was in *The Locket* with Marguerite Moreau, who appeared the following year in *Easy* with Naveen Andrews.

In 1988, O'Quinn was in the Western *Young Guns* starring Kiefer Sutherland, who now stars in *24*, which featured Daniel Dae Kim in seasons two and three as a SWAT officer. There are three alternate one-step links between O'Quinn and Kim as well: O'Quinn played real-life figure Howard Hughes in 1991's adventure/fantasy *The Rocketeer* with Jennifer Connelly, who also starred in 2003's *The Hulk*, which featured Kim as an aide; O'Quinn was in the 1996 psychological thriller *Primal Fear*, which starred Richard Gere, who also starred in the 1997 assassination thriller *The Jackal*, which also had Kim in a supporting role; Kim's appearance in *The Jackal* also links him to Bruce Willis, who played the title assassin and had also starred in the TV series *Moonlighting*, which had O'Quinn guesting in the 1987 episode "Take a Left at the Altar."

In 2000, O'Quinn was in the docudrama *Rated X*, about the pornography-making Mitchell brothers, one of whom was played by Charlie Sheen, who was the lead in *Spin City* when Jorge Garcia appeared on the sitcom in 2001.

O'Neill can be connected in two steps to Maggie Grace, who was in *Law and Order: SVU* with its regulars. Mitch Pileggi guest-starred in a different episode—he was a regular on *The X-Files* series and in the feature version; O'Quinn has a recurring role in the series and also appeared in the movie.

There are three different one-step connections between O'Quinn and Harold Perrineau. O'Quinn was in 1991's *The Rocketeer* with Paul Sorvino, who was Capulet in Baz Luhrmann's Miami-based *Romeo + Juliet*, with Perrineau as Mercutio; O'Quinn had a recurring role on *The West Wing*, where he worked with fellow guest Jesse Bradford in the 2004 episode "An Khe"; Bradford also was in *Romeo + Juliet*. In 1985, O'Quinn was in *An Early Frost* with John Glover, who as mentioned before worked with Perrineau in *Macbeth in Manhattan* and *The Tempest*.

O'Quinn went on to be a regular in the *X-Files* spin-off *Millennium*, which has Gregory Itzin as a guest in the 1997 episode "Walkabout"; in 1989, Itzin had appeared in the telefilm *Guts and Glory: The Rise and Fall of Oliver North* starring David Keith, who then starred in 2002's *Sabretooth* with Josh Holloway. Itzin also worked in the unaired 2004 pilot *Fearless*, which also starred Ian Somerhalder. More visibly, O'Quinn and Somerhalder can be connected through William H. Macy, who as noted worked with O'Quinn in *Ghosts of Mississippi* and with Somerhalder in *In Enemy Hands*. Maybe if an actor can be connected to his fellows in only one or two steps, that means his characters can miraculously take steps, like Locke? Except where does Yunjin Kim fit into this?

My workmates have begun exhorting me to get up and go to lunch. I ask someone to bring me back an airplane-sized portion of peanuts, to keep me in the mood.

Day 15

My colleagues at the office are looking at me strangely, suggesting that I have become obsessed with what I am doing. How ridiculous. I am sure there are plenty of people who go much longer than five days without showering while doing research.

I have found that certain actors seem to occur again and again as links between the lost players.

One is the already-mentioned John Glover, who also connects Perrineau to Jorge Garcia. Glover starred as the Devil in the 1998 TV series *Brimstone*, which featured Kristin Minter as a guest; in 2000, she did the feature *King of the Open Mic's* with Garcia. Glover's work on *Smallville* likewise provides a Perrineau/Ian Somerhalder connection, as Somerhalder appeared in six episodes of the series as Adam Knight in the 2002 season.

Gregory Itzin, who linked Perrineau to Somerhalder and Josh Holloway, also creates a path between Matthew Fox—Itzin guest-starred in two 1999 episodes of *Party of Five*—and Matthew David Kelley, with whom Itzin worked in the 2002 *Judging Amy* episode "No One Expects the Spanish Inquisition."

Actress Meagan Good connects Daniel Dae Kim (who worked with her in the 2003 action movie *Ride or Die*), Malcolm David Kelley (who worked with her in the 2004 comedy *You Got Served*), and Emilie de Ravin (who worked with her in the 2005 thriller *Brick*).

J. K. Simmons is at the center of a similar nexus. He was a series regular on *Oz* with Harold Perrineau and appeared in both *Spider-Man 2* and the baseball drama *For Love of the Game* with Daniel Dae Kim; Simmons was also in both *Spider-Man* films with Willem Dafoe, who costarred in *The English Patient* with Naveen Andrews.

There are two alternate connections between Kim and Andrews to be found—Kim was in season three of *24* with D. B. Woodside (who played the president's brother); Woodside was in 2003's feature film *Easy* with Andrews. Kim was also in the 2004 *Without a Trace* episode "Exposure" with Marianne Jean-Baptiste, who was in *London Kills Me* with Andrews.

John Rhys-Davies turns out to provide connections for more *Lost* actors than just his *Lord of the Rings* colleague Dominic Monaghan.

Rhys-Davies also starred in the 2002 monster movie *Sabretooth* with Josh Holloway, which means that Holloway is connected via Rhys-Davies not just to Monaghan but also to Sean Bean and thence to *Don't Say a Word* with Brittany Murphy and onward to *Party of Five* with Matthew Fox (or alternately to the McKellen/*X-Men*-James Marsden link to Fox). Rhys-Davies also worked in 2004's *The Princess Diaries 2: Royal Engagement* with Caroline Goodall, who was in *Easy* with Naveen Andrews, thereby connecting him back to Holloway.

I used to go for long walks, but I am now afraid to leave the computer, in case some question occurs to me that may fade from my increasingly clogged memory before I can return to my desk to research it. I am dizzy. I cannot tell if it is because I'm chasing these facts back and forth in my head or because I keep spinning my swivel chair around, clockwise and counter-clockwise, a form of exercise that does not require getting up from the computer.

My colleagues have given up on their pleas that I go to lunch and have begun bringing me food and beverages, which is kind of them.

Day 17

With six years on the air, *Party of Five* had a massive amount of guest stars, who turn out to connect Matthew Fox to almost all of his cast-mates on *Lost*. Daniel Von Bargen appeared in the 1998 episode "Love and War" and then in 2000 acted with Naveen Andrews in the feature film *Blessed Art Thou*, a fantasy about the testing of faith at a monastery.

In *Party*'s 1999–2000 season, Thomas Ian Nicholas had a recurring role as Todd Marsh, and then he worked in 2002 with Ian Somerhalder in *Rules of Attraction*.

Neve Campbell, Fox's onscreen sister in *Party*, was in the first *Scream* film with Skeet Ulrich, who went on to star in 2003's TV series *Miracles*, with Maggie Grace guesting in the "Mother's Daughter" episode.

There is a rather cumbersome link between Fox and Jorge Garcia. Lacey Chabert, Fox's *Party* sister, was in 2004's *Shadow of Fear* with James Spader, who guest-starred on the 1997 *Seinfeld* episode "Stanky Hanky." *Seinfeld*'s co-creator Larry David sometimes appeared on the show and went on to create and star in HBO's *Curb Your Enthusiasm*, with Jorge Garcia appearing as a drug dealer in the 2004 episode "The Car Pool Lane." I am sure there is a simpler connection between Fox and Garcia, but between chair-spinning and minor dehydration—I keep forgetting to avail myself of the office water fountain and the other employees for some reason are becoming increasingly reluctant to approach—I am too light-headed to look into it at the moment.

Fox also starred in a short-lived 2002 UPN series, *Haunted*, about a police detective whose near-death experience allows him to see visions. Eddie Cahill had a recurring role in *Haunted* and was in a 2002 episode of *Dawson's Creek*, which co-starred Joshua Jackson, who was in the 2001 feature *The Safety of Objects* with Patricia Clarkson, who was in *Carrie* with Emilie de Ravin. Again, there must be a shorter de Ravin/Fox route. Do these long routes signify the fact that the storylines of Jack and Hugo and Jack and Claire do not often intersect? If only I weren't so hungry—I wonder how the desk tastes…And I wonder if I will ever find a connection to Yunjin Kim….

Day 19

I have found another *Curb Your Enthusiasm*/Larry David/*Seinfeld* link between Jorge Garcia and another *Lost* actor—Daniel Dae Kim was in the 1998 *Seinfeld* episode "The Burning" as a college student. However, it's quicker to link Garcia and Kim via John Rubinstein, who played Kim's evil law firm supervisor in the third season of *Angel* and guest-starred on *Becker* during Garcia's tenure in 2004 in the "Subway Story" episode. *Angel* also connects Kim to Maggie Grace; Julie Benz played the vampire Darla during Kim's time on *Angel* and worked in the 2004 *Oliver Beene* episode "Idol Chatter" with Grace.

Day 20

I've found some more one-step-removed links.

Naveen Andrews was in 1996's *The English Patient* with Kristin Scott Thomas, who starred in 2001's *Life as a House* with Ian Somerhalder.

Josh Holloway was in *Sabretooth* with David Keith, who was in 2002's *Carrie* with Emilie de Ravin. De Ravin can also be connected via two different one-step routes to Harold Perrineau: either via Katherine Heigl, who starred with de Ravin in *Roswell* and with Perrineau in *The Tempest*, or through Harry J. Lennix. Lennix was one of the leads in *The Handler*, with de Ravin guesting in the 2003 episode "Dirty White Collar" and the 2004 episode "Acts of Congress," and Perrineau worked with Lennix in *The Matrix: Reloaded* and *The Matrix: Revolutions*.

Jorge Garcia connects to de Ravin in one step via her *Roswell* associate Jason Behr, who worked with Garcia in the 2004 film *Happily Even After*. Behr connects de Ravin and Garcia in one extra step to Ian Somerhalder, who was in *Rules of Attraction* with James Van Der Beek; Behr guested on *Dawson's Creek*, in which Van Der Beek was the Dawson of the title.

Garcia links to Josh Holloway through Vanessa Angel, who starred with Holloway in *Sabretooth* and worked with Garcia in the 2004 telefilm *The Good Humor Man*. Ted Danson starred with Garcia in *Becker* and with Malcolm David Kelley in the 2005 telefilm *Knights of the South Bronx*; Michael Boatman was a regular on *Spin City*, where Garcia guested as a cabbie in 2001's "The Arrival"; Boatman also guested in the same *Law and Order: SVU* episode, 2004's "Obscene," as Maggie Grace.

Grace worked with Chris Sarandon in the *Cold Case* episode "Volunteers"; Sarandon worked with Malcolm David Kelley in the 2002 *Judging Amy* episode "No One Expects the Spanish Inquisition" (which also features Kelley's Fox connection, Gregory Itzin).

As for Grace and Somerhalder, *Lost*'s lovers/stepsiblings who were respectively second and first casualties among the regulars, they are connected most directly through Tom Welling, who stars as Clark Kent in *Smallville* and starred with Grace in 2005's remake of the horror film *The Fog*. Does working with Tom Welling mean your character is fated to die on another show? Heck, it seems to mean that for most of the characters on *Smallville* and in *The Fog*....

Day 22

Just dredging up random connections now, still trying to find a unifying theory....

Daniel Dae Kim was in 24's second season with Thomas Kretschmann (though I cannot recall if they shared scenes), who was in *In Enemy Hands* with Ian Somerhalder.

Maggie Grace and Randy Oglesby were both guests on episodes of *Cold Case*, albeit not the same one; Oglesby is in the cast of *Blessed Art Thou* with Naveen Andrews.

In 1992, Andrews was in the thriller *Double Vision* with Kim Cattrall, who went on to star in *Sex and the City*. David McCallum guested in the HBO sitcom's 1999 episode "Shortcomings," then went on to star in *NCIS*, which featured Emilie de Ravin in the guest cast of the 2003 episode "Sea Dog."

Jorge Garcia has two different connections to Naveen Andrews, both via Andrews's *English Patient* costar Willem Dafoe, either through Dafoe's work with *Spin City* lead Charlie Sheen in the 1986 Oscar winner *Platoon* or through Dafoe's work with Ted Raimi in the *Spider-Man* films, as Raimi and Garcia both appeared in the 2002 feature horror parody *Tales From the Crapper* (I haven't seen the latter film, but *Platoon* seems the classier link).

While not in the same episode, Garcia and Richard Lewis were both on *Curb Your Enthusiasm*. Lewis guested on *7th Heaven* while Jessica Biel was a regular; Biel was in *Rules of Attraction* with Ian Somerhalder.

As mentioned, Sam Anderson, *Lost's* tailie Bernard, was in the same *Miracles* episode as Maggie Grace; he was also in the first season of *Angel*, though not in Josh Holloway's episode. Grace's work with Angus McFadyen on *Miracles* also provides a roundabout link to Harold Perrineau—McFadyen was in the 2000 Shakespearean drama *Titus* with Harry J. Lennix, Perrineau's *Matrix* sequels compatriot.

Perrineau and Holloway are likewise linked by several steps: Perrineau worked with Miriam Margolyes in *Romeo + Juliet* (she played the Nurse); Margolyes was in the 2004 comedy *Chasing Liberty* with Mark Harmon, who stars on *NCIS*, which featured Holloway as a guest in the 2004 episode "My Other Left Foot."

Holloway and Somerhalder are connected through the following route: Holloway was in the 2001 thriller *Cold Heart* with Nastassja Kinski, who back in 1982 was one of the title characters in the supernatural film *Cat People*, with John Heard as her human suitor; in

2003, he worked with Josh Holloway in the *CSI: Miami* episode "The Best Defense."

That's it—I've connected all the *Lost* cast...no, I still haven't found a link to Yunjin Kim. I collapse in my chair, sobbing. Has it all been for nothing? Is there no pattern? Do bears pirouette in the woods? I sit up. No, bears do *not* pirouette in the woods. They also do not play ping-pong there, though they do other things. This is not a futile quest. I shall persevere.

Day 29

Thank God for Aaron Sadovsky. I have never met this man, do not know what he looks like or sounds like and indeed I have little information about him. However, I know that he has held a variety of production jobs, including assistant director, segment producer, and production coordinator. I also know that he has had small roles in a variety of projects including the part of "Leering Man" in the 1996 comedy *Loose Women* with Charlie Sheen, an unaccredited bit as a train conductor in the 1998 supernatural thriller *Fallen* with Denzel Washington, John Goodman, and Donald Sutherland, and an appearance as a ticket counter in 2002's *High Times Potluck* with Jason Isaacs. With such costars, I connect Sadovsky in a few steps to anyone. Most important for my purposes, Sadovsky played a golf caddie in the 1996 South Korean miniseries *Beautiful Vacation* starring Yunjin Kim. The quest is saved (a line I've always loved from *Wizards*)....

Going through Kim's *Lost* comrades alphabetically by surname, always returning to Sadovsky and *Beautiful Country* as the first step, the connections are as follows, usually in four steps:

John Goodman of *Fallen* worked in the 2004 Bobby Darin biopic *Beyond the Sea* with Brenda Blethyn, who worked with Naveen Andrews in the 1993 miniseries *The Buddha of Suburbia* (four steps).

Goodman also worked with Pauley Perrette in 2001's comedy/drama *My First Mister*; Perrette is a regular on *NCIS*, which had both Emilie de Ravin and Josh Holloway as guests (four steps each).

There are two different connections between Yunjin Kim and Matthew Fox: either Donald Sutherland working with Sadovsky in *Fallen* and then with Fox in *Behind the Mask* or Dan Lauria guesting on *Party of Five* in the 1997 episode "You Win Some, You Lose Some" and then working with Sadovsky in *High Times Potluck* (three steps each).

Sadovsky worked with Charlie Sheen in *Loose Women*, which links him to Jorge Garcia via *Spin City*.

We're back to the Goodman connection for Maggie Grace—Goodman worked with Selma Blair in 2001's *Storytelling* and Blair costarred with Grace in *The Fog* (four steps).

Not surprisingly, the quickest connection between Yunjin Kim and Malcolm David Kelley is Denzel Washington in both *Fallen* and *Antwone Fisher* (three steps).

There is a fairly simple connection between Yunjin Kim and the actor playing her husband, Daniel Dae Kim (in addition to their surnames). Aaron Sadovsky was in *Loose Women* with Keith David, who was in the Oscar-winning 2005 *Crash* with Daniel Dae Kim, who plays a hit-and-run victim with a big secret (three steps). Hmm, a character with a big secret... maybe it will turn out that Jin and Sun have the *least* complicated pasts on the island?

We're back to the *Fallen* connection to link Yunjin Kim to both Evangeline Lilly and Ian Somerhalder. James Gandolfini (later to become famed for playing Tony Soprano) was in *Fallen*, and also in 1998's courtroom drama *A Civil Action* with William H. Macy, who's in *Stealing Sinatra* with Lilly (four steps) and as noted earlier, in *In Enemy Hands* with Ian Somerhalder (also four steps).

I have found two different four-step links between Kim and Dominic Monaghan, both via the Sadovsky/*Fallen*/John Goodman connection on her side and (not shockingly) *The Lord of the Rings* on his. Goodman was in both 2001's dark comedy *One Night at McCool's* with *LotR*'s Liv Tyler (Arwen) and in 2005's *Marilyn Hotchkiss' Ballroom Dancing and Charm School* with Sean Astin (Sam the hobbit).

There are three different three-step links (if not more) between Kim and Terry O'Quinn. There's a link via John Goodman, who worked with O'Quinn in the 2004 *West Wing* episode "The Stormy Present." In the same year, O'Quinn did another *West Wing* episode, "NSF Thurmont," that also guest-starred Jason Isaacs, who appeared in *High Times Potluck* with Aaron Sadovsky. Alternatively in 2001, O'Quinn was in *American Outlaws* with Muse Watson, who was then in the 2004 thriller *Season of the Hunted* with Sadovsky.

Finally, there are two different four-step connections between Kim and Harold Perrineau: either via one of the links between Perrineau and son Kelley (Denzel Washington in *Out of Time* with Sanaa Lathan, who worked with Perrineau in *The Best Man*) or through the Sadovsky/*Loose Women*/Keith David connection. David was in the 2000 football comedy *The Replacements* with Keanu Reeves, who worked with Perrineau in the *Matrix* sequels.

That's it. I've managed to connect all fourteen *Lost* actors to one another! I spring up from my chair and do the Dance of Joy, considerably startling my co-workers (I think they may have assumed I had lapsed into a near coma several days ago). Now all I have to do is analyze the connections and find a pattern. Should I start with the significance of whether the actors are separated by one, two, three, or four links, or should I begin by looking at what sort of parts they play at either end of the links? Could the word "links" be connected to the golf course Hugo constructed on the island, and if so, should I investigate whether any of the casts's previous roles included golf scenes? Or golf pants...?

143

Writer G. O. Likeskill is a journalist currently taking a sabbatical at the world-famous Arkham Asylum. Visiting days are Tuesdays and Thursdays, which are connected by Wednesdays.

Double-Locked

AMY BERNER

Years ago, when writing my own novel Ender's Game, *I needed to have one of my characters adopt a pseudonym for online use, a name suggesting political savvy, wisdom, and a nobility of outlook that would inspire trust. I had my character call himself "Locke," after the philosopher. But the character who was using that name was a sometimes violent, semi-wacko genius kid consumed with ambition and full of conspiracies.*

It's not just my own vanity that makes me wonder whether the writers of Lost *named their character John Locke only after the philosopher, or if at least one of them intended to insert an echo of my character Peter Wiggin. Because the Locke of* Lost *sometimes gets that demonic gleam in his eye....*

"If we will disbelieve everything, because we cannot certainly know all things, we shall do much what as wisely as he who would not use his legs, but sit still and perish because he had no wings to fly."
—British philosopher John Locke (1632–1704), *An Essay Concerning Human Understanding, Fifth Edition*, Book I, Chapter 1, Section 5

An Essay Concerning the Understanding of John Locke

By John Locke
TO THE RIGHT HONORABLE LORDS OF ENTERTAINMENT
IN THE NEW WORLD, PRINT, AND OTHERWISE

My Lords,

This essay, called into being because of your fictional creation which began its telling three centuries to the year following my demise, now exists to stand or fall on its merits and the reader's fancy alongside my prior works. With respect to your collective wisdom, which I am certain is held in high esteem among the populace, I have completed the task set upon me and applied my own Ideas to the subject at hand. I have endeavored to fully examine this single creation to the best of my ability based on my Knowledge and Experience, just as you, no doubt, also regularly advance your speculations in the most abstract Knowledge of things beyond ordinary reaches or common methods of your day.

From completing this analysis, I pray that all entertainment of your era shall be similar in scope and quality to this example, evolved further still from the gladiatorial contests and base-driven diversions of centuries past than even we ourselves, the society of my own time, have progressed. It is my fervent hope that fictional creations, such as this *Lost*, are the rule rather than the exception, and that you have filled your society with similarly multilayered, thought-provoking diversions that add positively to the entertainment experiences. The diversions of a society add to the collective Experience and thus help shape a nation. However, as I know not what Experiences will affect each mind in the coming years, I cannot know what the future will yield.

Your Lordships' Most Humble and Most Obedient Servant,
John Locke

Epistle to the Reader

I have put into thy hands an examination of a fictional character in so much as he mirrors my own philosophies as well as my name. Mis-

146

take this not as a commendation of myself, just as I have asked in the past, but rather a diversion of my idle hours that I hope will prove diverting to thine as well. Although I chose to spend much of my efforts examining the character that is my namesake, I find my ideas incorporated into this narrative concept in ways that extend well beyond this single fictional individual. As an example, I find it most interesting that each episode centers on the perspective of one character, and, more interesting still, that many of these episodes begin with focus on an eye.

It is through looking through the eyes and, less literally, from the perspectives of the characters' Experiences that we gain Understanding of the inhabitants of the island as well as Understanding the island itself. The island is enwrapped in mystery, and we cannot hope to gain Understanding of it without these perspectives, these glimpses of both their present and past. The flashes of the castaways' former lives prove especially enlightening, providing explanations of current actions and opinions, something available only in a fiction such as this. "If we could but see the secret motives that influenced the men of name and learning in the world and the leaders of parties, we should not always find that it was the embracing of truth for its own sake that made them espouse the doctrines they owned or maintained."[1]

But this Understanding is by its very nature remains limited. As I once wrote, "The Understanding, like the eye, while it makes us see and perceive all things, takes no notice of itself, and it requires art and pains to set it at a distance and make it its own object."[2] Each Experience is but a fragment of the whole, and we must distance ourselves from each fragment as we fit it into the aggregate in order to gain a full Understanding for the story. Indeed, without these glimpses of the past, we cannot fully understand actions on the island.

The quest for Knowledge and Understanding also appears in the guise of the Dharma Initiative, an organization that appears, at the time of this writing, to have been founded in order to create experi-

---

[1] Locke, John, *An Essay Concerning Human Understanding*, Fifth Edition, 1706, Book IV, Chapter 20, Section 17.

[2] Ibid, Epistle to the Reader.

ments on the island designed to broaden human Knowledge in several areas. This is just one of the mysteries of the island and the characters, all of which drive the collective interest of the populace in the ongoing story, for the discovery of Knowledge is reward in itself. The mind rejoices in each discovery: "Its searches after truth are a sort of hawking and hunting and hunting, wherein the very pursuit makes a great part of the pleasure."[3]

If I may beg your patience and give one additional example: I observe a continuing theme of comparative morality, in which a choice between what should or should not be done is determined by an individual's past Experience. The castaways demonstrate my theory that we are not born with innate principles, as such things would rely on innate ideas, which I do not believe exist. Thus, "The truth of all these moral rules plainly depends upon some other, antecedent to them and from which they must be deduced, which could not be if either they were innate or so much as self-evident....Hence naturally flows the great variety of opinions concerning moral rules which are to be found amongst men."[4] The choice to imprison or to torture can be considered moral if the deciding individual's gathered Experience, and therefore Understanding, considers the judgment to be moral.

Before I proceed with what I have thought regarding the fictional John Locke himself, I must here in the entrance beg pardon of my reader for the frequent self-references; such references are necessary when I must use my Understanding in examining his. In the pages that follow, I shall endeavor to examine his initial character state which led him to the journey, his Leadership Role and Interactions with the other castaways, his Instruction Methods, and his Faith in the island, and I presume to base these examinations on the parallels to myself.

Our first inquiry then shall be who this man was and how he came to be that man.

---

[3] Ibid, Epistle to the Reader.
[4] Ibid, Book I, Chapter 3, Sections 4–6.

Chapter I: A Discussion of John Locke, His Past, and His Arrival on the Island

1. The Roman satirist Juvenal is the first credited with "Mens Sana in Corpore Sano," or, as I once restated and expanded, "A sound mind in a sound body, (which) is a short but full description of a happy state in this world: he that has these two, has little more to wish for; and he that wants either of them, will be but little the better for any thing else. Men's happiness or misery is most part of their own making. He whose mind directs not wisely, will never take the right way; and he whose body is crazy and feeble will never be able to advance in it."[5] In what few glimpses that we witness of his life in a place called Tustin, John Locke lacked both a sound body and a sound mind before his arrival on the island, and he existed without family or a meaningful role in society. Indeed, he was neither a taxidermist nor a hit man, as the character Boone Carlyle surmised, but rather worked at tasks far below his level of intellect. It was his arrival to the island and his simultaneous restoration of the use of his legs that opened him up to Experiences that his fellows could not share to their full extent.

2. First, I shall examine the aspects of his body that are each unsound before his arrival. He gives up one of his kidneys, depleting him of an organ that thankfully is doubled in the human body, yet is still a vital organ and no small loss. Then, four years prior to the start of his time on the island, he loses the use of his legs, confining him to a wheelchair. The latter affected his daily life constantly, while the consequences of the former remained inside the mind.

3. It would make sense that both added greatly to the frustration and anger he once expressed regularly, as he once admitted to Sun Kwon while on the island. We witness one such past outburst in "Orientation, (2-3)": "Francine feels a little too much, if you ask me. You all do. I mean, seriously.... 'So-and-so never called me back, my mother stole thirty dollars from me'—I never even knew who my parents were....You want your damn thirty dollars back? I want my kidney back!"

[5] Locke, John, *Some Thoughts Concerning Education*, 1693, Section 1.

4. It was the circumstances of the former, the theft of his kidney by his natural father, who gained the kidney by duplicitous means and then discarded Locke as no longer useful, which led to this unsound mind and unhappy state, one obsessed with the man that ungraciously stole this organ. He turned to a group so that they might understand and help, and his relationship with Helen, a woman who becomes dear to him, sprang from this group. However, despite this new relationship, Locke remains less than whole, and the loss of the use of his legs likely amplified this. Due to his obsession, Helen leaves his company, after which Locke pays women to answer to that name, an even greater indication of his unsound mental state. At the time of his arrival on the island, he was a deeply unhappy man.

5. At the moment that his toe first moves following the crash, he regains his "sound body"; although he may still be without one kidney, he does miraculously regain the use of his legs and is therefore filled with joy, as evidenced by his citrus-enhanced mirth. This joy restores his strength of mind and spirit, and it is this restoration that triggers a "rebirth" due to his extraordinary recovery of mobility, thus rendering his mind all the more open to the island. As I have oft stated, I believe the human mind to be a blank slate at birth, "white paper, void of all Characters, without any Ideas. How comes it to be furnished...? To this I answer, in one word, from Experience, in that, all our Knowledge is founded, and from that it ultimately drives itself."[6] I refer to this theory by the Latin term *tabula rasa*, which I understand was borrowed by the writers of this fiction to entitle an early episode centering on this John Locke.

6. To be sure, his Simple Ideas remained intact, such as flavors and shapes, as did many of his Complex Ideas, such as practical Knowledge gained, but the more abstract Complex Ideas, like his concept of world order, became rewritten. While others on the island remained mired in the patterns of their past lives, Locke accepted the situation, incorporated the Knowledge into himself, and moved forward.

7. John Locke is often known to state, "Don't tell me what I can't do," and similar words to that effect. It is a wise man who does not

---

[6] Locke, John, *An Essay Concerning Human Understanding*, Fifth Edition, 1706, Book II, Chapter 1, Section 2.

accept limitations from others. Only an individual who is the sum of his Experiences can truly know of what he is capable, and only Experience can lead to a true Understanding of one's limitations before his arrival on the island. Although incapacitated compared to his prior state, he wishes to explore the limits of his capacity with an exploration of a vast wilderness, which is a wise course of action. "When we know our own strength, we shall the better know what to undertake with hopes of success."[7] He does not go into this situation lightly, but rather prepares by gathering stores of Knowledge regarding survival in such an environment. He works toward regaining a sense of self by these actions, and is understandably angered when thwarted.

8. In preparation for his endeavor, he studies at length about tracking, hunting, and other survival subjects, believing as I do that "The only fence against the world is a thorough Knowledge of it."[8] This study was to have increased the chance of his success in a wilderness environment, albeit a different one than he had intended to visit, and it was especially completed as both protection and to increase his potential contribution despite his limited mobility at the time.

9. The Locke of the island is a creation of his Experiences, as are we all, but his evolution since his arrival has been shaped more by island Experience than past Experience already imprinted onto his psyche. His gaze into the "beautiful" face of the island, although remaining mysterious to outside observers, changed him in a profound way, creating the basis for a strong faith, one that eschews deliberate rationality and instead accepts that the human mind cannot know all. He accepts that some things are not to be understood, which I shall discuss at length in the fourth chapter.

Chapter II: An Examination of the Evolution of Leadership in This New Community and the Role of John Locke within Its Government

1. Before I describe Locke's leadership role, I feel that I must address this contrived situation as a whole. The island represents the

---

[7] Ibid, Book I, Chapter 1, Section 6.
[8] Locke, John, *Some Thoughts Concerning Education*, 1693, Section 88.

original state of nature that I believe has existed in any locale without legitimate government, which was so well described in hypothetical terms by Thomas Hobbes (who indeed is not, as someone from the time of *Lost* inexplicably asked, a tiger). Every individual is free and equal in a state of nature, and in an uncivilized place, if left on their own, each would rely on their own strength and Experience for survival and would be under no obligation to obey another.

2. One example of a solitary individual in a state of nature is Danielle Rousseau, whose surname is a nod to Jean-Jacques Rousseau, a gentleman from the century that followed my own who believed that Man in his natural state is brutal and without morality. Although she does indeed act accordingly, by capturing Sayid Jarrah and, later, kidnapping Claire Littleton's child, I think that this need not necessarily be the case with every person in a state of nature. "The state of nature has a law of nature to govern it, which obliges every one; and reason, which is that law, teaches all mankind who will but consult it, that, being all equal and independent, no one ought to harm liberty or possessions."[9]

3. As the law of nature is unwritten, it is easily misapplied, for in the state of nature, each person becomes judge of what the law of nature requires and acts according to that judgment. In truth, the natural state of man is anarchy. In order to escape this primitive state and to ensure that the law of nature is applied correctly and impartially, both in the distant past and on this island, individuals leave this primitive state by entering into a social contract, under which the government provides protection.

4. However, the extreme freedom of the State of Nature appears advantageous, which brings up an important point. Allow me to restate what I once wrote so as not to paraphrase myself overmuch:

> *If Man in a State of Nature be so free, as has been said, and if he be absolute lord of his own person, equal to the greatest, and subject to no body, why will he part with his freedom? . . . To which it is obvious to answer, that though the state of nature he hath such a right, yet the enjoyment of it is very uncertain, and constantly exposed to the invasion*

---

[9] Locke, John, *Second Treatise on Civil Government*, 1690, Chapter II, Section 6.

of others: for all being kings as much as he, every man his equal, and the greater part no strict observers to equity and justice, the enjoyment of the property he has in this state is very unsafe, very insecure. This makes him willing to quit a condition, which, however free, is full of fears and continual dangers: and it is not without reason that he seeks out and is willing to join in society with others, who are already unit-ed, or have a mind to unite, for mutual preservation of their lives, lib-erties, and estates, which I call by the general name, property.[10]

5. Thus government is born from anarchy, and "the great end of men's entering into society, being the enjoyment of their properties in peace and safety, and the great instrument and means of that being the laws established in that society; the first and fundamental positive law of all commonwealths is the establishing of the legislative pow-er; as the first and fundamental natural law...is the preservation of the society, and (as far as will consist with the public good) of every person in it."[11] Indeed, the division and retention of property, both rightful and usurped, is a major theme of the early episodes. Gov-ernment on the island forms almost organically rather than by pur-poseful plan because of the desire for protection of life and property against both internal threats—both perceived and real—and proven, yet unknown, external foes.

6. Some, most notably the character known as James "Sawyer" Ford, do prefer the state of nature and resist the notion of govern-ment, especially as this island government exerts its authority early by taking extreme action against his person. Were it not for the incur-sions by the Others and the threat of the "monster," the society likely would not have formed as quickly, for "were it not for the corruption and viciousness of degenerate men, there would be no...necessity that men should separate from this great and natural community."[12]

7. As government emerged in this State of Nature, "the great ques-tion which in all ages has disturbed mankind, and brought on them the greatest part of these mischiefs which have ruined cities, depopu-lated countries, and disordered the peace of the world, has been, not

[10] Ibid, Chapter IX, Section 123.
[11] Ibid, Chapter XI, Section 134.
[12] Ibid, Chapter IX, Section 128.

whether there be power in the world, nor whence it came, but who should have it."[13] No natural hierarchy exists among humans, but social conventions have since created a hierarchy based on status of society brought about by Knowledge and Experience: professions. The individual whose profession naturally lends itself to respect, the medical doctor, is looked to in situations where these issues comes into question, and thus Jack Shephard becomes the head of this fledgling government.

8. Locke does not believe that Jack possesses absolute power; the island is in no way a monarchy, and Jack does not rule by any sort of divine right. When out of line, Locke challenges Jack, just as every citizen has the right to challenge his government, especially when leaders act contrary to public trust or ill-use their power. I believe that a right of revolution exists, going so far as that a group can declare their independence over atrocity or hardship. As an example, the Law of Nature forbids a government reducing one's fellows to a state of desperation, which is why Ana Lucia Cortez's "tribe" remnants left her behind to join the larger tribe that afforded more protection. They departed for the government that could better fulfill its basic role, protection of property, despite the fact that Ana Lucia had successfully fulfilled this role despite difficult situations previously.

9. Regardless of the small size of this newly formed society, a select group rules the whole, a representative government by general consent rather than election, and Locke naturally becomes a member of this group. Due to the nature of this environment, Locke understands the need for government, even though he is the best equipped to stand alone for survival in a state of nature. He instead turns his skills to the benefit of the common good.

10. Locke retains his own power in this "tribe" strengthened by his actions in three arenas. First, his mixes his labors with the island's resources, thus making the food he provides his own in the most basic of senses. As he shares his efforts with the others, he earns respect in exchange. Second, although a member of this ruling group, he answers questions forthrightly when asked and does not often keep secrets or his own counsel—with the exception of the hatch and mortal

---

[13] Locke, John, *First Treatise on Civil Government*, 1690, Chapter XI, Section 106.

injury sustained by Boone, as discussed in the next chapter—while others habitually dodge issues. Third, and most importantly, as his Experiences have led him to become the spiritual man of the island, he is the one sought after for wisdom. It is Understanding that sets us above other creatures, giving us advantage and dominion. So also does the John Locke of this fiction carry an Understanding that sets him apart from his fellows, a serenity brought about by his Experiences and his faith in the higher power of the island, which acts as a manifestation of the Almighty in his world view.

11. Many of the castaways turn to him when in distress or need, seeking advice or direction; new mother Claire, for one, often turns to Locke when in need rather than her eager suitor, Charlie Pace. At times, he will also seek out those he knows are in distress, such as when Sun Kwon believed her husband to be dead. He remains tranquil in this wild environment, trusting the island to provide, and his fellows are drawn to him due to this. To continue the tribal analogy, he is Shaman to Jack's Chief, but while Jack is in power by unspoken consent of the group, Locke has a position of power without being the de facto leader. As such, he also fills the role of mentor and teacher, as discussed in the next chapter.

Chapter III: Rationality Versus Revelation through Experience in the Teaching Methodology of John Locke

1. As stated, John Locke attained a position to instruct those that are lost on their own paths. Although often sought for advice by those of his community, his interactions with the self-destructive Charlie Pace and his protégé Boone Carlyle demonstrate the most extensive opportunities for instruction, and for both, he exemplifies that "It is one thing to show a man that he is in an error, and another to put him in possession of the truth."[14]

2. Rather than lecture or preach to his fellows, he leads others toward and into Experience as instruction. Experience, it must be said, is in actuality twofold: external and internal. External experience, or

---

[14] Locke, John, *An Essay Concerning Human Understanding*, Fifth Edition, 1706, Book IV, Chapter 7, Section 11.

sensation, gives us ideas of supposed external objects, such as color, sound, extension, or motion, while internal experience, or reflection, makes us understand the operation of the spirit on the objects of sensation, such as knowing, doubting, or believing. These two aspects must be combined in order to fully experience the lesson.

3. Early in the island's settlement, Locke discovers Charlie's drug addiction and deprives him of this drug during a hunting expedition, making it an Experience that serves as instruction.

> LOCKE: *I think you're a lot stronger than you know, Charlie. And I'm going to prove it to you. I'll let you ask me for your drugs three times. The third time, I'm going to give them to you. Now, just so we're clear, this is one.*
>
> CHARLIE: *Why? Why? Why are you doing this? To torture me? Just get rid of them and have done with it?*
>
> LOCKE: *If I did that you wouldn't have a choice, Charlie. And having choices, making decisions based on more than instinct, is the only thing that separates you from him* (the boar).
> —"The Moth (1-7)"

Locke understands the nature of humanity to err, and therefore gives Charlie the chances to err without repercussion, thus letting him Experience the lesson rather than merely hearing it. "All men are liable to error; and most men are in many points, by passion or interest, under temptation to it."[15] The drugs represent an extreme temptation to Charlie, but Locke does not lecture or reprimand, relying instead on Charlie experiencing this lesson for himself rather than imposing actions upon him.

4. His allegory of the moth also demonstrates the need for Experience as a learning tool in "The Moth": "This moth's just about to emerge. It's in there right now, struggling, it's digging its way through the thick hide of the cocoon. Now, I could help it, take my knife, gently widen the opening, and the moth would be free. But it would be too weak to survive. The struggle is nature's way of strengthening it." Charlie struggles through the lesson, fighting the urges of his

---

[15] Ibid, Book IV, Chapter 20, Section 17.

addiction, and in the end, he is victorious. Regrettably, his victory is temporary, as drugs become available to Charlie on the island, and Charlie errs again, but the Experience of Locke's lesson gives him the Knowledge that he has the power within himself to overcome his addiction.

5. Boone's tie to his life prior to the island wrapped around him stronger than any drug: the combined tie of family, fascination, and sexual attraction, all represented by his stepsister, Shannon Rutherford. However, Locke recognized that Boone was open to the island and all that it offers, perhaps more than any other castaway, and institutes extreme measures to break these ties. However, this also is a lesson that must be experienced and not something one can be told. He drugs Boone so that his mind could break the ties, and the resulting vision forces Boone to watch her die.

157

6. According to Locke in "Hearts and Minds (1-13)", this was "an experience that I believe was vital to your survival on this island," and it was what made him ready to follow in Locke's footsteps. Putting Boone's mind into an altered state to destroy the Shannon who existed in his mind gave him his own island rebirth. Logic and reason would not have yielded the same results. "Earthly minds, like mud walls, resist the strongest batteries; and though, perhaps, sometimes the force of a clear argument may make some impression, yet they nevertheless stand firm, and keep out the enemy, truth, that would captivated or disturb them."[16] Locke's serenity and faith are what prepares him as the font of wisdom on this island, an acceptance of what is and openness to what will be.

Chapter IV: Island Faith and Acceptance of Knowledge Existing Beyond Our Grasp

1. To his fellow castaways, and indeed, to many in the audience, Locke is an enigma. He bases his actions on Faith rather than Reason, accepting the island's gifts and commands without question. He does not demand explanation, knowing that he cannot know all things. "When we consider the vast distance of the known and visible parts

---

[16] Ibid, Book IV, Chapter 20, Section 12.

of the world, and the reasons we have to think, that what lies within our ken is but a small part of the universe, we shall then discover a huge abyss of ignorance."[17]

2. Locke looks into the face of the island, something that even we, as the outside observers, have not witnessed, and sees something Holy. This Experience stands alongside his restoration as the basis of his faith in the island. "When the spirit brings light into our minds, it dispels darkness. We see it as we do that of the sun at noon, and need not the twilight of reason to show it to us. This light from heaven is strong, clear, and pure...carrying its own demonstration with it; and we may as naturally take a glow-worm to assist us to discover the sun, as to examine the celestial ray by our own dim candle, reason."[18]

158

3. He does not share this Faith with others, for they have not shared this Experience, although he encourages others to pursue their Experiences, such as when he tells Jack to go after the ghost of his father in "White Rabbit (1-5)." Without their own Experiences, they cannot truly accept the island in their conscious mind. "Consciousness is the perception of what passes in a man's own mind. Can another man perceive that I am conscious of any thing, when I perceive it not myself? No man's Knowledge here can go beyond his Experience."[19] Nor can we, as an audience, fully understand his motivations, as we have not shared his Experience with him.

4. As the gift of the island, the restoration of his mobility, begins to fade, Locke looks for a way to appease that which gave him such a boon. What follows is a vision of Boone covered in blood that points the way to an aircraft. It is this aircraft's fall from the trees that costs Locke's young follower his life. One must wonder if Locke pondered whether he was required to trade Boone for his own boon (do pardon the play on words; under the circumstances, it simply could not be helped).

5. Locke firmly believes in "Man of Science, Man of Faith (2-1)" that "Boone was a sacrifice that the island demanded." He does not

---

[17] Ibid, Book IV, Chapter 3, Section 24.
[18] Ibid, Book IV, Chapter 19, Section 4.
[19] Ibid, Book II, Chapter 1, Section 19.

claim to understand the reasons, instead accepting that the reason transcends his Understanding. This acceptance is evidence of his faith, although it is both baffling and disturbing to his fellow castaways. "So that in effect religion…is that wherein men often appear most irrational and more senseless than beasts themselves."[20] I accept that his Experiences and Faith led him to his conclusions, although his fellows would likely not be as Understanding, as they based their existence on reason alone. Locke realizes how much more exists in this universe that is beyond our comprehension.

6. Although he is not a student of epistemology, his Experience has led him to the realization that many in my circle share. Since we cannot perfectly know the truth or falsehood of various religious beliefs and opinions, there is no justification for imposing beliefs on another. In the example of the opened hatch and the countdown situation of the bunker, Jack attempts to impose his logic on Locke, the belief that the countdown should be allowed to run down to zero. Locke's beliefs seem peculiar to some of the others, but "New opinions are always suspected, and usually opposed, without any other reason but because they are not already common."[21] But although Jack's opinion contrasts Locke's own, at the end of their confrontation, Jack stops disputing Locke's claim, obeying Desmond's instructions, and thus, per Locke's belief, those of the island.

7. It is this acceptance of what lies outside of human Experience and reason that drives him to allow the unseen force of the island to capture him (Jack stops this force despite his pleas) and to take charge of the button and its 108-minute countdown. It is his realization that others do not share his Understanding that drives him to indoctrinate Boone and keep the hatch a secret from the rest. It is this faith that gives him the secure Knowledge that the sacrifice of Boone is necessary as he believes it to be the island's wish, a belief strengthens when his legs, restored on the island, begin to fail him.

8. The powers of the island seem to transcend known science, and audiences and castaways both resist that Objects and Ideas exist that are beyond our Understanding. "Thus men, extending their inquiries

---

[20] Ibid, Book IV, Chapter 18, Section 11.
[21] Ibid, Epistle Dedicatory.

beyond their capabilities, and letting their thoughts wander where they can find no sure footing…never coming to any clear resolution, are proper only to continue and increase their doubts and to confirm them at last to perfect skepticism. Whereas, were the capacities of out Understanding well considered, the extent of Knowledge once discovered, and the horizon found which sets the bounds between the enlightened and the dark parts of things, between what is or is not comprehensible by us, men would…employ their thoughts and discourse with more advantage and satisfaction in the other."[22] Will there be an explanation of why Jack's father appears to his son, or how the numbers emanating from the island resulted in lottery winnings, or how Walt's mind seems to affect the world around him? John Locke does not need to know how or why, and instead accepts these things.

Conclusions

1. Though I have now come to a conclusion regarding my analysis of John Locke, I accept that more shall be revealed by the character's creators, and thus could prove my conclusions to be erroneous. Nevertheless, I state my summary for your deliberation, to be accepted or discarded as you see fit.

2. Locke is a rational man who believes in the value of Experience, the value of government that does not invade an individual's rights, the important role of Experience in improving the mind, and that all things in this world cannot be understood.

3. I find this Locke to be a fascinating creation, sharing my own views on the world, and were he not a figment of a creative contingent but rather flesh and blood, I believe that he and I would agree on a great many matters. However, as he is but a fictional character, I am obliged to you nonetheless for this creation, one that reflects so many of my own Ideas, and I am indebted that it has opened an opportunity to gain Understanding of my own Ideas through a single incarnation in your culture.

Finis.

[22] Ibid, Book I, Chapter 1, Section 7.

Double-Locked

Amy Berner attempted to fit seventeenth-century philosopher John Locke into her head for this essay, but she's a writer/event planner in real life rather than a writer/philosopher. Then again, keeping a philosophical outlook in event planning is never a bad thing. As a writer, she is best known as a columnist, reviewing and analyzing science fiction and fantasy films, books, and television shows—including, of course, *Lost*—for Dark Worlds (www.darkworlds.com). Amy's essays also appear in *Five Seasons of Angel*, *The Anthology at the End of the Universe*, *Alias Assumed: Sex, Lies and SD-6*, and *Farscape Forever! Sex, Drugs and Killer Muppets*. She lives in San Diego, California.

The Art of Leadership

GLENN YEFFETH

I've spent years observing, studying, and thinking about leadership. And I've come to two simple conclusions:

1. Leaders are leaders because for some reason other people follow them.

2. I'm not one.

The question, "Who ought to be boss?" is like asking, "Who ought to be tenor in the quartet?" Obviously, the man who can sing tenor.
—Henry Ford

I'm not a leader...I don't have what it takes.
—Jack Shephard

LEADERSHIP IS A TOPIC that never loses its interest, and we are continually searching for sources of insight into this difficult subject. For decades, management tomes have plumbed the great minds of history in search of wisdom, leading to such books as *Management & Machiavelli, Leadership Secrets of Attila the Hun, Winnie-the-Pooh on Management* and, a personal favorite, *Jesus CEO.*

But how impressive are these so-called leaders, anyway? One out of twelve people in Asia are direct descendants of Attila the Hun, which is an accomplishment of sorts, I suppose. Of course, this accomplishment was achieved through rape and pillage on a truly grand scale (or, in management-speak, a vision-based implementation of an unprecedented multinational involuntary impregnation process). But Attila was a cannibal (he ate two of his own sons) and a drunkard who drowned in a pool of his own blood in an alcohol-induced nosebleed (while attempting, apparently, to impregnate his new bride—he was consistent, anyway). Surely we can find a better model of leadership.

Machiavelli was, let's face it, an unemployed civil servant writing on spec white papers on leadership in the hopes of getting a job. A clever writer, yes, but a model of leadership? Not quite. Winnie-the-Pooh I won't even discuss. And Jesus, while certainly possessing good leadership skills, had a mere twelve disciples. Fine for its day, no doubt, but by modern corporate standards not really all that impressive (let's be frank; Paul did the heavy lifting, leadership-wise).

But Dr. Jack Shephard is another matter altogether. Not chosen by any electorate, not wanting any position of authority, Jack emerged as leader through sheer natural talent. And he faces challenges that dwarf those of any leader in history. He must deal with the dangerous Others, rampant polar bears/nanotech swarms, computerized doomsday machines, bad-luck numbers, and keeping Boone from having sex with his own sister. And then there are the challenges of survival on the island, the tail-section folk, uncovering the secrets of the Dharma Initiative, and keeping Hurley out of the ranch dressing....

Surely those of us seeking wisdom on the topic of leadership need seek no further. We should simply study the actions of the master. Let us ask: what would Jack do?

Lesson #1: Never Give Up

When Boone was clearly dying on the table, did Jack abandon his patently hopeless attempts to save him? No, he did not. Ignoring all reason, he shoved a tube in his arm, Rambo-style, *and gave his own blood to the dying patient.* This actually makes a lot of sense, because, well, they weren't *exactly* a blood-type match but they were kinda close, and it would have been too hard to find another match at that point. It's not like Jack had anything else to do; he could afford to be a little light-headed. Of course there was Claire's baby coming, but Jack had already delegated that to Kate, so what could go wrong? The point is, uh, that the proof of the pudding is in the eating, except not in this case because Boone does die despite everything. I'll come back to this one....

Lesson #2: The Ends Justify the Means

When the unpleasant Sawyer stole Shannon's medicine, did Jack hesitate? No, he did not. He authorized Sayid to begin a torture session that would turn stomachs at Abu Ghraib. Now, this might seem heartless, yes, but this is what's known in torture literature as a "ticking time-bomb case." Many lawyers agree that torture is justified when the torturer knows that the torturee has critical information that could save lives. This is a textbook example of justified torture because, you see, Sawyer had information that could save Shannon's life. Well, actually he didn't, but *Jack didn't know that.* Of course, Sawyer reveals nothing, and it turns out the medicine wasn't needed to save Shannon's life, and Sayid felt so guilty he decides to leave the group. When they captured the Other and Jack was willing to let the whole island (world?) be destroyed to stop his torture, that might *seem* inconsistent, but, as Ralph Waldo Emerson says, "consistency is the hobgoblins of little minds," and with the polar bears, nanotech clouds, or whatever, the last thing they need is hobgoblins, so we can all agree that these were good decisions. Right?

Lesson #3: Leave No One Behind

When Michael went searching for his son, did Jack think through the consequences of racing after him? No, he did not. He led his team into the woods, despite the reservations of less-hardy souls, until they were soon surrounded and outnumbered by the Others...

...um...

...I'm sure there's something....

What luck for rulers that men do not think.
—Adolf Hitler

JACK: *Hurley, they're numbers.*
HURLEY: *What's that thing where doctors make you feel better just by talking to you?*
JACK: *Bedside manner.*
HURLEY: *Yeah, that. Yours sucks, dude.*

Surely Jack did something right. Didn't he?

As leaders go, Jack is a great doctor. While the survivors unquestionably do look to Jack as their leader, it's not at all clear why. Upon examination it's increasingly obvious that *everything Jack does is wrong*. Reluctant to lead yet irrepressibly bossy, stubborn but wishy-washy, too scientific to accept the realities of the survivors' situation yet irrational on a myriad of issues, Jack is the ultimate anti-leader. He makes Winnie-the-Pooh look levelheaded.

Need more proof?

Jack opposed the golf course as frivolous, but it turned out that it was a huge morale boost for the whole island (and let's remember the critical importance of morale in the survival rate of disaster victims). Jack refused to read at the funeral ceremony, despite its importance to the survivors (did I mention the importance of morale?). He failed to convince the survivors to move to the cave, resulting in a splitting-up of the tribe. He didn't believe Claire when she claimed to be attacked even though just *pretending* to believe her would have calmed her (and her anxiety was quite risky for the baby). As a result, she was kidnapped and Jack relieved his guilt by (yet again) storming into the woods to do something, however ineffective (he winds up walking in circles until Locke finds him).

He put Hurley in charge of the food, which is like putting Michael Jackson in charge of a day-care center. He continually behaves in an irrational, hostile manner, particularly when anyone challenges his arbitrary opinions. He was furious with Locke for entering the hatch for reasons that aren't the least bit clear. He conspired with ex-police officer/psychopath Ana Lucia to build an army.

Jack is supposed to be a man of science, but he rarely tries to figure anything out. Sayid is the man of science. Jack is the prototypical arrogant doctor, knowledgeable and authoritative, expecting to be obeyed and respected by virtue of his superior knowledge. Of course, most of the problems on the island aren't medical.

He is a good doctor, though (except for the crappy bedside manner and the tendency to make promises he can't keep)....

> *If the blind lead the blind, both shall fall into the ditch.*
> —Matthew 15:14

> *A leader is a dealer in hope.*
> —Napoleon Bonaparte

So who is the real leader on this island? The obvious alternative candidate is Locke, the man of faith. Like a master Jedi, Locke reveals a real talent for enrolling the young and feeble-minded into his vision. Walt quickly succumbed to his charms, as did Charlie and Boone. He even wins over Claire. He supplies food—always popular on a desert island—and the best tracking skills of the group. He works hard to build relationships with all the key players, building a crib for Claire and a dog whistle for Michael, warning Boone not to antagonize Sayid, and saving Jack's life at least once (not that it helped much with Jack's irrational dislike of Locke).

But Locke's style of leadership is less Mahatma Gandhi and more David Koresh. He does have a true spiritual sense, leading Charlie away from heroin and to a belief in his own potential, helping Sawyer release his guilt (remember the vindictive boar?), and forcing Boone to let go of the incestuous[1] relationship with Shannon. But he's a bit too, well, *intense*.

He manipulates and controls Charlie to an extent that would be unacceptable to anyone *but* a junkie. And his willingness to tie up and drug Boone in order to help him achieve some kind of realization about his sister was just a wee bit over the top.

More to the point, none of these apprenticeships last very long.

---

[1] Literally, I'm afraid.

Charlie goes over to the dark side when he drops Locke to become Sawyer's apprentice. And we all know what happened to Boone.

Locke's good nature and impressive survival skills almost make one forget the fanatical gleam in his eyes. Almost. His determination to break into the hatch (and to keep pressing the button once in) is a bit too much of a faith-based initiative for most of the survivors. He's a little too weird, a little too mystical, to appeal to most of the islanders. He's respected, and he has his followers, but he isn't really a leader. He knows it, too, as revealed by his anger at the imprisoned Other for asking why Jack was in charge. This anger, belying Locke's usually calm countenance in the face of Jack's ravings, reveals that the competition between them is real, and that he knows that Jack is winning. Locke's intensity and fanatical faith makes it impossible for him to take the leadership reins from Jack, however incompetent Jack may be.

(Not that I'm telling Locke what he can't do. . . .)

So does the island have any leadership? Perhaps we're looking at the question too narrowly. Perhaps we are looking for a Karl Rove, not a George W. Bush. Perhaps leadership, in the context of *Lost*, is the ability to get other people to do what you want them to, whether or not they see you as a leader. The ability to be effectively in charge, if not visibly in charge.

One has to consider Sawyer. He does get his way. He manages to seize control of most of the unclaimed goods on the island. He wants to get on the raft, and he does. He wants a kiss, and he gets one (although the price is a bit high). He wants the guns, and he gets them too. Is he the leadership mastermind we've been searching for?

Not quite. Despite Sawyer's clear successes, mostly accomplished through a combination of force and trickery, he is frustrated at every turn. Kate (with Jack's help) gets the suitcase from him. Jack and Sayid tie him up and torture him. His "leadership skills" led to a longer stay in the pit than either Michael or Jin, not to mention getting shot by Ana Lucia (she does that a lot). While he is a good manipulator, he can rarely get anyone to do things without trickery . . . and everyone is increasingly suspicious and wary of him. He has burnt so many bridges that it is impossible to imagine him rallying the survivors on anything.

The Art of Leadership

A leader is best
When people barely know he exists.
Not so good when people obey and acclaim him,
Worse when they despise him.
Fail to honor people,
They fail to honor you
But of a good leader who talks little,
When his work is done, his aim fulfilled,
They will say "We did this ourselves."
—Lao-Tse

The real leader has no need to lead—he is content to point the way.
—Henry Miller

HURLEY: *Everyone's going to hate me, Rose.*
ROSE: *Now that's just plain silly—you're about the only one on this is-*
land that everybody loves.

Sawyer is too blatantly antagonistic to be the secret leader of the *Lost* gang. No, we are looking for someone below the radar screen. Someone who never seems to make waves, but always seems to get their way. Someone who influences things without seeming to. Someone who everyone likes.

Are you thinking what I'm thinking?

Could Hurley really be the leadership mastermind of *Lost*? Let's consider this. It's Hurley who builds the golf course that turns around island morale. It's Hurley who conceives and executes the census that reveals the existence of the Others and identifies Ethan Rom as the mole (including obtaining an important item[2] from Sawyer without resorting to either torture or sexual favors). He managed to be put in charge of the food—complaining about it the whole time—and uses this authority to cement his relationships with everyone on the island (while allowing himself an unlimited supply of ranch dressing).

That's not all.

Hurley, for all his good nature, has a streak of ruthlessness. He's

---

[2] The passenger manifest.

willing to let Locke enter the wrong code into the computer. He defies everyone to obtain the batteries from Rousseau. He decides, on his own, who to tell about the hatch (note that he's one of the first to know about it) despite the wishes of the "leaders." And no one calls him on any of it.

He carefully steers the "leaders" through friendly conversation. He tried to refocus Boone on hunting, leading to the crisis between Boone and Locke. He kids Jack into letting go of some of his seriousness (JACK: I'm not really in the mood, Hurley. HURLEY: Really? Wow, usually you're, like, Mr. Ha ha.). He was instrumental in improving the raft's potential for success (by obtaining radio batteries from Rousseau, a task Sayid had declared impossible). He stopped Charlie from hurting Aaron. He formed a "love connection" with Libby; was it true love or did he suspect her of being an Other (how does he step on her foot while boarding if she's in the tail section and he's in the middle?). He comes up with a new radio for Sayid, both to cheer him up and restore his value to the group, not to mention increasing their chances of rescue.

So what does Hurley want?

He wants first dibs on the food supply, and he has it.

He wants to be liked and trusted by everyone, and he is.

He wants to be in a position to influence the other "leaders": Jack, Sawyer, Locke, Sayid, and Rousseau, and he does.

He wants to solve the mystery of the cursed numbers. He hasn't yet.

Care to bet against him?

Glenn Yeffeth is the best-selling editor of such Smart Pop books as *Taking the Red Pill*, *The War of the Worlds*, and *Navigating the Golden Compass* and co-editor of *Finding Serenity*. He currently resides in Dallas.

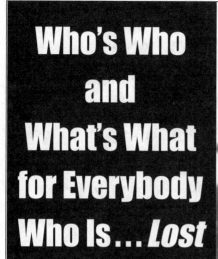

Who's Who and What's What for Everybody Who Is... *Lost*

WAYNE ALLEN SALLEE

As Aristotle once said, "You can't tell the players without a program." Admit it—this Lost Encyclopedia *is the reason you bought this book. You're going to bookmark the first page of this section and keep it by the television on Wednesday nights, so you can look stuff up during the commercials. And if you're truly obsessive, you'll memorize whole sections of it so you can dazzle your friends at parties. "You know, 'Kate Dodd' is the name Kate was using at the point of her capture in Australia by the U.S. marshal." Wow, dude, you actually know stuff like that?*

However, I'm annoyed that Sallee didn't mention, under the entry for Katey Sagal, that she played Peg Bundy for many years on Married...with Children. *(Not to mention recurring roles on* Futurama *and* The Shield.*) (And she was also Bette Midler's backup singer during her 1979 appearance on* Saturday Night Live.*) Anybody who doesn't understand the significance of the fact that John Locke nearly proposed marriage to Peg Bundy is never going to get a handle on* Lost, *and that's a fact.*

A

Aaron

Claire Littleton was eight months pregnant when Oceanic Air Flight 815 crashed, and her baby was born forty-one days later. She visited a psychic to see what the future held for her after her unborn child's father left her and she decided upon adoption. Claire is at first rebuffed and the psychic returns her money. She returns to him, and he tells her that "danger surrounds" the child, and he tells her that he has found a couple in Los Angeles who want the baby and shoves a ticket for the ill-fated flight into her hands. There are conflicting images of this ticket, thanks to modern marvels like TiVo and PhotoShop, and the date on the ticket is either September 22, 2004 (the original air date of the *Lost* pilot, or 2009 (which would make things interesting because this would ensure that the show's flashbacks are all occurring in present-day settings). Note: In the Bible, Aaron was the brother of Moses.

Abductions

Claire and Charlie were abducted by Ethan Rom, but it became known that Claire was the sole intended target. Almost a dozen of the tail-section survivors, including two children, were taken roughly from their base camp within two weeks of the crash. At this writing, it is not known if any of those abducted are alive or dead.

Abed-Jazeem, Noor

Nadia's given name at birth. Sayid tells Agent Cole that she no longer uses that name.

Abrams, J. J.

Executive producer of *Lost*.

Accident, The

The reason Hurley was institutionalized by his mother was because of an accident that killed two people. Already overweight, he climbed onto a crowded dock that collapsed on twenty-three people, causing two fatalities.

Acolyte

One who assists a minister in a liturgical service.

Adam and Eve

Nicknames given to two skeletal bodies found on ledges in the caves Jack discovers. Jack makes the assumption that the bodies have been there at least half a century; one held tight to a pouch containing two rocks, one white and one black.

Adams, Richard

The author of *Watership Down*.

ADF

Automatic Direction Finder. Henry Gale claims his balloon was equipped with an ADF beacon.

Adoption

Claire planned to give her unborn baby up for adoption. Michael was pressured by his ex-wife, Susan, to give up his parental rights so that Walt could be adopted by her new husband, Brian Porter.

Aguilar, Father

The priest who held service over Hurley's grandfather's funeral. He was struck by lightning while administering blessings.

Airplane

Kate had buried a pale blue, palm-sized toy airplane in a time capsule with her childhood sweetheart in Iowa back in 1989. It was subsequently unearthed at the time Kate's mother was dying. It was the only item in the safety deposit box in the New Mexico bank Kate robbed, and she retrieved it from the U.S. marshal's Halliburton case after he died on the island.

Akinnuoye-Agbaje, Adewale

The actor who portrays Mr. Eko.

Alcohol

Tiny bottles of alcohol are used by Jack to sterilize wounds, including his own, in the aftermath of the crash. Sawyer saves several bottles in his "stash" for drinking, which he shares with Kate during a drinking game. Later, Jack proffers one of Sawyer's tequila bottles to Ana Lucia on the day Shannon's body is buried.

Alex

Danielle Rousseau claimed that after her French expedition crashed on the island sixteen years ago, the Others took her baby daughter away from her. This was the show's first reference to the significance of babies or children on the island. And adult Alex is with the group led by Mr. Friendly that abducts Kate after Jack, Locke, and Sawyer follow Michael into the jungle.

Al-Jazeera

Arabic television station. Scenes of Sayid on a television screen in a flashback may be from an Al-Jazeera clip. Early in season one, Sawyer uses this as one of several ethnic derogatory terms when he argues with Sayid.

Aloe

Succulent plants having rosettes with spikes of showy flowers. Sun shows Walt how to use aloe leaves like toothpaste, rather those finger strips they give kids for school nowadays, and presumably Mr. Eko showed the tailenders a similar method. How else can Ana Lucia's sparkling-white smirk be explained?

Amarillo Slim

Nickname Sawyer gives to Jack in order to goad him into playing cards.

Amnesia

Partial or total loss of memory in one's cognitive state of mind. After Claire was rescued from her abduction by Ethan Rom, she could not remember any details of the two weeks she was missing in the jungle.

Amsterdam, the Netherlands

Michael's wife Susan moved there to work overseas with Brian Porter, and on the way to see Walt for possibly the last time, Michael was hit by a car and suffered leg injuries.

Anagram

A word or phrase spelled by the rearrangement of letters. A frivolous example is by rearranging Oceanic into the word Cocaine. A better example, and one the clinical-thinking fans of the television show use, shows that Ethan Rom can be juggled into the words "Other man."

Ancillary

Relating to something that is added but is not essential. Many island survivors and characters in the various flashbacks of the core group of survivors can be considered ancillary to the show, e.g., it is not necessary to know much about Claire's boyfriend or Charlie's brother's family.

Andrews, Naveen

The actor who portrays Sayid Jarrah.

Ann Arbor

This midsized city harbors the University of Michigan.

Annie

The alias Kate uses when she is on the farm in Australia.

"An Occurrence at Owl Creek Bridge"

When Sawyer arrives in the bunker to tell Locke that Jack is on his way to retrieve the guns, Locke has just flipped through the pages of this book, presumably looking for any notes or film clips. The story, by Ambrose Bierce, is about a soldier who is hanged from the above-named bridge, yet the man believes that the rope breaks and he escapes to run off to return to his wife. Very much the opposite of "your life flashing before your eyes" tales, the story ends when the soldier's neck breaks from the fall. Yet another "dead or alive?" literary reference. The shelves look like the inventory at the Marquis de Sade's closing-out sale.

Antarctica

The southernmost continent, location of the South Pole and Southern Magnetic Pole. Michael has to sail his raft before the northerly winds of monsoon season end, as the only place south is, well . . .

Anxiolytics

Tranquilizer used to relieve anxiety and reduce tension and irritability.

Apollo candy bars

Several boxes of these "full o' nuts" bars are in bright purple wrappers and are found by Kate in the Section #3 pantry after Desmond puts her in the room and holds Locke at gunpoint. Each box of candy bars has the Dharma Swan logo, and the bar she unwraps has a consumption date of October 23, 2004.

Armory

A side room which can be locked that has held, at various times, guns, the Virgin Mary statues, and the man using the name Henry Gale.

Arrow, The

A Dharma station found by the tail-section survivors; unlike the bunker, it seems more like a storage shed, as the only entrance is through a camouflaged tree. The station has limited electric power, and on a bench or shelf in the corner, they find items wrapped in something like burlap: a glass eye, a Bible, and a two-way radio. The Bible, it is later learned, is hollowed out, and a key-missing section of the "Orientation" film is rolled up inside. The Arrow seems to have been abandoned, perhaps used by the Others.

Artisan, Paul

The private investigator in the novel *Evil Twin*.

Arzt, Dr. Leslie

One of the mid-section survivors who was not introduced until the last episodes of the first season, he was a ninth-grade science teacher. His knowledge helped Michael decide when to set sail with his raft and then helped Jack, Locke, Kate, and Hurley find explosives in the *Black Rock*. He showed the others how to handle sweating dynamite in order to blow open the mysterious hatch, but blew himself up in the process.

Asiana Hotel

Jin had been employed here as a busboy, and was promoted to waiter.

Asclepion

A temple of healing, from the Greek name for the god of medicine, Asklepios.

Asklepios

The Roman god of medicine, known in Greek literature for his holistic remedies and humane treatment of the mentally ill. A snake curled around a staff (or rod) is a symbol on the Dharma hatch where Ethan and his gang kept Claire captive for almost two weeks. The symbol on the Dharma bunker looks very similar to that used by the American Medical Association.

Astin, Mackenzie

177

Portrayed Kate's childhood sweetheart, Tom Brennan.

Atari 2600

This electronic game program was the first documented interactive media to implement the phrase "Easter Eggs" to describe clues to further enhance the games' enjoyment.

Atomic Tobacco

An early '70s rock band, supposedly an influence on the early works of Geronimo Jackson.

Atonement

Compensation for a wrong, particularly when appeasing a deity.

Austen, Katherine "Kate"

After finding out that her stepfather, Wayne, was in fact her biological father, and believing that he could never be any better than a drunken wife-abuser, she kills him by setting their Iowa farmhouse on fire. She confessed to her mother, but her mother called the police, causing Edward Mars to pursue her for more than three years, from Iowa to New Mexico and finally Australia. Various flashbacks reveal her aliases to be Kate Ryan, Joan Hart, Annie, Maggie, and on the Oceanic Air Web site, Katherine Dodd.

Austen, Sam

The man Kate thought was her father, but who had been with her mother before Kate was born, an army sergeant who works as a recruiter in an Iowa U.S. Army recruiting office.

Aviary, The

Code name for the building at Fort George G. Meade, Maryland, that housed the remote viewing experiments.

Ayers Rock

A large magnetic rock in central Australia, near Alice Springs, which extends three and a half miles beneath the surface of the Earth.

B

Backgammon

A board game for two players, with moves decided by the roll of the dice. Locke finds a backgammon game and teaches Walt to play. The backgammon pieces are black and white, a recurring color scheme on the show.

Background survivors

These non-core survivors—many have no speaking parts—are usually seen in the background collecting firewood or doing laundry. Here are their names in alphabetical order: *Marcia Ardino, Armado Cacho, Chris Candella, Judy Chamness, Paul Edney, Faith Fay, Wayne Geiger, Juliette Goodell, Becky Goodman, Adelina Gregor, Kavika Isaac, Dane Justman, John Karaya, John Ludwig, Marjorie Mariano, Jim Mazzarella, Natalie Mei Lau, Beth Merritt, Tony Natoli, Kathleen O'Neill, Ryan Satch, Ivana Smith, Aden Stay, Jason Triplett, Dustin Watchman, Rand Wilson, John Yee, and Happy Zurowski.*

Backpacks

These items are more common as carry-on luggage than briefcases on some flights. The fuselage survivors use backpacks to carry water bottles and fruit. The tailenders carried no backpacks as much of the luggage was lost when the tail section crashed offshore on the south end of the island.

Backstory

Slang for a quick recap on someone's past, a phrase commonly seen in books of fiction. Also allows for development during current events in said fiction, and can be used to trick one into believing the wrong thing about an individual's true intentions.

Bad Twin

A private-eye procedural involving a wealthy heir's search for his evil brother. The manuscript was delivered by the author to Hyperion Books, owned by ABC, days before boarding Flight 815. In truth, it would be more likely that the writer would be delivering the pages or disk to his agent, unless he was sending the novel out on speculation.

Ba-Gua

The eight trigrams of the I-Ching, and its importance also relates to nature. Each of the Dharma logos is in the shape of a Ba-Gua octagon.

Bane, Jimmy

An individual who confronts Locke after his father fakes his own death. Anthony Cooper had swindled $900,000 from Bane as part of a retirement-fund scam.

Banofee pie

Before Claire tells Charlie that she misses peanut butter, Charlie tells her he misses this treat, a sweet pie made with toffee and cream.

Baptism

A Christian sacrament signifying spiritual cleansing and rebirth. Charlie has recurring dreams involving Aaron in danger. Mr. Eko explains that the dreams may signify that a baptism is necessary.

Baum, L. Frank

The author of *The Wizard of Oz*.

Bedside manner

Jack's father tells him that a doctor must always provide hope, even if that hope doesn't really exist, as the patient will always need to feel uplifted. Jack was also pointedly made aware he hadn't learned much when Hurley tells him, "Dude, your bedside manner sucks."

Beechcraft

Walter Herschel Beech co-founded in 1924, along with Clyde Cessna and Lloyd Sherman, the Travel Air Manufacturing Company, the world's largest producer of both monoplane and biplane aircraft. For those viewers who wonder how a plane from Nigeria might end up in the South Pacific, perhaps you should know that Beech's slogan was "The world is a small place when you fly in a Beechcraft."

Behemoth

Someone or something that is abnormally large and powerful. One of the names given to the island monster.

Bernard

Husband to Rose, he was in the tail section using the bathroom when Flight 815 broke apart.

Bicentennial

Of, relating to, or completing a period of two hundred years. The envelope containing the letter the young James Ford (known on the island as "Sawyer") wrote to the man who swindled his parents bore an embossed image for American Bicentennial.

Bierce, Ambrose

The author of the short story "An Occurrence at Owl Creek Bridge."

Big Dipper

The constellation Ursa Major, or Big (Polar?) Bear has a pattern of six stars that form a dipper and handle; the foremost stars point directly to Polaris, the North Star. When Hurley is watching Sam Toomey play Connect Four, the pattern he makes mimics a reverse version of the Big Dipper. From Hurley's point of view, it is seen as it would look in the northern hemisphere during the spring and summer.

Bissone, Angelo

An elderly man who passes away from heart failure after Jack operates on him.

Bissone, Gabriela

Angelo's daughter, who said she came to Jack after consulting many medical journals and believes that he performed miracle surgeries. After learning of her father's death, she embraces Jack and kisses him, and Jack allows it.

Black and white

The colors comprising the yin-yang symbol. This color scheme recurs throughout the show, i.e., the backgammon board, the Dharma logos, and the stones found with "Adam and Eve." Also, in Claire's dream, Locke had one black eye and one solid white eye.

Black Box

181

There are two of these devices on board each airplane; one records flight data, the other cockpit conversations. Made to withstand the worst of crash conditions, each device's recordings are protected by bright orange casings. Aside from planes that crash over water, the only cases of black boxes not being recovered were after the terrorist hijackings of 9/11.

Black Rock

A slave ship which was sitting amidst trees with land all around the hull; skeletons were shackled in the hold, and the survivors make use of dynamite that was found on board. The ship is settled in an area Rousseau has referred to as the "Dark Territory," and likely ended in its current position from a tsunami from centuries past.

Black smoke

According to Rousseau, the smoke will appear on the horizon as a signal that the Others are approaching. The smoke appeared a week after her daughter was born, and again the day the raft departed the island. Later that night, Mr. Friendly and his motley crew abducted Walt.

Blast doors

Examining the walls and ceiling in one section of the bunker, Michael makes Jack aware of their design and purpose, as he was an architect before the plane crash.

Blurry thing

The psychic Claire visits refunds the money from her first visit, claiming that his initial reading only produced a vision of a "blurry thing."

Boars

Uncastrated male hogs, having narrow bodies and prominent tusks. After several swine are found rutting in the fuselage wreckage, Locke forms a hunting party in search of boar meat.

Bollocks

British slang for the word $#!t.

Bonneville

This make of car, manufactured by Pontiac, appears in several flashbacks. This was the type of car that was involved in Kate's car crash in Iowa, and similar models were used in two separate pedestrian accidents, when Michael is struck while crossing the street and when Locke is trying to catch up to his mother in the parking lot.

Booby trap

An explosive mine hidden underground. Rousseau had set several such devices around her camp.

Book of Law

When Mr. Eko tells Locke the story of Josiah, he refers to the Old Testament with this term.

Boston Red Sox

Jack's father had a saying, "And that's why the Sox will never win the World Series," as a way to delegate blame away from human error and put it in the hands of fate and circumstance.

Bottitta, Ron

The actor who portrays Leonard Sims.

Bowen, Julie

The actress who portrays Sara Shephard, Jack's wife.

Bowman, Christian

The actor who portrays background survivor Steve Jenkins.

Box man

Desmond's nickname for Locke, referring to where Locke had been employed at the time of the crash.

Bpo-Bpo

Korean for the word "kiss," this was the name of Sun's shar-pei puppy.

Brennan, Tom

The childhood sweetheart of Kate. He's a doctor and schedules a fake procedure so Kate can see her mother on her deathbed. He dies during Kate's escape attempt. At the time she was wanted for the murder of her biological father.

Brothers Karamazov, The

Locke gives the fake Henry Gale this book about a feuding family, and the prisoner soon taunts Locke about why he lets Jack boss him around.

Brown, Clancy

The actor who portrays Joe Inman, the U.S. soldier who leads Sayid to his future role as torturer for the Hussein regime.

Bunker

A fortification of earth, mostly or entirely below ground. The hatch Locke and Boone discover leads to a huge bunker built into the shape of a geodesic dome with several hallways, one of which exits from the trunk of a huge tree within the jungle.

Butties diapers

Charlie had hoped for his band's comeback when DriveSHAFT had the opportunity to sing "You All Everybody" in a commercial. The four band members dance in diapers in an oversized crib with a teddy bear and a polar bear in opposite corners of the bedding. They lose the job because Liam is high on smack and cannot keep the rhythm and then falls through the bars of the crib.

C

C-4

Powerful plastic explosive. 300 pounds were stolen from a Melbourne army base by a terrorist cell Sayid helped infiltrate.

Cairo University

Sayid Jarrah attended this school with Essam, who later joined a terrorist cell group based in Sydney.

Canada

Ethan Rom tells Hurley that he is from Canada when the manifest list is being cross-checked. While the tail-section survivors' story is being told, a man named Nathan tells Ana Lucia that he is a Peace Corps worker from Canada.

Candle, Dr. Marvin

Narrates the "Orientation" film, which was created by the Hanso Foundation as part of a group of clinical programs which included the Dharma Initiative. Viewed in the bunker of Station #3, first shown by Desmond to Jack and Locke. Viewed from the waist up and wearing a white lab coat, Candle's left arm does not move throughout the film, and he might be an amputee. There is a scale model of the geodesic dome that makes up Station #3, and Candle gestures at the structure several times during his speech.

Calderwood

The name of the Sydney police officer who reviews Sawyer's file and tells him he will be deported and not allowed on Australian soil again.

Caldwell, L. Scott

The actress who portrays Rose.

Cardiopulmonary Resuscitation

Commonly known as CPR. An emergency procedure consisting of external cardiac massage and artificial respiration. Jack performs this act on Rose after the crash, and Ana Lucia does the same for Emma. Lucky kid.

Carlyle, Boone

One of the few survivors seated in the first-class section, along with stepsister Shannon Rutherford, according to the seating chart posted at www.oceanic-air.com. His mother, Sabrina, ran a wedding-consultation company, Carlyle Weddings, and he had recently been given a high-paying position as chief of overseas operations. He died forty-one days after the crash, after investigating a crashed Beechcraft. Using the cockpit radio for a distress signal, the added weight caused the lightweight plane to fall from a tree. Boone sustained several rib fractures but died from compartmentalized bleeding in his right leg.

Carpe Diem

Latin for "seize the day." In his own words, prior to the crash, Charlie had this type of attitude.

Cassidy

A woman who received a $600,000 divorce settlement. Sawyer and a man named Gordy set her up for a "long con," and Sawyer stayed with her for six months, eventually screwing both Cassidy and Gordy out of the money.

Cave

After days with little sleep following the crash, a fatigued Jack follows an apparition of his late father, whose casket was in the cargo hold of Flight 815 en route to interment in Los Angeles. The ghost gestures for Jack to follow him deeper into the jungle and at one point Jack's attention deviates toward the sound of rushing water. He finds an enclosed cave with fresh water from a nearby waterfall. The survivors from the fuselage eventually break into two groups, those watching for rescue at the beach and those who choose the safety of the enclosed cave.

Census

A period count of a given population. After Claire's abduction, Hurley creates a census based on the plane's passenger manifest.

Central Intelligence Agency

CIA agents interrogate Sayid in London, telling him that he can have the whereabouts of his beloved Nadia if he assists them in spying on a former college schoolmate.

-centric

Each episode of *Lost* involves flashbacks of a key survivor, and has been given sub-headings using the above hyphenation. The first part of the Pilot episode was Jack-centric. Certain flashback scenes have been deleted and only appear on the DVD collections, in a Claire-centric episode, a flashback involved Claire and the pilot making small talk about psychics prior to the flight.

Cephalexin

An oral cephalosporin commonly prescribed for mild to moderately severe infections, ranging from ears and throat to the urinary tract. This is one of the antibiotics that Jack uses to treat Sawyer after Sayid stabs him in the arm.

Cephalosporin

One of several broad-spectrum antibiotic substances obtained from fungi and related to penicillin.

Cerberus

A mythical monster. According to Greek mythology, a three-headed dog guarding the gates of Hell. Cerberus was the son of Typhon, one of the whirlwinds.

Cerberus System

The storm-door map shows indications that primary access to the system is near Station #3. This might be the actual name for the Monster, or Security System, as Rousseau calls it.

Chau, Francois

The actor who portrays Dr. Marvin Candle in the 8mm film titled "Orientation."

Chernobyl

This nuclear plant was located eighty miles north of Kiev in the former USSR (now the Ukraine). On April 25, 1986, the fourth reactor went out of control and a fireball blew off the heavy steel and concrete lid. Thirty people were killed instantly, and there were high radiation levels for a surrounding twenty-mile radius. In the bunker of Station #3, Sayid is attempting to break through concrete into a sealed room and tells Jack that the last time he saw something sealed in such a manner was at Chernobyl.

Chief of Surgery

Jack's father, Christian, was head of the surgical department at St. Sebastian's hospital until he was stripped of his medical license.

187

Chief Resident

Jack's title at St. Sebastian prior to his father's dismissal.

Chung, Byron

The actor who portrays Mr. Paik, Sun's father and Jin's employer.

Church

A place for public (and especially Christian) worship. After his "confession" to the fake Henry Gale, Mr. Eko starts building a church, eventually being helped by Charlie.

CIA

The Central Intelligence Agency.

Cindy

One of the tail-section survivors, Cindy was the flight attendant who serves Jack his drink in the first of the show's flashbacks, giving the doctor an extra bottle, which he places in his jacket pocket. She also pounds on the lavatory door as Charlie Pace tries to flush away his stash of heroin in the minutes preceding the plane crash. Cindy has an Australian accent, and she disappears as the tailenders, Jin, and Michael struggle to carry a stretcher holding a delirious Sawyer up a sharp incline.

Clinical psychology

The branch of psychology that studies abnormal mentation—the process of thinking carefully—and behavior. Gerald and Karen De-Groots were social scientists in the 1970s, and Libby, one of the few tailenders to survive both the plane crash and subsequent attacks by the Others, has said on several occasions that she is a clinical psychologist.

Clock

A numerical clock with numbers that flip over, reminiscent of 1970s alarm clocks, the minutes with a grey background and the seconds on a white background, count down to zero. The clock, when restarted, restarts its countdown to zero at 108 minutes. It does not reflect the passage of seconds until the four-minute point.

Clonazepam

An anti-convulsant drug given as treatment for epilepsy or panic attacks. One of the milder narcotics, with withdrawal symptoms consisting of abdominal pain and sweating.

Clones

A group of genetically identical cells or organisms derived from a single cell or individual by some kind of asexual reproduction.

Cluck's, Mr.

Hurley had been working at the "flagship branch" of Mr. Cluck's Chicken Shack when he won the Mega-Millions lottery. He quits after being confronted by his supervisor, Randy, about eating a box of chicken while on duty. A meteor later hits the restaurant, and Randy is also seen working at the same box company that employs John Locke. The official Web site of Mr. Cluck's hails the soon-to-be grand opening of a new restaurant at 1623 North 42nd Avenue in Los Angeles.

Cockpit

Compartment where the pilots sit while flying an aircraft. The cockpit crashed inland from the fuselage.

Coconut Internet

Sawyer-slang for the method in which information makes its way amongst the survivors.

Code

To reset the computer countdown to 108 minutes, the user has to type in the numbers 4, 8, 15, 16, 23, and 42, and then press the Execute button.

Coffin

A box which holds a body for burial or cremation. When Jack follows the supposed ghost of his father into the jungle, he discovers the caves. He also finds his father's casket, which is open and empty.

189

Coincidence

After Locke marvels at the fact that the two pieces of the "Orientation" film were found in different bunkers on the island, Mr. Eko warns him "do not confuse faith with coincidence."

Collision

Shannon's father, Jack Rutherford, is killed in a head-on accident with the SUV driven by Jack's future wife Sara. Also, when the paths of the tailenders and the other survivors cross rather suddenly, tragedy occurs when Ana Lucia shoots Shannon, mistaking her for one of the Others.

Collusion

A secret agreement. Locke and Boone were in collusion when they hid the discovery of the hatch from the rest of the survivors.

Colonel, The

Locke's nickname at the box company, bestowed by younger employees with whom he played strategic board games at lunch or on break. Locke admits to Randy (see separate listing) that he has never seen military service.

Columbus, Theo

The actor who portrays Jimmy Bane.

Commitment

The trait of sincere and steadfast fixity of purpose. Jack's father tells him that commitment is what "makes him tick" and this is why Jack has trouble with letting go.

Compartment syndrome

A medical condition where pressure or bleeding builds in certain areas of a body's limb after trauma, keeping needed nourishment from the affected area. Boone's right leg was crushed in such a manner that Jack could not save his life.

Compass

A navigational instrument for finding directions. Sayid uses a compass to locate magnetic north.

Computer

The computer in Station #3 is an old, beat-up Apple II computer which was manufactured in the early 1980s. The Apple II could be considered one of the first PCs, or personal computers, and it had a standard 16K ROM, although most were upgraded to 48K. The computer could only perform one function at a time.

Confession

The act of a penitent disclosing his sinfulness before a priest in the sacrament of penance in the hope of absolution. Charlie was a religious man, and wanted to confess his stealing property to support his drug habit.

Confidence man

More commonly known as "con man," an individual who gains another's trust and hopefulness and runs grifts to bilk people out of their money or property.

Connect Four

While Hurley quizzes him in the sanitarium, Leonard Sims plays this game while repeatedly reciting the number sequence.

Console to Console Communication

The manner in which Michael instant-messages his son on the Apple computer.

Cooper, Anthony

Locke's biological father, who he did not know for much of his adult life. He was on dialysis and conned his son into donating one of his kidneys, then abandoned him once again.

Coral Island, The

Several references are made to William Golding's novel *Lord of the Flies* on *Lost*, particularly a comment Charlie made toward the tailenders' tale of survival. In Golding's apocalyptic book about a group of schoolchildren surviving nuclear war, *The Coral Island*, a book by nineteenth Century novelist R. M. Ballantyne, is mentioned a number of times. The book is about three British boys on a deserted island with unrealistic depictions. Golding read the book as a young man and found Ballantyne to be racist, as the book's main tenet is that evil is associated to those who have black skin.

191

Coral Sea Islands

Declared as Australian territory in 1969, these uninhabited islands cover a million square kilometers of Oceania. The only population is in the Willis Islets area, where a staff of meteorologists work at a weather station. Several other weather stations are automated in this area.

Cortez, Ana Lucia

Once a Los Angeles police officer, Ana expected the remaining tail-section survivors to allow her to take charge, though she makes several bad judgment calls when uncontested. Seated in 42-F, the last row of the plane, she flirted with Jack at the bar in the Sydney airport. Ana chooses to believe that fellow survivor Nathan is one of the Others, holding him in a makeshift pit with bamboo bars until he confesses. Nathan is freed, and then killed by Goodwin, who was the actual "plant," just as Ethan Rom was at the other survivors' camp. She is key to keeping Jin, Michael, and Sawyer imprisoned after their raft is blown apart in the first-season cliffhanger, then allows them to lead the tailenders back to the main group, primarily because the tailenders have little in the way of supplies and medicine. Cutting back into the jungle to save time reaching the other camp, Cindy (see separate entry) disappears, a sudden downpour and strange background whispers from the jungle puts all on edge, and Ana fatally shoots Shannon in the chest as she stumbles out of the trees.

Corvus

The crow. Apollo had an affair with Corvus and they had a son, Asclepius, the founder of medicine, who is immortalized in the sky as Ophiuchus. Corvus was a spy for Apollo. Several articles have been written comparing elements in *Lost* to Stephen King's *The Stand*, and in King's apocalyptic plague book, bad guy Randall Flagg often takes the shape of a crow.

Countdown

Counting backward from an arbitrary number to indicate the time remaining before some event. The protocol at Station #3 is to enter a password into the compound's computer every 108 minutes. Klaxons begin blaring at three-second intervals at the four-minute mark.

Cowboy

One of the terms Ana Lucia uses to refer to the deathly ill Sawyer as the tailenders carry him in a makeshift stretcher.

CR 4-81516-23 42

Desmond injects something into his bicep from a vial in the drug cabinet. Each vial has this same batch of letters and numbers.

Crater

A constellation in the night sky shaped like a goblet. Corvus the crow carried this cup to Apollo.

Cremation

The incineration of a dead body. At the main crash site, dead passengers are cremated as the fuselage burns so as to keep away the rotting smell and disease, and Mr. Eko burns the Beechcraft drug-smuggling plane as a matter of cleansing the remains of his dead brother, Yemi.

Crossword puzzles

A pastime of Locke's as he handles monitor duty at the computer. He fills in words to fit his needs—"Gilgamesh" instead of "scripture" is an example—but this might be explained away by him as taking a "leap of faith."

Cryogenics

The branch of physics that studies the phenomena that occur at very low temperatures.

Cryogenics Development Imperative

One of the active programs listed on the Hanso Foundation Web site.

Cullen, Brett

The actor who portrayed Goodwin, the Other who infiltrated the camp of the tail-section survivors.

Curiosity

A state in which you want to learn more about something. Mr. Friendly quotes Alvar Hanso (as posted on the Hanso Foundation's Web site) to Jack, Sawyer, and Locke: From the dawn of our species, Man has been blessed with curiosity. Our most precious gift, without exception, is the desire to know more—to look beyond what is accepted as the truth and to imagine what is possible.

Curse

An appeal to some supernatural power to inflict evil on someone.

Curse of the Numbers, The

Hurley believes that he has been cursed by winning the lottery and that he is at fault for Oceanic Air Flight 815 crashing a thousand miles off course. It doesn't help that the winning numbers were etched into the cover of the hatch, along with the word QUARANTINE.

Cuse, Carlton

Executive producer of *Lost*, he has also written several episodes. Cuse also created the TV series *Nash Bridges*, starring Don Johnson and Cheech Marin, and *The Adventures of Briscoe County, Jr.*, whose ubiquitous star was Bruce Campbell.

Cusick, Henri Ian

The actor who portrays Desmond, one-time keeper of the computer countdown.

Cygnus

The constellation Cygnus, which holds two bright stars Altair and Deneb, is commonly called the Swan. In Greek mythology, Cygnus repeatedly dove into the river Eridanus trying to save his friend Phaeton, the son of Apollo. Cygnus is a prominent summer constellation in the Northern hemisphere.

D

Daddio

Jin laments to Sun that he can understand no one on the island, and after she tells him that she is pregnant, Jin recalls that Sawyer gave him this new nickname.

Damaged goods

Jack tells Kate that the Others will not abduct them because they are not "good."

Danny

Ana Lucia had a relationship with this man, likely the father of the child she lost, and he leaves her at some point after she was shot on duty.

Dark territory

The area that Rousseau tells Sayid where the other members of her expedition became infected with the sickness. There is also a slave ship, the *Black Rock*, perched amidst tree trunks, presumably tossed there by a tsunami hundreds of years ago.

Date of accident

Damon Lindelof told *TV Guide* that the writers "have never said exactly when the plane crashed. The assumption is that it happened in 2004 when the show premiered, but we've never said that." Case in point: when the psychic gives Claire her ticket, a screen capture shows the date on the ticket to be September 24, 2009.

Dave

Hurley sees this bald guy on the island after freaking out because Libby shows her attraction to him. Supposedly, Dave was an imaginary friend that Hurley invented during his stay at the Santa Rosa Mental Hospital, and Hurley had created him as a way to justify his eating disorder.

Dawson, Michael

Survived the crash with his ten year-old son, Walt Lloyd, and his Labrador, Vincent. He had just regained custody of his son after his ex-wife died of cancer. He sustained leg injuries after being hit by a car, and walked with use of a cane when Walt was younger. He uses his skills as an architect to design a system in the caves to allow showers, and also builds a raft that he attempts to leave the island on, joined by Walt, Jin, and Sawyer.

195

Daystrom Data Concepts

One of the *Lost* fan Web sites lists this company as owning several other companies, including Oceanic Airlines.

DC

A comic-book company that published a Spanish version of *Green Lantern/Flash: Faster Friends*. Hurley is reading the comic as Flight 815 taxis for take-off, and at a later date, Michael questions his son Walt's reading of the book even though he cannot understand the words. The story revolves around the governmental retrieval of a crashed UFO post-WWII, and a polar bear is seen in several panels. Later in the same episode, a polar bear is shot and killed, leaving the possibility that the creature was manifested by Walt.

Dean, Monica

The actress who portrays Gabriela Bissone.

Decryption

The activity of making clear or converting from code into plain text. Sayid steals maps of the island made by Rousseau, but the images and words make little sense.

DeGroot, Gerald & Karen

As seen in the "Orientation" film, the two doctoral candidates at the University of Michigan created the Dharma Initiative in 1970, a program that would present scientists with a place to study electromagnetism, meteorology, parapsychology, psychology, and utopian social studies.

Deposit Box 815

Kate stages a heist at a bank in New Mexico, pretending to be one of the customers. She later shoots a robber and allows all but her to be arrested by police. The only item she wanted was in Box 815, a pale blue toy airplane. She tells Jack that "it belonged to the man I loved, the man I killed."

de Ravin, Emilie

Portrays Claire Littleton, one of the core characters.

Desmond

Scotsman who encountered Jack while both were running in the stadium. Prior to the hatch being opened, with Kate and Locke descending into the bunker and geodesic dome, it is apparent that Desmond must inject himself with something from the drug cabinet and to punch in the number code every 108 minutes on the computer. He asks them if they are sick, but also, in checking to see if they are indeed his replacements, asks, "What did one snowman say to the other snowman?" (Note that in season one, Hurley poses the same riddle to Walt, saying that the answer is "Freeze!" Another purported answer is "Do you smell carrots?") Desmond claims he was in a boat race and after his craft had run aground on the island, Kelvin came running from the jungle asking for his help. Kelvin died soon after.

Desmond's photograph

There is a 4 x 6 photo that Desmond has on a shelf near the bunk beds, and he takes this with him when he scampers from the bunker, thinking the computer has been shot to bits. The man in the picture is obviously the happier, tanned pre-bunker Desmond, yet the blond woman in the photo is never in full view, as the photo curves away.

Destiny

An event that will inevitably happen in the future. Locke believes it was his destiny to be on the island.

Details

When working his cons, both on and off the island, Sawyer refers to clues always being in the details.

Dharma

Basic principles of the cosmos. Also, an ancient sage in Hindu mythology who is worshiped as a god by several lower castes.

Dharma Initiative

A research projected founded by the Hanso Foundation.

Diary

A journal of personal thoughts. Claire's diary is found by Sawyer after her abduction by Ethan Rom. On the official ABC Web site, under the entry for *Lost*, a link can allow the diary of an ancillary survivor named Janelle to be read.

Diazepam

Generic name for Valium. Prescription drug commonly prescribed for anxiety and depression, can also be used for drug or alcohol withdrawal.

Dickens, Kim

The actress who portrayed Cassidy, who lived with Sawyer during one of his "long cons."

Dictatorial decisions

As the tailenders trek toward the other group of survivors, Ana Lucia's judgment is questioned to the point that she feels that she is an outcast, and must live on the island alone after she accidentally shoots and kills Shannon.

Distillation

The process of purifying a liquid by boiling it and condensing its vapors. One way to convert salt water to fresh water.

Distress Signal

The French science team followed the source of this signal to the island. The transmission repeated the numbers and could conceivably refer to the island's coordinates. Rousseau changes the transmission to be a warning as well as a call for help. She warns that she was forced to kill the other members of her team because of a sickness, and that whoever picks up the transmission should head to the *Black Rock*.

Doctor, The

The tailenders are only aware that there is a doctor in the ranks of the other group of survivors. His identity comes as a surprise to Ana Lucia, as she shared a drink with Jack at the airport bar prior to flight, and during their banter she gives him her seat number, asking him if he wanted to change seats.

Dodd, Kate

The name Kate was using at the point of her capture in Australia by the U.S. marshal.

Donald

One of the survivors from the tail section, he had a compound fracture of his right leg. Libby adjusted the bones while telling one of her loopy stories about breaking her leg in Vermont while paying more attention to the ski instructor than the ski path. He dies, presumably from septic shock, within the first week of the crash.

Donkey Kong

When Sawyer is typing the numbers into the computer ever...so...slowly, he tells Jack he can't answer his question yet because he is about to get his high score on Donkey Kong, an arcade game from the 1980s.

Doomsday button

Hurley's nickname for the Execute button on the computer.

Dostoevsky, Fyodor

The author of *The Brothers Karamazov*.

Double take

Look at Jack's face when he realizes it is Desmond he meets in the bunker and after Mr. Eko tells him "Ana Lucia…made a…mistake." You'll get the idea.

Dream quest

Also known as a vision quest, it is an initiation based in Native American tradition but is in use worldwide in which one becomes more aware of the connection to a creational source. When Boone considers telling the other survivors about the discovery of the hatch, Locke hits him on the back of the head, then rubs a type of natural pseudylic, perhaps a substance similar to the South American Iawaska plant, which causes Boone to dream "in the third dimension." He sees his half-sister Shannon mauled to death by the monster that only a few of the survivors have seen.

199

A true dream quest will give confidence to a person and stronger connections to creation. The true purpose of Locke's actions toward Boone was to make him change his mind about making the discovery of the hatch public.

DriveSHAFT

Charlie was bass guitarist for this band and it was fellow band member, and brother, Liam who enabled Charlie's addiction to heroin. The band was known as a one-hit wonder for their song "You All Everybody." Initially, Charlie believes that most survivors recognize him or know of the band, when in fact Locke is the only one who acknowledges the band. At one point, believing Shannon would be impressed, Charlie sings the lyrics to the song, and she shrieks that she never wants to hear that song ever again.

Drug cabinet

There is a shelf of antibiotics in Station #3. Desmond injections some type of drug into his system on a regular basis, as he takes a huge quantity with him upon fleeing the hatch. There are other drugs there that Jack instructs Kate to look for so that Sawyer can be treated after he goes into septic shock.

Duckett, Frank

A con man who ran a shrimp truck in Sydney. Sawyer murdered him, tricked by Hibbs into thinking the man was the one who conned his parents. In truth, Duckett had owed money to Hibbs, who simply had Sawyer do the dirty work.

Dunn, Kevin

The actor who portrays Gordy, a partner in Sawyer's "Long Con."

Dynamite

An explosive containing nitrate sensitized with nitroglycerine absorbed on wood pulp.

Jack, Locke, Kate, and Hurley use dynamite from the *Black Rock* to blow open the hatch. They act carefully, as Arzt accidentally blew himself up moments earlier.

Dystopia

The state in which the condition of life is extremely bad as from deprivation or oppression or terror. Rousseau lives in fear of the Others and those with "the sickness."

E

Easter egg

A virtual Easter egg is a hidden message in an object such as a movie, book, DVD, computer program, or Web site. The basic idea is of a plastic Easter-egg hunt, where one cracks the egg in half and finds candy or money. In the case of *Lost*, any Easter egg found on the Web sites or on the show itself furthers the mysteries of the numbers, the Others, the bunkers, and why Hurley never seems to lose any weight.

Eko, Mr.

One of the tail-section survivors. As a teenager in Nigeria he was recruited by a thug captain to join his criminal militia, whose primary concerns were drug running, with one major market being Morocco. His younger brother, Yemi, who became a priest, tries to keep Mr. Eko from being arrested as the Beechcraft takes off. Yemi is shot and pulled onto the plane; the Nigerian police mistake Mr. Eko as the priest. Claire and, to a lesser and more selfish extent, Charlie inform Mr. Eko of the plane in the jungle. At the wreckage site, Mr. Eko stares down the smoke monster, which provides visions in the form of electric impulses, and the smoke retreats. He carries a staff that he has been carving scripture on for the entire stay on the island, keeps Yemi's cross, cremates the body by setting the plane afire, and when asked by Charlie, he admits that yes, he is a priest. Mr. Eko also killed two of the Others with a rock and his bare hands, and took a forty-day vow of silence.

Electromagnetic Research Initiative

One of the experiments funded by the Hanso Foundation. This experiment is currently in progress in Station #3.

Emerson, Michael

The actor who portrays Henry Gale.

Emma

One of the child survivors of the tail section, along with her brother Jack, who was abducted by the Others two weeks after the crash. Their parents were in Los Angeles.

Endometriosis

The presence of endometrium—a mucous membrane—elsewhere than in the lining of the uterus, causing menstrual pain. Sun displays these symptoms at a time when she and Jin are attempting to have a child.

Enforcer

One whose job it is to execute unpleasant tasks for a superior. Jin takes a job with Sun's father as a precondition to marriage. In one instance, he was required to beat a government official into submission after the closing of one of the father-in-law's businesses for safety reasons.

Eucalyptus

A tree with leaves that produce a gummy substance. Sun uses these leaves to help ease Shannon's asthma.

Execute

To act or perform an action. After entering the number sequence on the computer, the keyboard button labeled Execute must be pressed.

Experiment

The act of conducting a controlled test or investigation. Jack initially argues that the process of entering the number code on the computer every 108 minutes is nothing more than an experiment, an inquiry to see if someone would actually type in the code.

F

Faith healer

One who relies on holistic therapies for treatment of medical conditions.

Fallopian tubes

Either of a pair of tubes conducting the egg from the ovary to the uterus. Sun's doctor lies to her, saying that these organs are scarred and the reason she cannot become pregnant.

Fate

Charlie writes this word on four finger bandages on his left hand. The bandages are later left as a false trail by Ethan when he abducts Charlie and Claire.

Fay, Faith

One of the background survivors with no speaking lines of note, most noticeable for wearing a blue and white striped shirt with her midriff exposed. A fan base at the official *Lost* Web site has listed her character as SBSSG—Sexy Blue-Striped Shirt Girl. In a recent post on the site, Ms. Fay states that there are plans for more speaking roles for the background survivors. This, of course, will lead to new nicknames for Sawyer to invent.

Federated States of Micronesia

Using Hurley's numbers as coordinates—4.81500 degrees North, 162.34200 degrees East—an uninhabited area of the Pacific between

Papau New Guinea and the Marshall Islands is pinpointed. The closest mapped islands are Palikir and Majuro.

Fish 'N Fry

The fast-food restaurant Claire worked for; her wages were five dollars an hour.

Flame, The

The map on the blast door shows a drawing for Station #4, between the Swan and the medical station where Claire was being held captive. The flame icon could signify either Apollo or a Phoenix-like comparison to death and rebirth.

Flashbacks

203

Each of the main characters are allowed specific episodes where the individual is allowed to ponder events in current time on the island through reflecting on their own past decisions, both good and/or bad. Each flashback sequence will frame a character's actions and give justification to his/her role in the group of survivors.

Flatiron Building

A triangular building in lower Manhattan. Michael tells Walt that he will show him this building when he comes to live with him in New York City.

Flightline Motel

Locke's father is hiding out in this joint next to one of the runways at LAX as he waits for his son to bring him the money he had embezzled. During a scene of Locke in the hotel parking lot, an Oceanic Air Flight comes in for landing.

Fong, Larry

Executive producer and writer for *Lost*.

Ford, James "Sawyer"

As a child, he watched his parents die in a murder/suicide after they had been swindled of their life savings. When he became older, he ironically became a con man himself, adopting the name of the man responsible for his parents' deaths. He began hoarding anything salvageable from the crash site and seems to enjoy making the rest of the survivors dislike him. He worked his own con on the island, making other survivors suspicious of each other so that he might get the chance to gain control of the guns, a higher commodity now than when Flight 815 first crashed.

Fort Lewis

An army base near Tacoma, Washington. At one point in his career, Kate's father was stationed here.

Fox, Matthew

The actor who portrays Dr. Jack Shephard, the Alpha Male of the fuselage survivors.

Frainey

The name of the private investigator who Locke hired to locate his father.

Freckles

A nickname Sawyer commonly uses when flirting with Kate.

Frivolous Lawsuits

A group of fans filed a class-action suit against the Oahu Police Department after Cynthia Watros and Michelle Rodriguez, who portray Libby and Ana Lucia Cortez, respectively, were arrested on drunk-driving charges. The fans claim that they were still watching the first season on DVD and hadn't watched any part of season two, which is when the two characters are introduced. Their attorney argued that "It was a massive spoiler to reveal these actors are in the show, and we blame the police department for creating such a tragic consequence....They were well aware that thousands of fans were still getting through season one, and, yet, the irresponsible officers still went ahead with their arrests." The plaintiffs are, at this writing, seeking $350 million dollars in damages for "cruel spoiler activities" and "pain and suffering." It would be nice to know the attorney's name; he could have been listed under P for Pathetic. This writer can't make it through an El ride into the Loop without having at least three television or cable shows spoiled by people yapping on cell phones or to their fellow commuters.

Furlan, Mira

The actress who portrays Danielle Rousseau.

Fuselage

The center portion of a passenger plane. This portion of Oceanic Air Flight 815 crashed on the south side of the island, and was submerged after the tide rose in a strange manner, making the survivors move farther inland.

G

Gabriel, Andrea

The actress who portrays Sayid's lost love, Nadia.

Gaea

In Greek mythology, the mother of the earth.

Gago, Jenny

The actress who portrays Agent Alyssa Cole, the woman who promised to provide Sayid with the whereabouts to Nadia in exchange for his help infiltrating a terrorist cell.

Gainey, M. C.

The actor who portrays the bearded man in the boat in season one's cliffhanger. This character's name is listed as Mr. Friendly in the second season.

Gale, Henry

A man captured by Rousseau who is an Other. Held captive in the armory, his story was that he was from Minnesota—hey, it's *close* to Canada—and was hot-air ballooning with his wife, Jennifer, when they crashed on the island. He supposedly sold his company, which mined nonmetallic ores. Henry Gale was also the name of Dorothy's uncle and caretaker in L. Frank Baum's *The Wizard of Oz*.

Gallion, Billy Ray

The actor who portrays Randy, who worked with both Hurley and Locke in supervisory conditions.

Garcia, Jorge

The actor who portrays Hugo "Hurley" Reyes.

Geothermal energy

Sayid believes that the bunker's power system is derived by utilizing heat and steam from within the earth.

Geronimo Jackson

An obscure band from the early 1970s. Charlie and Hurley discover er one of the band's albums in the bunker. There is no record of this band on the Internet, and so might prove to be a clue to a future event. There is a band named Geronimo Black, per www.allMUSIC. com, and on one of their albums, a song is titled "Other Man," which is an anagram for Ethan Rom.

Giacchino, Michael

Composer of the show's musical score.

Gilday, Michael

The actor who portrays Gerald DeGroot in the "Orientation" film.

Gilgamesh's Irisglance

A book published in 1992, and written by Wolfgang Wackernagel. The poem is written in verses that form both the iris and the whites of an eye, with an opening line: "His eye beneath the eyelid was of divine descent." The only relation to this book is that the Bible that Mr. Eko (Gilgamesh) shows Locke (Enkidu's friend) was found in a steamer chest in the Arrow bunker along with a glass eye.

Ginter, Lindsey

The actor who portrays Kate's father, Sgt. Sam Austen.

GL-12

Code name that Locke (aka The Colonel) uses for his co-worker when playing strategic games during breaks and lunch hours while working at the box company.

Glass eye

A glass eye was found in the Arrow supply bunker by the tailenders, along with a Bible and a shortwave radio.

Glue

Locke makes glue from animal fat; one of its uses is to build the cradle for Claire's baby.

Golf course

207

Upon finding equipment in luggage found in the jungle, Hurley builds a golf course that initially consists of only two holes.

Gordy

Sawyer's partner in the "long con," he was the one who discovered Cassidy as a good mark because she had received a $600,000 divorce settlement.

Grace, Maggie

The actress who portrayed Shannon Rutherford, who was shot accidentally by Ana Lucia while looking for Walt.

Granger, Janelle

One of the "background" survivors, her diary can be found at www. ABC.com under the listing for *Lost*. She traveled to Australia to scuba dive with Joanna, who drowned several days after the plane crash. At the time of this writing, she might have been abducted by the Others, as the diary ends on day forty-three post-crash.

Graue, Mickey

The actor who portrays Zack, Emma's brother; both were survivors from the tail section and were then abducted by the Others.

Grill Flame

Code name for the remote viewing project based at Fort Meade, Maryland during the 1970s and 1980s. The project name was changed to Center Lane in late 1983. *The Washington Post* broke the study of the government's funding to so-called psychic spies in the mid-1990s.

Grillo-Marxuach, Javier

Writer and supervising producer for the television show *Lost*.

Grunberg, Greg

The actor who portrayed the pilot of Oceanic Air Flight 815.

Gunpowder

208

A mixture of potassium nitrate, charcoal, and sulfur used in gunnery, time fuses, and fireworks. To heal one of Charlie's injuries, Sayid pours gunpowder in the wound and lights it for a brief time.

H

Had arm

An anagram for Dharma. There are several characters missing an arm or having no mobility in a limb, most notably, Dr. Marvin Candle.

Haddad

The head of the terrorist cell Sayid infiltrates in Sydney.

Halperin, Ken

Hurley's accountant. One of the investments Halperin makes on Hurley's behalf is buying the box company in Tustin, California, where Locke was employed as a regional collections manager.

Halyard

Sawyer barters a spot on board the raft by offering Michael cable from his stash, thus enabling Michael a way to raise the sails.

Hamel, Veronica

The actress who portrays Jack's mother, Margo Shephard.

Han, Byung

Korea's Secretary for Environmental Safety, this man endures a beating at Jin's hands, even though Mr. Paik had wanted one of Jin's co-workers to kill the man.

Handler, Evan

The actor who portrays Hurley's possibly imaginary friend, Dave.

Hanso, Alvar

Billionaire of Danish-Norwegian descent, he made his money from defense weaponry development. Hanso funded various projects and experiments listed on his company's Web site, www.TheHansoFoundation.org. The Dharma Initiative is a hidden link.

Harrison Valley Police

Listed on the slate Kate is holding in her mug shot.

Hart, Joan

An alias Kate gives to a motel clerk when checking to see if she had received any mail.

Hatch, The

A window to the lid of the hatch was uncovered by Locke and Boone on one of their boar-hunting expeditions. They spent several weeks digging around it; eventually the lid was blown by dynamite found at the Black Rock. The hatch leads into a vertical passageway with rungs of a ladder that have started to rust away. The word QUARANTINE and the number sequence are etched on the square lid of the hatch, which leads into a bunker. Much of what occurs in the bunker can be explained by reading the entry for the "Orientation" film. Computers and machinery from different eras are scattered throughout this underground geodesic dome. Libby tells Hurley when they are doing laundry that the washer and dryer seem to be the newest item in the bunker. Most items, including the food in a well-stocked pantry, have a logo for Dharma Industries with a Swan in the center. There are blast doors that separate the dome from the rest of the bunker.

Havelock, Kristen

The actress who portrays Emma, Zack's sister.

Heatherton, Francis Price

Charlie dated his daughter, Lucy, and was given a job selling copiers at one of the many companies Heatherton owned. Charlie is fired after suffering drug withdrawal and vomiting while attempting to make a sale.

Heatherton, Lucy

A girl Charlie seduces so that he might steal something from her family to pawn for drugs.

Helen #1

Locke has known two women with this name and neither involves the Hanso Foundation's attempts at cloning: the first Helen was an operator on, well, a certain phone line which Locke paid $89.95 an hour to call, which makes me wonder what kind of salary he was making at that box company. They had been talking for eight months with some regularity, but Helen #1 declines Locke's offer to join him on his walkabout trip in Australia, even though Locke had already purchased two tickets in anticipation of a meeting.

Helen #2

In between Helens, Locke donated a kidney to his biological father, who then abandoned him. He joins an anger management group, and it is this woman who suggests he take "a leap of faith," a word Locke uses often once on the island, usually in counterpoint to Jack's logic.

Hepatic artery

The major artery that is attached to the liver. Jack's father severs this artery in a patient while operating drunk, causing the patient's death and the eventual loss of his own medical license.

Herbal remedies

Medicines derived from herbaceous plants. Sun uses such knowledge in several instances, particularly in cases where Jack does not have the proper pill vials he culled from the fuselage after the crash.

Heroin

A highly addictive morphine derivative. Charlie gets addicted to heroin after watching his brother use the drug.

Hewitt, Robby

British agent with the ASIS who enlists Sayid's help in infiltrating a terrorist cell by gaining the confidence of his old college roommate.

Hexagram

A regular polygon formed by completing two equilateral triangles from a regular hexagon.

Hibbs

Sawyer's former partner-in-crime. He sends Sawyer to Australia believing he will finally avenge the con man who caused his parents' death by murder-suicide. The truth was that the man Sawyer killed was a man who owed a gambling debt to Hibbs.

Hieroglyphics

A writing form dating to ancient Egypt that involves symbols being used to tell a story. Locke briefly sees this type of symbol in the split second he is late hitting the execute button on the computer. The symbols might be for the as-yet-unknown other Dharma station logos.

Holloway, Josh

The actor who portrays the character James "Sawyer" Ford.

Hope

The one-word response Locke gives to Hurley when he is asked what he believes is at the bottom of the hatch before they blow the lid with dynamite.

Hopkins, Neil

The actor who portrays Charlie's brother, Liam Pace.

Horan, James

The actor who portrayed Kate's biological father, although he did not know this.

Hurley

The name Hugo Reyes uses on the island, although he has not explained the significance for the moniker as of this writing. He admits the nickname to Jack, saying that it is not important to explain at that specific time.

Hurst, Lillian

The actress who portrays Carmen Reyes, Hurley's mother.

Hyperopia

Farsightedness. Sawyer develops this condition after spending the first weeks after the crash reading paperbacks and pamphlets. He suffers headaches and sensitivity to sound and light, thus allowing Jack to offer a correct diagnosis.

Hysterics

A state of violent mental agitation. Michael was wide-eyed and crazier looking than Desmond when he orders Locke and Jack at gunpoint to back into the armory, after which he locked them in, regardless of the computer countdown.

I

I-Ching

Also known as the Book of Changes. Chinese philosophy used in the studies of Buddhism and Confucianism. The I-Ching is comprised of sixty-four hexagrams comprised of trigrams, each with their own meaning.

IMDb

Internet Movie Database. Any of the cast and recurring characters can be looked up by name at this Web site, www.IMDb.com. If one is curious about other movies or television appearances, it might be worth checking out, e.g., Terry O'Quinn's recurring role on FOX's *Millennium*, Jorge Garcia's one-shot on HBO's *Curb Your Enthusiasm* (which landed him the *Lost* audition) or Cynthia Watros's Daytime Emmy—winning appearances on the soap opera *The Guiding Light*.

Incident, The

During the "Orientation" film, Dr. Marvin Candle refers to an enigmatic occurrence that happened at Station #3. Since this time, a sequence of numbers must be typed as a computer command every 108 minutes.

Infiltration

A process in which individuals penetrate an area. The Others have disguised themselves as castaways in each of the plane-crash survivors' camps.

Infirmary

A health facility where patients receive treatment. Jack allows his shelter to double as a treatment center.

Inhaler

A dispenser that produces a chemical vapor to be inhaled in order to relieve nasal congestion. Shannon's asthma inhalers were lost at sea. Sun's knowledge of herbal remedies allows Shannon to avoid asthma attacks by placing eucalyptus leaves across her neck.

Initiative

Readiness to embark on bold new ventures; the commencement of a series of actions.

Inman, Joe

A high-ranking U.S. officer during the Gulf War who was in charge of locating a downed helicopter pilot. He leads Sayid toward the art of torture and interrogation.

Insurgents

A group of people who take part in an armed rebellion against the constituted authority. They witness the suicide bombings in present-day Iraq; prior to Saddam Hussein's capture, the Republican Guard would capture insurgents and torture them in order to find out future plans or the identity of other group members.

Interrogation

Formal systematic questioning. Sayid uses torture as a form of inquiry when questioning Sawyer about the whereabouts of Shannon's asthma inhalers, while Ana Lucia throws Nathan into solitary confinement in the belief that he is an Other and will crack from the pressure.

Inventory

An itemization of resources. Hurley's job in the bunker is to keep a list of food and prior to the discovery of Station #3, which contains an armory, Jack kept count of the guns and ammunition the survivors had on hand.

Ionosphere

The outer region of the earth's atmosphere; contains a high concentration of free electrons. Sayid explains to Hurley that radio transmissions bounce off the ionosphere and can originate many miles away.

Iraq

Middle Eastern country situated between Iran and Syria. The United States staged Operation Desert Storm in 1991 after dictator Saddam Hussein invaded neighboring Kuwait. Hurley mistakenly believes that Sayid was an American citizen who was involved in this military intervention.

Iraqi Republican Guard

A main branch of the Iraqi army, its members identified by maroon berets, knowledgeable in torture techniques against prisoners. Sayid worked with this unit during the Gulf War of 1991 as a communications officer.

Isaac

An Australian physical therapist who treats Rose for symptoms possibly similar to Locke's.

Ischemia

Local anemia in a given body part sometimes resulting from thrombosis or an embolism. Jack is able to perform successful surgery on an elderly man named Angelo, but then his heart gives out on the operating table. Later that night, Jack finds out that Sara, his wife, is leaving him.

Iteration

In computer science, a single execution of a set of instructions that are to be repeated, or looped, a given number of times or until a specified result is obtained. Sayid is able to determine that the French transmission has been running for sixteen years, through his calculations of the number of iterations.

ITR Reports

Inpatient Treatment Records. Jack's father passes on a stack of folders to him, reminding him of his duties at the hospital.

215

J

Jackson, Scott

Killed by Ethan Rom, who had sworn to murder one fuselage survivor per day if Claire was not returned to him. He worked for an Internet company in Santa Rosa, California, and was returning home from a two-week vacation to Sydney that he had won in a contest.

James, Henry

The author of *The Turn of the Screw.*

Jansen, Diane

Kate's mother, who died of cancer.

Jarrah, Sayid

A veteran of the Iraqi Republican Guard, he is a master at both torture techniques and building electronics from scratch. He is met by a CIA agent and a member of the British ASIS and told to infiltrate a terrorist cell in Sydney in exchange for the whereabouts of his long-lost love, Nadia.

Jaunty cravat

On one of the podcasts, Bernard is described as wearing a jaunty cravat. Someone suggested to me that there might not be enough entries under J. I now have him looking up entries for the letter Y.

J Boat

A sailing vessel. In an attempt to get a spot on the raft, Kate informs Michael that she had spent two summers crewing on this type of boat.

Jenkins, Steve

One of the background survivors. Hurley laments that he kept screwing up the names between this guy and Scott, who was killed by Ethan Rom. Also, Sawyer notes that he sleeps close to a woman named Tracy, who has a husband and child in Fresno, California.

Jesus Stick

Charlie's nickname for the stick that Mr. Eko scratches scripture on.

Jethro

One of Sawyer's nicknames for Hurley.

Joanna

The second of the original forty-eight survivors from the fuselage to die. She drowns after being caught in the riptide. Boone, who had lifeguard skills, attempts to save her but in turn is saved by Jack. The doctor agonizes over the fact that it had been several days since the crash; most of the survivors were looking to him as leader, yet he couldn't remember the name of the drowned woman.

John The Baptist

Mr. Eko tells Claire that when John the Baptist baptizes Jesus Christ, the clouds opened and a dove flew out. By cleansing his sins, "John had freed him," Mr. Eko said, adding, "Heaven came much later."

Joop

A British orangutan harvested by British explorers in the early part of the twentieth century, also referred to as Experimental Subject 626. A link that shows a memorandum about Joop's age and progress can be found on the Hanso Web site, under Life-Extension Project.

Joseph, Kimberly

The actress who portrays Cindy, the flight attendant from the tail section.

Jungle Boy

Sawyer's nickname for Ethan, once his true identity is known and he evades capture in the jungle.

K

Kalgoorlie

A small town in Australia's outback. Sam Toomey moved to this town so that he could remain isolated after he gained the bad luck that came with knowledge of the Numbers.

Kate's Horse

This black stallion makes several appearances in Kate's recent life. After the U.S. marshal arrested her at a bus station purchasing a ticket to Jacksonville, Florida, his car swerves to avoid a horse in the road, the car hits a tree, and Kate escapes. She sees the horse on the island while picking fruit, and later Sawyer sees it outside the tree entrance to the bunker before Kate does. She nuzzles the horse, proving it is not a shared hallucination.

Kelley, Malcolm David

The actor who portrays Walt Lloyd.

Keshawarz, Donnie

The actor who portrays Sayid's college roommate Essam Tasir.

Kelvin

According to Desmond, Kelvin raced from the jungle to help him after Desmond's boat hit a reef, after which he shared duties typing in the computer code. Kelvin died three years before Locke and Jack talk with Desmond. All Kelvin told Desmond about why the code had to be typed every 108 minutes was "to save the world."

Kevin

Sara's fiancé at the time of her crash, who could not deal with the extent of her partial paralysis. Sara eventually was healed of her injuries and married Jack.

Kim, Daniel Dae

The actor who portrays Jin-Soo Kwon. His television wife had to help him with his Korean as Kim was born in the U.S.

Kim, Je-Guy

The doctor who lies to Sun, telling her she cannot have children, but later guiltily admits that it is Jin who is impotent and he was afraid of family reprisals.

Kim, Yunjin

The actress who portrays Sun Kwon.

Knoxville, Tennessee

The letter Sawyer carries around as a reminder of his intent to execute the man who bilked his parents of their life savings bore a postmark from this city near the Georgia border, as well as an embossed image for the American Bicentennial.

Korea

An Asian peninsula separating the Yellow Sea and the Sea of Japan. Jin and Sun are both Korean, and Jin speaks only Korean, while Sun secretly learned English years ago.

Kurtz, Swoosie

The actress who portrays Emily Annabeth Locke, John Locke's biological mother.

Kwon, Jin-Soo

Married to a subservient Sun and worked for her father, Mr. Paik. Felt dishonored by his wife after learning that she knew how to speak English; they have fallen deeper in love ever since Sun realized Jin had not died after the raft set sail, and the message bottle floated back to shore. Jin had part of a handcuff attached to his wrist for several weeks and Locke eventually cut it off, but not until after Jin and Sun were reunited and, well, the thing had to have rubbed against something on someone. Locke could have taken care of that a little faster, I'm just saying, is all.

Kwon, Mr.

Jin's father, a fisherman living in a poor village.

Kwon, Sun-Soo (nee Paik)

Jin's wife. She thought they were going on a vacation when in fact she was actually accompanying him on a mission for her father to deliver a watch. She secretly took English lessons after believing her marriage was failing. She has expert knowledge of herbal remedies and has started a vegetable garden.

L

"La Mer"

"La mer" is the basis for the song "Beyond The Sea," made famous as a signature song by Bobby Darin (along with "Mack The Knife") in the 1950s. These words are written on several pages that Sayid stole from Rousseau, and Shannon helps decipher the lyrics. The French version was written by Charles Trenet and Leo Chauliac. Shannon knows the song because she heard the lyrics in the closing credits of *Finding Nemo*.

Lance

While taking his census, based on the plane manifest, Hurley mistakes Ethan Rom for this individual, who is actually a thin red-haired man who wears glasses.

Lancelot

Sawyer is reading this book by Walker Percy, set in 1970s New Orleans. The theme of the book is that it is a time when chivalry is dead and the idea of goodness is muddled. A recurring theme in Percy's novels is the idea that his characters can only compare their lives to similar events in film or other media.

Laptop computers

The power cell from a laptop contains a battery which would be extremely useful in powering up electronic equipment Sayid makes from scratch.

Late

Charlie originally had the letters FATE written on white bandages around his fingers, and he later changes the word.

Latitude

The angular distance between an imaginary line around the Earth parallel to its equator at the equator itself. Sayid believes that the numerical sequence might relate to coordinates on the island. It could also relate to the location of the island in regards to its location in the South Pacific Ocean.

Lava lamp

220

A lamp filled with lumps of tallow that float in oils, a huge fad in the early 1970s. One of the items in the bunker that seems to pinpoint the era in which it was constructed.

Lee, Jae

Son of a hotel owner who Sun believes she will form a relationship with until discovering he plans to marry a woman in the U.S. After leaving the blind date, Sun literally bumps into her husband-to-be, Jin.

Lehne, Fredric

The actor who portrayed the U.S. marshal who had tracked Kate to Australia for her arrest.

Le Territiore Fonce

Rousseau's description of the area of the island where the slave ship resides. She believes the other members of the French expedition team were infected in this area.

Libby

A clinical psychologist who dropped out of medical school after one year. She was in the tail section of the plane and helped perform triage after the crash. The fact that she babbles a lot and gives sudden wide-eyed expressions makes one think she might be a part of the original group and trying her best to fit in. Then again, her crazy look might just be her "bedside manner." At one point, it will occur to Hurley that he recognizes her from somewhere else. I doubt it was at Mr. Cluck's.

Life-Extension Project

One of the experiments funded by the Hanso Foundation. Access to this link on the Hanso Foundation's Web site is denied.

Lilly, Evangeline

The actress who portrays Kate Austen.

Lindelof, Damon

Executive producer for *Lost*.

Listening post

Several of these small military bases were scattered throughout the Pacific during WWII, for the use of eavesdropping on a given subject and then sending the information on for decoding. Lenny Sims and Sam Toomey worked at the same post while in the United States Navy, and it was here that they heard the Numbers for the first time. Present-day listening posts include the Pine Gap military installation, jointly run by the U.S. and Australian militaries, located in Woomera, Australia, and the NSA post hidden in the Blue Ridge Mountains surrounding Sugar Grove, West Virginia. The knowledge of the latter was discovered in the early 1970s after a remote-viewing plan proved to be too successful.

Littleton, Claire

She was eight months pregnant at the time of the crash of Flight 815. Wanting to give up the baby for adoption—the father, Thomas, left her, and she was working for five dollars an hour at a fast-food restaurant—she goes to see a psychic, who tells her that danger surrounded the baby, and he provides her with the plane ticket, claiming that there is a couple in Los Angeles waiting to adopt. Claire was kidnapped by Ethan Rom and was missing for almost two weeks in the jungle; she reappeared with no memory after the crash.

Liturgy

A rite or body of rites prescribed for public worship. The throwing of handfuls of dirt onto Shannon's grave by the survivors is such an example; another would be the cremation of the dead passengers in the fuselage and Mr. Eko's brother in the Beechcraft.

Living trust

A trust created and operating during the grantor's lifetime. After Shannon's father died, her stepmother stopped giving her any kind of monetary allowance.

Lockblade knife

Ana Lucia grabbed this knife off one of the dead Others—or "them," as the tailenders referred to the children's abductors—and later shows Goodwin that the knife had the words U.S. ARMY stamped on the tang. She tells him that this type of knife hadn't been seen in about twenty years.

Locke, John

Often referred to as the island mystic, Locke had been paralyzed in his right leg for four years, until the crash of Flight 815. He learned survival expertise and hunting and tracking knowledge from his biological father, who persuaded Locke to donate his kidney for him, after which he abandoned him again. Locke feels it is his destiny to be on the island and was willing to let the black smoke pull him down into a hole, but Jack saved him instead by throwing dynamite into the crater.

Long con

A scam that involves gaining the confidence of a mark over months of time. Sawyer is involved with one that takes six months to complete.

Longitude

An imaginary great circle on the surface of the earth passing through the north and south poles at right angles to the equator. See listing for latitude.

Lost lands

Islands or continents that may have existed in the past, now submerged into the sea due to geological catastrophe. Atlantis and Lemuria are examples. Compare this entry with that of Phantom Islands, which refer to land masses named by cartographers in the current historical age.

Love Connection

A television dating show from the early 1990s hosted by Chuck Woolery. Sawyer mentions this phrase when Hurley asks him how much he knew about Libby.

M

Madame Nutso

Arzt's nickname for Rousseau. If he had met Locke's mother, I'd bet the same name would apply.

Madison

The Labrador that portrays Vincent, Walt's, well, dog.

Magnetic anomaly

An unexplained fluctuation in the magnetic field. On the island, the compass strays from true magnetic north several times.

Magnetic field

The lines of force surrounding a permanent magnet or a moving charged particle.

Magnetite

The first magnetic substance, given the nickname "the Black Rock."

"Make Your Own Kind of Music."

A song recorded by "Mama" Cass Eliot, formerly of the 1960s band The Mamas & The Papas.

Mala beads

There are 108 mala beads on a thread, symbolizing the 108 mental conditions or sinful desires that one must overcome to reach enlightenment or nirvana.

Mango

Large, oval, tropical skinned fruit with a juicy aromatic pulp and a large hairy seed. Sun plants a grove that includes mango trees.

Manifest

A customs document listing the contents, passengers included, that are put on a ship or plane. Hurley eliminates the dead passengers from the manifest, and starts an informal census so that each survivor can provide his vital statistics. This information could be used in case Jack needed to treat anyone for injuries and to keep no one a stranger to the group. Hurley later finds that the Other who gave his name as Ethan Rom could not be matched to the passenger manifest.

Manipulandum

A word coined by B. F. Skinner which is defined as "manipulation by deception."

Mapother, William

The actor who portrayed Ethan Rom.

Marasco, Ron

The actor who portrays Ken Halperin, Hurley's accountant.

Mars, Edward

The U.S. marshal who tracked Kate for three years before her arrest in Australia. He was severely injured by a piece of wreckage which Jack removed from his abdomen. Sawyer tried to play Dr. Rambo Kervorkian by shooting him, but only perforated a lung; Jack then euthanized him through asphyxiation. Mars had a Halliburton case which contained four guns and at least one hundred rounds of ammo, and he wore a Sig Sauer in an ankle holster.

Mathematical Forecasting Initiative

One of the experiments funded by the Hanso Foundation. Access to this link at the company's Web site is currently forbidden.

McCormick, Jason

The man who shot Ana Lucia, causing her miscarriage. After being arrested for assaulting a woman in Echo Park, he confesses to the shooting. Ana Lucia denies it was him, and soon afterward, waits for him to finish hustling at pool and shoots him as he tries to open his car. She tells the survivors that his body was never found.

M'Cormack, Adetokumboh

The actor who portrays Yemi, Mr. Eko's younger brother.

Memoirs of A Geisha

A novel written by Arthur Golden and published in 1997. The tale is of an orphaned girl in 1929 who becomes a geisha, a traditional oriental servant and, at times, an entertainer. As Sun was taking care of Jin after spilling his coffee in the Sydney airport, a woman observes to her male companion that it was like observing a scene from the book.

Mental Institution

A hospital for mentally incompetent or unbalanced individuals.

Mercado deal

When Cassidy thought she was part of Sawyer's con, she thought it was called the Mercado deal.

Merrick Biotech

This company is operated by PB-SALES, which also owns Oceanic Airlines, Yoyodyne Propulsion Systems, Geocomtex, and Daystrom Data concepts. This is not a fan Web site, but there is little correlation to the various companies other than a statement that Merrick has performed cloning on human test subjects.

Message bottle

Before Michael, Jin, and Sawyer leave on the raft, most of the survivors write personal messages on scraps of paper and place them in this long-necked bottle. Claire and Shannon find the bottle washed ashore and Sun buries it near the garden she planted.

Miller, Barbara Joanna

The full name of the crash survivor who drowned. Her full name is learned after Kate steals her passport, hoping to disguise her true identity if she did qualify for a spot on Michael's raft.

Mind's eye

The imaging of remembered or invented scenes. When Locke is teaching Walt to throw a knife, he told him to envision the target in his mind's eye before he threw it.

Miracle worker

Sara tells Jack with much resignation that someone with his medical abilities will never have a normal home life.

Mitigating circumstance

A law that does not exonerate a person but which reduces the penalty of the offense. Kate kept calling the U.S. marshal about the charges she was wanted for, presumably wanting to explain how Wayne beat her mother with regularity, and eventually these calls led the marshal to set a trap; he told Kate that he was keeping the toy airplane in a safety deposit box in a bank in New Mexico.

Mokule'ia Beach

The fuselage of the plane crash was placed on this beach, one of the remotest areas on Oahu. It is near Dillingham Airfield, once a U.S. Air Force base.

Molotov cocktail

Named for a nineteenth-century Russian statesman who has a city in Eastern Russia named for him, this is an incendiary bomb made of a bottle filled with flammable liquid and fitted with a rag wick. A blond-haired woman in the speedboat's cabin, possibly Alex, throws one at the raft, setting it afire, moments after Mr. Friendly makes his demands that Michael "give [him] the boy."

Monaghan, Dominic

The actor who portrays the character Charlie Pace.

Monsoon

A seasonal wind in Southern Asia and Oceania which brings heavy rains, also defined as any wind that changes direction with the season. There are periods of rapid, heavy rains on the island, much like here in Chicago.

Monster

A force on the island, seen by only a few survivors, and which Rousseau calls a "security system." It appears to be massive, by the thrashing sounds and the amount of foliage that is moved or torn apart in its path. It appears to be a huge cloud of smoke supposedly made up of tiny nanobots. The cloud appears near Mr. Eko and amidst flashes of light, he can see images of the last two months on this island as well as images from his youth and of his younger brother, Yemi, as a priest.

Montaud

A member of the French scientific team; Rousseau told Sayid that he lost his arm while in the Dark Territory.

Moonbeam

One of Sawyer's nicknames for Libby.

Morrocan

Mr. Eko was going to get involved with drug trading with neighboring Morocco, but chose instead to kill the dealers.

Moses

When Claire tells Mr. Eko that she named her baby Aaron, Mr. Eko tells her that Aaron was the brother of Moses, and as Moses did not speak well, Aaron did most of the talking.

Mothership

In an interview in the January 31, 2006, *Detroit News*, executive producer Carlton Cuse says: "The show is the mothership, but I think with all the emerging technology, what we've discovered is that the world of *Lost* is not basically circumscribed by the actual show itself." Cuse is referring to the podcasts and various fan Web sites.

Mozambique

Republic on the southeastern coast of Africa. Locke believes that the *Black Rock* likely set sail from this country, based on the fact that it carried mining supplies.

Mr. Clean

Sawyer's nickname for Locke when he gets angered during a treacherous climb.

Mullen, Ray

Kate stays with this Australian sheep farmer for a period of time, calling herself Annie, until she is turned in by Mullen to the U.S. marshal for a $24,000 reward.

Mural

A painting that is applied to a wall surface. There is a mural on the wall of the bunker; the numbers and the total 108 are painted prominently.

Murder

Unlawful premeditated killing of a human being. Sawyer murdered Frank Duckett in Australia. Kate believes she murdered Tom Brennan in Iowa when in fact it was her actions that caused him to be shot by the police trooper; Kate did not kill her child fiancé herself.

Muslim

A follower of Islam. The CIA was going to cremate Sayid's friend Essam, and he stayed behind in Sydney an extra day to ensure the proper burial.

N

Nadia

A friend of Sayid's. She is to be interrogated as belonging to a group of insurgents. Sayid allows her to escape. Her birth name is Noor Abed-Jazeem. Sayid learns that she is living in Irvine, California, and working at a medical research institute, and he is on Flight 815 because he had finally learned her whereabouts after seven years of searching for her in both England and the Middle East.

Naira

Domestic monetary unit of Nigeria, circulated in banknotes and coins, introduced in 1973 to replace the pound at a ratio of two to one. Nigeria was the last country in the world besides Britain to stop using the pound as legal tender.

Najaf

An Iraqi religious capital. Nadia was accused of having involvement in a bombing in Najaf.

Namaste

Candle signs off the "Orientation" film with this word, and it is also mentioned on the Hanso Foundation Web site. It is a Hindu word that tells one to pay homage to the inner light of all living things.

Namhae

Jin's hometown, a small fishing village on the south coast of Korea.

Nanotechnology

The branch of engineering that deals with things smaller than 100 nanometers—a unit of length equal to one billionth of a meter—especially with the manipulation of individual molecules.

Narvek, Norway

The hometown of Alvar Hanso. In the "Orientation" film, the photo of Hanso has him standing in Narvek's city hall. In UFO mythology, a flying saucer crashed on the island of Spitsbergen, off Norway's coast, on September 9, 1952. The debris was brought back to Narvik.

Nathan

One of the tail-section survivors. Initially suspected of being a member of a group of people—the fuselage survivors would soon know them as the Others—he is imprisoned in a pit by Ana Lucia. Another assumed survivor named Goodwin lets Nathan out of the makeshift prison, then breaks his neck, knowing that if the others eventually believed Nathan, the suspicion would shift toward Goodwin himself.

Navaho, Lars

An anagram for Alvar Hanso. This name has shown up on several Web sites, and the individual can be e-mailed. Occasionally a response can be elicited.

Neosporin

Trade name for a topical drug containing several antibacterials; used as an ointment for minor skin irritations. Jack tells Libby a tube of this could heal a cut, but the going bartering rate from Sawyer is several loads of laundry.

New Kids On The Block

A boy band in the late '80s and early '90s. Kate and Tom's "time capsule" was a NKOTB lunchbox.

Nexus

The means of connection between things linked in a series. This island is described as a nexus for its inhabitants.

Niagara Falls

Bernard proposes to Rose in a restaurant overlooking the waterfalls when she tells him that she is dying of cancer.

Nickname

A designation given to a person. Sawyer uses pop-culture references with just about everybody on the show. It could be said that by allowing himself to be called Sawyer, even after Locke and others know him to be James Ford, he has also assigned himself a nickname.

Nigeria

A country in western Africa. A map and official currency of this country was found in the Beechcraft plane that Locke and Boone discovered in the jungle.

Noetic

Of or associated with or requiring the use of the rational mind.

Norma Rae

A nickname Sawyer gives to Bernard, when he attempts to enlist help in building the S.O.S. Sawyer's implication is that Bernard is having trouble with the help at his "Sand Factory."

NSA

The National Security Agency, based at Fort George G. Meade, Maryland.

Numerical sequences

Several of Hurley's winning lottery numbers appear, in part or in whole, throughout flashback sequences of various episodes. Several examples follow:

4

Quite a few inconsequential connections, some involving hours or days.

8

Number of shots shared between Sawyer and Christian Shephard.
Sawyer's age when his father and mother died.
Shannon's age when her father married Boone's mother.
Channel 8 was the news station that spotted Hurley as the lottery winner.

15

There were fifteen members of the French science team.
The raft was fifteen miles out to sea when the blip appeared on the radar.

16

Rousseau's distress signal has been playing for sixteen years.
There were sixteen Virgin Mary statues on the table when Eko spoke with the nun about buying them.

23

Flight 815 taxied from this Gate.
Jack sat in row 23, across the aisle from Rose and (assumedly) Bernard.
The number of survivors from the tail section of the plane.
Mr. Eko recites the 23rd Psalm as he cremates his brother Yemi.

42

Ana Lucia sat in the last row of the plane.
Number of spaces in a game of Connect Four.

108

The computer in Station #3 must be reset every 108 minutes.
The number is prominently seen in a painted mural on the wall of
the bunker at Station #3.

815

The doomed Oceanic Air flight bore this flight number.

Jack Rutherford, Shannon's father and Boone's stepfather, is pro-
nounced dead at 8:15.
The safety deposit box that held Kate's toy airplane was numbered
815.
Charlie was trying to sell a photocopier with a model number of
C815 while fighting drug withdrawal.
Kate and Tom buried their time capsule along with a cassette re-
cording, identifying the date as August 15, 1989.
Michael and Walt's hotel room number.

2342

Hurley's hotel room in Sydney.

O

Obits

The Helen who stayed with comb-over Locke reads the obituaries because they are the only part of the newspaper that does not depress her.

O'Brien, Flann

The author of *The Third Policeman*.

Oceanic Flight 815

The plane that left Sydney was a Boeing 777. Six hours into the flight
to Los Angeles International Airport, the pilots encountered prob-

lems with radio transmission and turned back to Fiji, the nearest airport with the largest runway. Two hours after turning back, Flight 815 hit massive turbulence and broke apart into three pieces.

Oceanic World Airlines

Headquartered at 1642 Airport Loop, Los Angeles, CA 90048. Web site http://oceanicworldair.com/. Flight 815 of this airline company was flying nonstop from Sydney to LAX (Los Angeles International Airport) when it crashed on an island in the South Pacific.

Ofloxacin

The generic ingredient in Floxin, one of the fluoroquinolone anti-infectives. Prescribed for infections of the lower respiratory system. Jack treats Sawyer's wound with this drug after Mr. Eko brings him to the bunker.

233

Oil Change

The title of DriveSHAFT's only album.

Operandum

Another word for operant conditioning, as coined by B. F. Skinner.

Ophiuchus

A constellation in the summer skies. Ophiuchus, or Serpent Handler, was known to the Romans as the god of medicine. He was the son of Apollo, and as his medical skills of healing herbs grew, Ophiuchus learned to revive the dead. Zeus killed him with a thunderbolt after Hades became worried that there would be no new souls in Hell.

O'Quinn, Terry

The actor who portrays John Locke.

Organic phenomenon

Another term for xenogenesis (see separate entry).

"Orientation" film

Desmond tells Locke and Jack that all the answers to the bunker can be found in this film. Narrated by Dr. Marvin Candle, who explains in detail, accompanied by photographs, that the bunker, or Station #3, was built in the 1970s and it is one of six stations, though it is unclear if the other five are on the island. Additional funding came in 1980 from the Hanso Foundation, run by a wealthy Danish industrialist, Alvar Hanso. The monies were channeled toward the Dharma Initiative, the idea of the husband-and-wife team of Gerald and Karen DeGroot, doctoral candidates at the University of Michigan. There is a computer in Station #3 into which a series of numbers must be entered every 108 minutes. The station was to be manned by two people, working for 540-day shifts. Station #3 has unique magnetic properties and Candle makes mention of "an incident," which may be the reason for the computer countdown. Mr. Eko finds a Bible in one of the Arrow supply lockers; inside is a portion of the film that had been sliced out. He and Locke watch it and find that the missing section is a cautionary tale to not attempt to use the computer for anything other than typing in the number sequence.

Orion

The son of Poseidon, king of the seas. In one Roman legend, Artemis, goddess of the Moon, fell in love with Orion and neglected her duties of illuminating the night sky. Artemis's twin brother, Apollo, watched Orion bathing in the seas, and by shining the sun brightly upon him, turned him into a blur. Apollo then dared Artemis to shoot an arrow at the blur. After realizing that she had killed her lover, Artemis lost all interest in life, and this is why the moon will always be cold and lifeless.

Osteoma

A slow, benign tumor consisting of bone tissue, usually on the skull or the mandible. Sam Toomey's name is an anagram for "my osteoma."

Others, The

This group of island inhabitants are enigmatic; they leave no tracks as they move through the jungle and converse in backward whispers. They keep a list of survivors that they feel are "good" and therefore worthy of abduction. Ethan Rom infiltrated the main survivors, and Goodwin did the same with the tailenders. Mr. Eko and Ana Lucia killed three of the Others, Charlie shot Ethan, and Ana Lucia later impaled Goodwin (Good One?) as they fought. There seem to be two factions of Others, some well dressed and others barefoot and wearing pale clothing with no identifying tags.

Outlaw of Cave-in-Rock

James Ford (the real name of Sawyer on *Lost*) was a pirate also known as Satan's Ferryman at the turn of the nineteenth century. Living in the vicinity of Cave-in-Rock, Illinois, Ford was known as a counterfeiter river pirate and serial killer. He also headed up the Ford's Ferry gang and was assassinated in 1833 in Elizabethtown, Illinois.

Oz

A common nickname for Australia, as the natives pronounce is OZ-stral-ya.

235

P

Pace, Charlie

Bass player for the U.K. band DriveSHAFT; also plays the piano. His father was a butcher and looked down on his sons' musical enthusiasm. Soon after Charlie penned what he had hoped would be the band's comeback song, a ballad about two brothers, Liam sold the piano in order to buy tickets to Australia.

Pace, Liam

Charlie's older brother and lead singer of DriveSHAFT. Once a heroin addict, he moved to Sydney with his wife, Megan, and newborn daughter to find employment and enter a rehab clinic.

Paik, Greg Joung

The actor who portrays Dr. Je-Guy Kim.

Parodies

Several musical parodies have appeared on the Internet, including one sung to the tune "Wreck of The Edmund Fitzgerald." A very unique effort in Flash animation was made to the tune of Weird Al Yankovic's "Bohemian Polka" (after Queen's "Bohemian Rhapsody"), which incorporates many scenes from the first season.

Patrick, Robert

The actor who portrays Sawyer's partner-in-crime, Hibbs.

Patterson, David

The actor who portrays Agent Robbie Hewitt, who enlists Sayid's aid in Sydney.

Payback

While Hurley is flipping out and seeing his imaginary friend Dave, he attacks Sawyer, punching him and repeating every nickname the hick cowboy wannabe ever used on the island: Jabba. Bam! Sta-Puft. Bam! Pillsbury. Bam! Hurley. BAM! Wait, that last one *really* is Hugo's nickname, he just hasn't explained how he got it.

Peanut Butter

Charlie makes a futile attempt to find peanut butter for the pregnant Claire, and instead brings an empty jar, telling her its contents are indeed peanut butter, and Claire's imagination takes over. Actual peanut butter is later found in the pantry of Station #3.

Pearl

Bernard forgets Rose's birthday and hopes to find her a pearl, attempting to ask Jin like it's a game of charades. In addition, the map drawn on the blast door has a reference to a possible station called the Pearl.

Peninsula

A large mass of land protruding into a body of water. The tailenders follow the beach until it juts out into the ocean. Mr. Eko tells Ana Lucia that the land may not be passable, and they venture through the jungle, leading them into a situation where Ana Lucia shoots Shannon as their paths cross during a huge rainstorm.

Percy, Walker

The author of the book *Lancelot*, he was a practicing physician before becoming a writer in the 1950s.

Perdidos

In Mexico, *Lost* is renamed as *The Lost Ones*.

Perrineau, Brittany

Harold's wife, she portrayed Mary Jo, the woman who pulled Hurley's winning lottery numbers, and later appears as Sawyer's one-night stand. The general theory is that she was actually playing the same role for both parts.

Perrineau, Harold

The actor who portrays Michael Dawson.

Phuket

Jack tells Sawyer that he learned to play cards in this resort town in Thailand. The implication is that this is where the doctor had the tattoos placed on his left shoulder. See the related entry, Tallahassee.

Pilot, The

Never named, he was found in the cockpit by Jack, Kate, and Charlie. He was concerned to know that after sixteen hours there had been no rescue attempt; he explains that "six hours in, our radio went out, no one could see us. We turned back to land in Fiji. By the time we hit turbulence, we were a thousand miles off course. They're looking for us in the wrong place." Immediately after this, he was yanked from the cockpit by the Monster, and his body was found mangled high up in a tree.

Pine Gap

A joint U.S./Australian facility located near Alice Springs. Described as a Joint Defense Research Facility, the CIA and NSA both show affiliation with this facility, also used for intelligence gathering. The United States has been conducting experiments into electromagnetic propulsion at Pine Gap since the base opened in 1966.

Podcasts

Podcasting is a term coined in 2004, when the use of RSS syndication technologies became popular for distributing audio content for listening on mobile devices and personal computers. There are several *Lost* podcasts available, including *Lost* "diaries" that will be available by subscribing to Verizon mobile phone service. Most podcasts can be downloaded to iPods. I'm still not certain how iPods work, as I am just now changing over from 8-track to spool-tape recorder.

Polar bear

White bear found in the polar regions. Several polar bears have been seen on the island and may relate to Walt's ill-defined powers. Polar bears are encountered by the Flash and Green Lantern in the comic book of Hurley's that Walt looks at (it is written in Spanish). Walt likely latched on to the threatening images without making the connection that the comic was set near the Arctic Circle in the late 1940s.

Polaris

The earth's axis points toward this star, providing true magnetic north, in the northern hemisphere. It is located in Ursa Minor, and two stars in the "Big Dipper" segment of Ursa Major serve as pointers toward the star. It is in a fixed position in the night sky throughout the year. While Claire was held captive, Ethan showed her a mobile of four Oceanic planes circling a big silver star.

Porter, Brian

Michael's wife Susan leaves him and lives with Porter, her business partner, and they eventually gain full custody of Walt.

Porter-Lloyd, Walt

Son of Michael Dawson and Susan Lloyd, he has the ability to manipulate probabilities, ranging from his winnings at backgammon games to various events that occur when he gets angered. Since his abduction by Mr. Friendly's crew, he has shown a kind of backward-remote viewing technique. Shannon is able to see him and he can converse by speaking backward; presumably because Walt's dog Vincent was left in Shannon's care.

Portsmouth, England

The *Black Rock* mining ship has this port of call written under its name. In the 1800s, ships based in Portsmouth transported convicts to Australia.

Prosthetics

Artificial limbs. The farmer who turned Kate in had an artificial right arm, as Kate pulls it off while trying to pull him from his wrecked vehicle. It also appears that Dr. Marvin Candle has an artificial left arm. Perhaps there should be a listing for David Janssen as Dr. Richard Kimble, who spent four years looking for a one-armed man who killed his wife.

Psychic

A person apparently sensitive to things beyond the natural range of perception. Claire is given the tickets for Flight 815 by a psychic who apparently is aware that the plane will crash. In a deleted flashback scene, Claire is talking with the pilot about psychics, who tells a story about a relative who didn't heed one's advice. The relative considered dating Bernard, from the tail section of the plane, who sold his computer company for $39 million and later married Rose.

Psychosomatic response

Relating to the influence of the mind on the body. For example, a person with chronic pain feeling in better health after taking a placebo instead of actual pain medication. There are instances where physical symptoms are caused by mental or emotional causes. There is some belief that Locke's paralysis and recurring leg stiffness prior to Boone's death might be "all in his head."

239

Punishment

The imposement of a penalty for some action or deed. There are several instances where the survivors, memorably Sun talking with Claire in the caves, think that perhaps they survived the crash as a punishment for a past misdeed.

Purgatory

In theology, a place where those who have died in a state of grace undergo limited torment to expiate their sins. One of the first theories about the island was that everyone on Flight 815 had died, but those surviving were being put through tests to determine their worth. Now that the bunker and "Orientation" film have been discovered and watched, respectively, the survivors' state of being may reside more in the hands of science and clinical psychologists than in the faith of an afterlife.

Pygram, Wayne

The actor who portrays Isaac in the Rose-Bernard-centric episode in season two.

Q

Quarantine

Enforced isolation to prevent the spread of infectious disease. The word is etched into the metal of the hatch leading to the bunker. It is also painted on the inside of the camouflaged door to the Arrow bunker that the tailenders found.

Queens Cross

The section of Sydney where Christian Shephard's body was found in an alley. A tox screen by the medical examiner showed that he died of a myocardial infarction.

Quest for Extra-Terrestrial Intelligence

An experiment funded by the Hanso Foundation. Access to the link provided at the foundation's Web site is prohibited.

Quit

Locke tells Sun that he was lost in his life's direction, and is content on the island, believing he is on the island because he "quit looking."

R

Ranch Dressing

Locke teaches Michael target practice on a gallon bottle of Dharma Ranch dressing. There goes a nice dip for the Apollo candy bars. Nice job, Locke.

Randall, Josh

The actor who portrayed Nathan, one of the survivors in the tail section.

Raymonde, Tania

The actress who portrays Danielle's daughter, Alex.

Remedy

A notation on the blast door map near the medical station where Claire was held captive states that "the remedy is worse than the disease."

Remission

An abatement in intensity or degree (as in the manifestations of a disease). After Bernard proposes, Rose tells him that her cancer had been in remission for six months, but after it returned, her doctors gave her one year to live.

Remote Viewing

This term came into use in December 1971 as a frame of reference denoting long-distance experiments in which the "target" was far beyond the range of any of the five physical senses. Evidence from the experiments was largely used during the waning years of the Cold War era, examples being the "viewing" of Soviet submarine bases and other East European sites. On the island, Walt seems to be performing a type of reverse remote viewing, where others can see him, instead of the opposite.

Resources

Available sources of wealth; a new or reserve supply that can be drawn upon when needed. The dead passengers are treated as resources, e.g., Kate takes a pair of hiking shoes off of a corpse so that she has sturdier footwear. Jack and Sawyer also find resources in the passengers' luggage, both using their "source of wealth" in different ways.

Reyes, Carmen

Hurley's mother. She felt he was wasting his life working at Mr. Cluck's, but was similarly unhappy after her son had won his millions.

Reyes, Diego

Hurley's brother, whose wife, Lisa, left him for a waitress.

Reyes, Hugo "Hurley"

Won $114 million in a Mega-Millions Lottery with numbers he later thinks to be cursed. He was working at Mr. Cluck's Chicken Shack at the time of his winnings.

Robert

A member of the French expedition and Rousseau's lover. Rousseau claims to have killed him and the other members of her team after they became infected with "the sickness."

Rodriguez, Michelle

The actress who portrays the character Ana Lucia Cortez, the Alpha Female of the tailenders.

Roebuck, Daniel

Portrayed Dr. Leslie Arzt for several episodes during the first season of *Lost*.

Rom, Ethan

Was discovered to have infiltrated the camp after Hurley could not match his name to the passenger manifest. Claimed to be from Canada, and offered no information about his occupation, other family, etc. Rom—along with Goodwin, were more well-dressed and powerful than the Others, who seem to dress like the Flintstones—kidnapped Claire and Charlie, hung the recovering smackhead from a tree, and made good on a promise to kill a survivor a day unless Claire was returned to him when Scott Jackson was found with his neck broken. Once captured, Charlie shot him six times in the chest, though it was not likely Rom would have given any information to the survivors. Ethan Rom is an anagram for "Other Man."

Rose

Bernard's wife. She was separated from him after he went to the tail section to use the bathroom. Sits across the aisle from Jack, who later performs CPR on her after the crash. She is from the Bronx.

Roseola

A red eruption of the skin. Claire's baby is given this quick diagnosis by Jack when she worries over his fever. It can also be described as the flushing of the cheeks in Ana Lucia's and Libby's respective real-life mug shots.

Rousseau, Danielle

Member of a French science team that departed from Tahiti. Ran aground on the island after following the distress signal broadcasting the numbers. She was seven months pregnant at the time of the shipwreck; her daughter, Alex, was taken by the Others a week after she gave birth. She changed the distress signal, which has been broadcasting in a continual loop for sixteen years, and claims to have killed all the members of her expedition after they contracted "the sickness."

Royalties

Payment to the holder of a patent, copyright, or resource for the right to use their property. Although Malcolm David Kelley (who portrays Walt) has been seen only twice since the raft burned, he should be allowed to make a certain amount every time Michael cries out his name. Let's face it; the last time we heard someone's named shouted repeatedly on the screen was either Jack calling for Rose or vice versa in the film *Titanic*.

243

Rutherford, Adam

Father to Shannon and stepfather to Boone, he was involved in a head-on car accident with Jack's future wife, Sara. He was brought to St. Sebastian's hospital three to four years prior to the plane crash, and was fifty-seven when he was pronounced dead at 8:15 that morning.

Rutherford, Shannon

Her stepbrother was Boone; she turned twenty-one on the island. Portrayed as self-centered, helpless, and useless early on, partly because she clings to the belief that the survivors will be rescued. She is able to translate Rousseau's distress signal because she spent a year as a nanny in France, babysitting a boy named Laurent. She was cut off from receiving any money from her late father's trust after she turned eighteen.

S

Sacrifice

This word has several meanings, one of which is a loss entailed by giving up or selling something at less than its value, which occurs after Charlie burns his heroin stash and finds his guitar intact. Another, more sinister, meaning is the act of killing an animal or person in order to propitiate a deity. It seems as if Locke was losing the strength in his legs until Boone dies when the Beechcraft plummets from the tree canopy.

Sagal, Katey

The actress who portrays Helen, the one-time lady friend of Locke who suggested he needed to take a "leap of faith."

Sagitta

The name of the arrow with which Apollo slew Cyclops. Also the name of a small constellation seen in the southern hemisphere.

Santa Rosa Mental Health Institute

Hurley was treated as a patient at this hospital, and may have been treated by a doctor named Curtis.

Sarin

Isopropyl methylphosphonoflouridate. A colorless and oderless nerve gas, it evaporates quickly and becomes a nerve agent that is used in warfare and terrorism. When the United States bombed Iraq during the Gulf War of 1990–1991, Sayid was told to interrogate his own countryman after being shown an account of sarin being used in the town of Habaja, where Sayid had family.

"Save the world."

The only explanation Kelvin gave to Desmond for typing in the numbers on the computer before the clocked counted to zero was "to save the world."

Sawyer, Frank

The man who bilked James Ford's parents out of their life savings, causing James's father to commit murder-suicide when he was almost ten. In later years, Ford took the name Sawyer as his own.

Schizophrenia

A psychotic disorder categorized by distortions of reality and withdrawal from social contact. Locke's mother suffered from this malady and was placed into the Santa Rosa Mental Health Institution, the same place that Hurley met Leonard Simms.

Screen caps

Short for a captured still from a video. One of the most stellar Web sites devoted to *Lost*, www.thetailsection.com, provided viewers with various scene of the bunker, the mosaic, the Dharma logos, and even the collective images in the smoke monster that Mr. Eko stood down. The viewing of the screen caps has helped those sad few of us, myself and maybe a few people in West Virginia, who still record on VHS, do not have high-definition TV, DSL, and other inventions I'm not even aware of yet. On the other side, I do have an 8-track player that can record blank 8-tracks. *The Best of Tom Jones*, anybody?

245

Seabilly

A nickname for the bearded Mr. Friendly, back when he was piloting the boat when Walt was abducted. Surprisingly, this is not a sobriquet that Sawyer came up with.

Security System

Called this by Rousseau as she helped several survivors go to the *Black Rock* for dynamite, though she refuses to elaborate. More commonly referred as "The Monster," or "the smoke monster," it makes both mechanical sounds—reminiscent of the sounds a roller coaster makes—to biological sounds such as roaring. It can suck trees into the ground, and makes booming, thrashing sounds when in pursuit of someone.

Seeds, The

Their signature song, "Pushin' Too Hard," is heard playing in the bunker while Henry Gale is held prisoner.

Seoul Gateway Hotel

Jin was hired as a doorman at this prestigious hotel; after he quit because he was reprimanded for letting "lower-class" people into the hotel, he literally bumps into Sun, his future wife.

Shaving cream

After Jack sees Locke in the bathroom after Jack had showered, Locke explains the steam opens his pores and allows him to shave cleanly, as there is no shaving cream. At least, that's his story.

Shephard, Christian

Jack's father and former chief of surgery at St. Sebastian's. He lost his medical license for operating while drunk. Sawyer meets him in a seedy Australian honky-tonk within days of the former doctor's death.

Shephard, Jack

Followed in his father's footsteps as a spinal surgeon. He later caused his father's dismissal from St. Sebastian's by reporting to the Mortality Board that his father had been operating while under the influence of alcohol. His father flew to Australia soon after and Jack's mother implores Jack to go after him. Upon his arrival, Jack discovers his father has died of a heart attack brought on by his years of drinking, and he boards Flight 815 with his father's body for burial. He is the reluctant leader of the survivors, and tends to put the crash survivors' future in the hands of science, not in faith or fate.

Shephard, Margo

Jack's mother. She insisted that her son fly to Australia to bring his father's body back to Los Angeles.

Shephard, Sara

Jack's ex-wife. He had operated on her spine after an auto accident, and she married him after her recovery. She started having an affair with someone she met at the gym where she does her rehabilitation exercises.

Shin, John

The actor who portrays Jin's father.

Sims, Leonard

A patient in the same psychiatric ward as Hurley who passed on the series of numbers in which Hurley eventually used to win the lottery.

Sioux City

Sawyer tells Cassidy he will meet up with her in this town on Iowa's border with Nebraska. They must have been very close to Kate's hometown, because Kate's mother is the waitress when Sawyer and Gordy are parting ways. Sawyer wants her to wait for him at the Sageflower Motel, off Highway 29.

Skinner, B. F.

Mentioned as a visionary in the "Orientation" film, Skinner was a clinical psychologist and author of several books. He wrote several controversial articles in which he proposed widespread use of psychological behavior modification in order to improve society. His term for this was "operant conditioning," and it became known as a Skinner box. He created this as a graduate student at Harvard University in 1930. It was used to study animal cognition and how long it would take them to realize that pressing a certain lever or button would release food or water, which Skinner called a "primary reinforcer."

247

Solipsism

The philosophical theory that the self is all you need to know to exist.

Somerhalder, Ian

The actor who portrayed Boone Carlyle

S.O.S

An intentionally recognized distress signal in radio code. Bernard wants to make a giant S.O.S sign on the beach filling it in with black rocks, hoping that a passing plane or satellite might see it.

Sousveillance

Inverse surveillance. The recording of an activity from the perspective of a participant in the activity. On a larger scale, one might consider Desmond's series of mirrors to watch the hatch; another example might be the knowledge someone like, say, Libby, might gain to pass on to the Others.

Spiritual insurance

Locke tells Claire that in its simplest form, this is the definition of baptism.

Staff, The

According to the map on the blast door, this is the location of the Cadaceus Medical Station and that it is too far from Station #3 for anyone to investigate and return to the hatch within the 108 minutes needed to reprogram the computer.

State of Nature

A theory developed by English philosopher John Locke (1632-1704), in which he explained how people could live together without any laws or government.

Steve

Hurley apologizes at Scott Jackson's burial, saying he was sorry he called him Steve all the time. That is, when he wasn't calling him "Dude."

Stewart, Arlene & Joseph

Claire backed out of signing an adoption agreement with this Melbourne couple.

St. Sebastian Hospital

The Los Angeles hospital where Jack was on staff as a spinal surgeon.

Sullivan

One of the background survivors who seems to be a bit of a hypochondriac.

Swaddling

A binding of clothes in infants, particularly newborns. Locke shows how to calm Aaron by wrapping a blanket around the baby, restricting his movements. There are numerous references to the Christ child in swaddling cloth.

Swan

The code name for Station #3. In the night sky, the constellation Cygnus, containing a Sun-like star named Vega that is only fourteen light-years from Earth, is nicknamed The Swan. Cygnus also appears in Roman mythology (see separate entry).

Synchronicity

The relation that exists when things occur at the same time. Not to be confused with either fate or coincidence.

T

Tahiti

The most important island in French Polynesia. The French science team departed this island and changed course when they heard the repeated radio transmission of the numbers. Their boat crashed on a reef on the opposite side of the fuselage wreckage.

Tailenders' last names

Are they just being snobs, or will any of the survivors from the tail section, aside from Ana Lucia, ever bother to mention their last names?

Taini, Jayne

The actress who portrays Martha Toomey, widowed wife of Sam. Part of her leg is a prosthesis—after Toomey moved away from a larger city, not wanting the curse of the numbers to harm innocents, he was involved in the car accident, causing severe injuries to his wife's lower leg.

Tallahassee

While playing cards, Sawyer tells Jack that he knows what certain medicines are because, while he wasn't in Phuket, he was in Tallahassee, and something was burning and it wasn't the sunshine.

Tampa Job, The

One of the cons that Sawyer and Hibbs were involved in together.

Tariq

Sayid's former commanding officer who is tortured by Sayid. He cannot believe that Sayid would work for the Americans, but Jon Inman showed Sayid a film on how sarin nerve gas was used on his hometown.

Tartarus

In Greek mythology, place where the wicked are punished after death.

Tasir, Essam

A member of a terrorist cell in Sydney and former college roommate and friend of Sayid. He is coerced by Sayid, who is working with the CIA in hopes of learning the whereabouts of his beloved Nadia, to use a large amount of the explosive C-4 to blow up an unnamed government building. Tasir kills himself when he learns that his friend betrayed him over a woman.

Taylor, Tamara

The actress who portrays Walt's mother.

Tequila

Jack is at the airport bar before Flight 815's departure with Ana Lucia drinking tequila, suggesting that the next drink be shared during the flight. Jack offers Ana that second drink five weeks later on the island, after Shannon's burial.

Territoire Fonce

French translation for the Dark Territory, the area surrounding the *Black Rock* slave ship.

Terry, John

The actor who portrays Dr. Christian Shephard.

Them

The phrase the tailenders use to describe the Others. Ana Lucia still uses this word after the two surviving groups have merged together.

Therapeutic

Tending to cure or restore to health. Locke tells Jack that he has kept the heroin stash in the Virgin Mary statues for "therapeutic value," should Charlie need it.

The Third Policeman

Desmond shoves this book into his backpack with quite a bit of antibiotics as he prepares to flee the bunker. Written by Flann O'Brien in 1940, it was not published until 1967, after his death. The novel is a story about academic obsession and a commentary on Einsteinian physics.

Ticotin, Rachel

This actress portrays the character of Ana Lucia's mother, a police captain in the Westwood area of Los Angeles.

Tighe, Kevin

The actor who portrays Anthony Cooper, Locke's father.

Tikrit

Home town in Iraq of Sayid, located northeast of Baghdad.

Titanium

A light, strong, gray, and lustrous corrosion-resistant metallic element used in strong lightweight alloys (such as *airplane parts*); the main sources are rutile and ilmenite. There are pieces of girder in the bunker, and Sayid tells Jack that he might be able to break through a sealed section of the bunker because titanium is nonmagnetic.

Tito, Grandpa

Hurley's grandfather, who dies of a heart attack during a live television feed once reporters know that Hurley is the winner of the MCGA-Millions lottery.

Tokyo Rose

Sawyer's nickname for Sun, when he is talking to Locke about how the others feel after the faked attempted abduction.

Toomey, Martha

Wife of Sam Toomey, who explained the story of the numbers to Hurley.

Toomey, Sam

Was stationed at an Australian listening post in the Pacific during WWII. Leonard Sims told him about the repetition of the numbers amidst the normal static they encountered. He eventually used the numbers in a bean-guessing contest, and then encountered repeated bad luck, and eventually he committed suicide.

Tour de Stade

A course one takes in an emptied stadium by running up and down each of the steps in the arena. Jack met Desmond, who had actually been training, whereas Jack was fighting his anger and frustration at not being able to bring progress in Sara's recovery from the spinal operation.

Tracy

Was alone on Flight 815, and when messages were collected for a "message bottle" to be taken on the raft Michael builds, she writes a note to her husband and two children. Sawyer reads her message at random in the aftermath of the raft burning by the people in the boat. He also notes wryly that she has been sleeping next to Steve for several weeks.

Transference

In psychoanalysis, the process whereby emotions are passed on or displaced from one person to another. During a conversation with Jack, who is chopping firewood, Hurley explains that it was a word he learned at the mental hospital.

Trebuchet

Medieval artillery used during sieges. A heavy war engine similar to a catapult used for hurling large stones. Locke and Boone build such a device on a smaller scale in hopes of breaking the glass casing of the hatch.

Triangulation

A method of determining the position of a fixed point from the angles to it from two fixed points a known distance apart. Sayid fashions a way to try and determine the source of a radio signal by use of bottle rockets being shot into the air from various positions around the crash site.

Triple-A

A nickname for the real name of the actor who portrays Mr. Eko.

Troup, Gary

One of the passengers on Flight 815 who did not survive the crash. He had just turned in a mystery manuscript to his agent prior to leaving Australia.

Truss, Warren

Australia's Minister for Agriculture, Fisheries and Forestry. Sawyer was arrested for head-butting this man in a Sydney bar. The policeman in charge, Calderwood, reads James Ford's police record jacket and then informs him of his official deportation and hands him a ticket for Flight 815.

Tsunami

A destructive wave caused by an underwater earthquake. The shoreline will be exposed by as much as several hundred feet, and the resulting wave will build to a speed of 600 mph as it crashes back to land.

Turn of the Screw

The "Orientation" film is hidden behind this book in the bunker. Written by Henry James and serialized in *Collier's Weekly* between January and April of 1897, the essence of the story is a governess who sees the ghosts of children in an old mansion. Literary arguments over the last century suggest either the governess's madness or the true existence of ghosts.

Twenty dollar bill

The real Henry Gale had written a note to his wife Jennifer on the back of the only writing paper he had, the money in his wallet. He describes leaving the crash site of the balloon to find the beach, cryptically ending the note with "If you are reading this, I must be dead."

Typhon

In Greek mythology, a monster with a hundred heads, one of the whirlwinds, and father of Cerberus, the Chimera, and the Sphinx. His parents were Gaea and Tartarus.

U

Uluru

The healer that Bernard brings to in Australia is called Isaac of Uluru. Uluru is the Aboriginal name for Ayers Rock.

Unexplained

Having the reason or cause not made clear. The survivors have encountered several bizarre living things or objects as the island is explored, e.g., the polar bear, the Beechcraft plane, the *Black Rock* mining ship, and the smoke monster.

Unix command

A function of the decades-old computer in the bunker of Station #3.

Unknown Logo

A third Dharma imprint can be seen on the shark when viewed beneath the waters as Sawyer flounders next to the remnants of the raft. The image seems to be a horizontal line, much like the Arrow. One possibility is that, since the logo is on a shark, that the design might be that of the island itself; the smoke monster could be the security system on land, "tagged" sharks might be the water-based protection.

U.S. Marshals

The government agency that had an agent tracking Kate for three years, following her from Iowa and New Mexico, eventually finding her in Australia.

V

Validation

The cognitive process of establishing a valid proof. While Hurley and Libby are doing laundry in the bunker, she mentions this term used commonly by psychologists. Hurley then asks if he had ever met her before; Libby replies that Hurley stepped on her toe, that he was wearing headphones and was the last one boarding, but neglects to mention how he could have been near her as she was in the tail section.

Video diaries

Verizon cell phones offer two-minute episodes that chronicle stories of the background survivors of Flight 815. For those with *really* short attention spans?

Vincent

Walt's dog, he spends quite a bit of time in the jungle. The producers have said that he will prove to be a very important part of the show, and I am assuming that it is not a reference to the dwindling boar population. Before leaving on the raft, Walt gave Vincent to Shannon, knowing she still grieved over Boone's death. Presumably, Shannon was the one who saw visions of Walt because of the connection he had with his dog.

Virgin Mary

Boone found several statues of the Madonna on the Nigerian drug smugglers' plane. They were hollowed out and filled with bags of heroin.

Vodka

Unaged, colorless liquor originating from Russia. Jack was given several bottles by Cindy, the flight attendant, before Flight 815 hit turbulence. When he awoke in the jungle in the opening scene of the pilot episode, the vodka in his pocket jogs his memory of the crash.

Vortex

The shape of something rotating rapidly. In metaphysics, there are several energy grids mapped, including the Bermuda Triangle in the Atlantic, and the Devil's Triangle off the coast of Japan, sites of many plane and ship disappearances going back centuries. Another energy grid covers the area where the island most likely can be found.

W

Walkabout

Nomadic excursions into the Australian bush by an aborigine. Locke is infuriated when he is not allowed to join a busload of travelers for a walkabout because he is in a wheelchair. The travel company refunds his money with a ticket on Flight 815. In a deleted scene, the tailenders find a box floating to shore; Nathan, Goodwin, and several others struggle with the box, and when it is opened they find only souvenir boomerangs from the same company that denied Locke his spiritual tour.

War wound

Locke tells Sayid that the scar from where his kidney was removed was from an old "war wound."

Watchman, Dustin

The actor who portrayed Scott Jackson, a survivor killed by Ethan Rom.

Watership Down

Sawyer is reading this book, originally in Boone's luggage. There are various similarities to island life, as the book is about a warren of rabbits who feel threatened.

Watros, Cynthia

The actress who portrays Libby, the only main character to not have given out her last name to anyone. Might it be DeGroot? Then again, with those crazy eyes, Norman Bates might've had a younger sister we never knew about. Does anybody else hear the lambs screaming?

Wayne

Kate's biological father, a drunken wife-beater. He was killed by Kate when she blew up their home in Iowa; her mother was working at night as a waitress at the time.

Wayzata

Henry Gale's wallet held a driver's license showing his address as 815 Walnut Ridge in this Minneapolis suburb.

Welcome Home

Name of the home inspection company Locke is owner of when he tells Nadia that it is okay to move in with her husband, after which she tells him that she is single.

Westhills baseball cap

One of the items Kate and Tom placed in their time capsule.

Wexler, Judith Martha

Listed among the dead during the service held before the fuselage is set on fire and the passengers within are cremated.

Wheelchair

Locke was confined to a wheelchair prior to the plane crash for at least four years. When the chair was found in the wreckage of the fuselage, Locke makes no mention of it, and it is used to move heavy objects. The chair burns when the corpses in the fuselage are cremated and a permanent signal fire is created. Locke's leg paralysis is learned during a flashback detailing Locke's reason for coming to Australia.

Whistle

Locke carves a dog whistle from a branch and uses it to get Vincent to return to the camp on the beach.

"Who the hell is Wayne?"

The first thing Sawyer says in the bunker, after regaining consciousness as Kate spills her guts about killing her father. With this line, maybe now people will stop coming up to me and yelling "Wayne's World! Party time!" That is so 1992.

Widmore Construction

A sign on the wall of a London construction site during the aborted filming of the "You All Every-Butties" video.

Widmore Laboratories

Maker of the home pregnancy test that Sawyer offers to Sun. Widmore Labs is also seen beneath the air tanks on the hot air balloon that crashed into trees on the island.

Wit's Basin Mineral Industries

A Minneapolis-based company dealing in nonmagnetic iron ore pellets, they have interests in South Africa, Colorado, and Canada. The fake Henry Gale told Sayid that he sold a company that mined nonmagnetic ore. This company actually exists; I was idly Googling while searching for Easter eggs.

Wizard of Oz, The

Everyone knows L. Frank Baum's novel, even Sawyer. The point to be made is that, like the possible "Other," Henry Gale, the Wizard arrives in Oz by a balloon, and Dorothy leaves in the same manner.

Wrinkle in Time, A

A novel about three children who are taken to various inhabited planets in the galaxy by three entities and also one of the books read by Sawyer. The book's implications reflect several key aspects of the DeGroots' clinical experiments. In the novel by Madeline L'Engle, the children are shown planets where the inhabitants have flourished after fighting off a dark cloud and one planet where the cloud won and reduced the planet to a world of people with two-dimensional actions. This latter planet reflects the repeated actions of Desmond keying in the numbers at Station #3, thus taking away any individuality he previously had.

WXO

The call letters of the radio station Sayid and Hurley hear using the transmitter Bernard took from the Arrow bunker. The "W" would mean that the station is east of the Mississippi River. A song by Duke Ellington has just ended, and after the call letter announcement, Glenn Miller's "Moonlight Serenade" begins.

X

Xenogenesis

The alternation of two or more different forms in the life cycle of a plant or animal. Also known as heterogenesis. The island monster might be explained in such a way.

Y

Yanks

Charlie occasionally refers to the American survivors with this word.

Yebnan kelb

259

A derogatory term in Arabic used by Sayid, which translates to "son of a dog."

Yemi

Mr. Eko's younger brother, he chooses priesthood as an adult after Mr. Eko keeps him from executing an old man on orders of a thug captain. Mr. Eko kills the man instead and leads a life of crime and intimidation. Yemi is shot dead prior to the Beechcraft plane with the cargo of Virgin Mary statues takes off, and his body is pulled on board the plane. Years later, Mr. Eko has Charlie take him to the site where the drug smugglers' plane lies upside down on the jungle floor. He finds his brother's mummified corpse, takes the cross from his neck, and burns the plane, cremating him.

Yin-Yang

The interdependent relationship, as well as inherent conflict, between opposites.

"You All Everybody."

The title of DriveSHAFT's one hits.

Yusef

Member of a terrorist cell in Sydney, along with Essam Tasir.

Z

Zack

Emma's brother. Both were survivors from the tail section of Flight 815 and were abducted by the Others.

Zahra

The wife of the college roommate Sayid betrayed. She was killed by a stray bomb while shopping for clothing.

Zeke

After the confrontation with Mr. Friendly, Sawyer sneers like Elvis and says "We ain't through, Zeke."

Zoology

Writer and supervising producer Javier Grillo-Marxuach mentions in *Lost Magazine* that the Dharma Initiative was "a communal research facility on the island. A lot of scientists and free-thinkers got together to do a lot of different kinds of research [including] psychiatry [and] zoology."

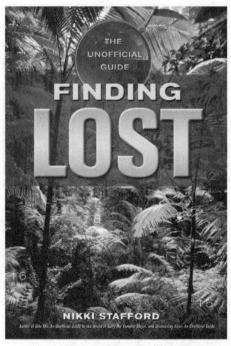